BUSBY: ARCHITECTURE'S NEW EDGES

Busby: Architecture's New Edges

An Ecotone Publishing Book/2015
Copyright © 2015 by Peter Busby

Ecotone Publishing – an Imprint of the International Living Future Institute

For more information write:

Ecotone Publishing
International Living Future Institute
721 NW Ninth Avenue, Suite 195
Portland, OR 97209

Author: Peter Busby
Graphic Design: Pablo Mandel, Circular Studio
Edited by: Fred McLennan
Back cover photograph: Paul Baur
Front cover photograph: Nic Lehoux

Library of Congress Control Number: 2014950438

Library of Congress Cataloging-in Publication Data

ISBN: 978-0-9827749-3-9

1. Architecture   2. Environment   3. Philosophy

First Edition

Printed in Canada on FSC certified paper, Processed elemental chlorine-
free, using vegetable-based inks.

BUSBY: ARCHITECTURE'S NEW EDGES

Gord,

I hope you enjoy this book — and I trust you are doing well.

Best.

[signature] 5·2015

ECOtone publishing company

Energy. Environment. Experiential Learning (EEEL); University of Calgary; Calgary, AB; 2011

VanDusen Botanical Garden Visitor Centre; Vancouver, BC; 2012

Contents

Foreword

Centuries from now, when historians look back to the beginning of the Anthropocene, a time when we realized that human beings had become the dominant influence on living systems, we will be particularly interested in what is happening at this time: a burst of design, technology, and social awareness coming together led by a particular sector of the population: architects, builders, redevelopers, and resilient urbanists. Writers constantly remind themselves to use the simplest word possible to convey meaning. However, there is an offshoot of a word we rarely see that might name this current era: the Cladogene. Cladogenesis is when a species population branches off in evolutionary terms, and that is what has happened in the field of the built environment. It is similar to what Jason F. McLennan refers to as zugunruhe, the agitation and restlessness found in species before long migrations to a different environment. Far ahead of any other profession or industrial sector, architects and designers, planners and developers, all inspired by farsighted cities, are restlessly agitating, discarding assumptions, demonstrating the possibilities of reimagining the relationship between human systems and living systems in their work. A Cladogene era is a breakaway in human evolution.

Architecture's New Edges traces the beginning of this era through the eyes of one of its foremost practitioners, Peter Busby. His life illustrates and created this paradigmatic shift in understanding. Given the fundamental gravity of our time, the fact that we stand at the cusp of overwhelming forces brought about by human ignorance and rapacity, from ocean death to climate change, from the sixth extinction to resource wars, the design lineage traced herein is vastly greater than a portfolio review. The reimagination of architecture and design is recognition that the entire earth is like the Galapagos, an island chain with limited resources and real constraints. The designs described and illustrated here, with their responsiveness to culture, place, water, climate, and function, are like Darwin's finches, each structure modified and adapted to thrive in its environment and make its environment thrive. The infectious repetitis of post-war architecture is not gone yet, but it is withering in the face of human need. Structures like the Nicola Valley Institute of Technology and developments such as Dockside Green become an expression of heritage, resource frugality, place, and human well-being, imitating biological heterogeneity in their diverse form and function.

For the reader, the modesty of this book is a balm. We are so beset by the litany of our current and looming losses that we rarely get to see how humanity is learning to heal. Peter is not alone, and he would be the first to make note of it. He joins and is joined by tens of thousands of others, including students coming out of our schools who now have a very different worldview than the previous generation. They are emboldened and informed by Peter's oeuvre, and enlivened by the ideas of Ray Cole, Ian McHarg, Sym Van der Ryn, Ed Mazria, sometimes without even realizing the source. As this paradigm shift unfolds, we see how evolution occurs in one generation. Darwin was never to know that his famed finches did not evolve over centuries but over single lifetimes. The same is true of human beings. We can change quickly. When we read Peter's work and his sincere and straightforward stories of the evolution of his awareness and design, we know that a compassionate and livable future is possible, a future that surpasses anything we can yet imagine in its capacity to nurture life and humankind.

—Paul Hawken, Mill Valley, California, September 2014

Paul Hawken has written seven books published in over 50 countries in 28 languages including four New York Times bestsellers, *The Next Economy, Growing a Business, and The Ecology of Commerce, and Blessed Unrest*. Bill Clinton called his book *Natural Capitalism* one of the five most important books in the world. He has appeared on numerous media including the Today Show, Larry King, Talk of the Nation, Charlie Rose, and he has been profiled in articles including the Wall Street Journal, Newsweek, Washington Post, Business Week, and Esquire. His writings have appeared in the Harvard Business Review, Resurgence, New Statesman, Inc., Boston Globe, Christian Science Monitor, Mother Jones, Utne Reader, Orion, and other publications. He founded the first natural food company in the United States that relied solely on sustainable agriculture, Smith & Hawken, OneSun Solar, and Drawdown.org. He has served on the board of many environmental organizations including Point Foundation (publisher of the Whole Earth Catalogs), Center for Plant Conservation, Trust for Public Land, and National Audubon Society.

Courtesy Paul Hawken

Acknowledgements

Like all design, writing is not a solitary art. It is necessarily collaborative. I want to recognize those who have inspired, conspired, and generally supported me in large measure during the process of bringing this book to completion.

Thank you first to the designers and all of my team members from Peter Busby Architects (1984-1986), Busby Bridger Architects (1986-1996), Busby + Associates Architects (1996-2004), and Perkins+Will. Over the years my colleagues have inspired me with their ideas, their values, and their commitment to the greater good. I would also like to express my appreciation for some of my most longstanding colleagues and collaborators: Paul Bridger, Ray Cole, David Dove, Robert Drew, Paul Fast, Susan Gushe, Jim Huffman, Kevin Hydes, Rod Maas, Blair McCarry, Cornelia Hahn Oberlander, Sören Schou, Adam Slawinski, and Kathy Wardle. Working with each of you has elevated my thinking, expanded my understanding, and greatly improved my design work. I thank you.

Without a great editorial team, good ideas can get lost in the shuffle. For their help getting the ideas from my head to the page with persistence and good humor, a special thank you to Cora Palmer and Mary Adam Thomas; Mary for long hours of discussion, insightful organization, and awesome delivery of the main text; Cora for patience and perseverance, organization and meticulous attention to the completion of the project, over thousands of hours. Thank you to Pablo Mandel for helping my ideas stand out on the page. Many thanks to Michael Berrisford and the rest of the team at Ecotone Publishing for their thoughtful editing.

Perkins+Will have made this project feasible with their moral and financial support, which is deeply appreciated. Perkins+Will is much more than just support, of course. While I have helped shape and change the nature of the firm, my partners at Perkins+Will have influenced and changed me with new ideas and practices that widened my thinking, all for the better. Thank you all. It's been a wonderful journey.

I would also like to express my gratitude to Paul Hawken for contributing his valuable time to authoring the Foreword. I admire Paul and his work immensely, and I am deeply honored to have his thoughts in this book.

Finally, I want to acknowledge the commitment of our clients, past and present. Our thoughts are nothing without you. Thank you for the opportunity to bring our shared visions and ideas to life.

I hope you all enjoy the fruits of all our efforts.

About the Author

Peter Busby, a founding member of the Canada Green Building Council, is internationally recognized for his contributions to architecture and planning. Busby's award-winning portfolio embodies his philosophy of social responsibility and commitment to sustainable design. Since opening his Vancouver practice in 1984, Peter's body of work has gained a reputation for design excellence and innovation, becoming a powerful catalyst in the growth of the green architecture movement in North America and abroad. After merging his firm with Perkins+Will in 2004, Peter became a driving force across the company, compelling its industry-leading sustainable design initiatives. In 2012, Peter relocated to be the Managing Director of Perkins+Will's San Francisco office, bringing his focus on sustainable communities and regenerative design to all Perkins+Will's West Coast offices, directing teams working on projects locally and internationally. Peter's dedication to design advocacy remains steadfast; he lectures frequently at academic institutions and professional engagements around the world.

Peter holds a bachelor's degree in architecture from the University of British Columbia and a bachelor's degree in political science from the University of Toronto. In recognition of his professional and community contributions, Peter was admitted to the College of Fellows of the Royal Architectural Institute of Canada (RAIC) in 1997. In 2005 Peter was invested as a member of the Governor General's Order of Canada, the highest civilian award in Canada that recognizes a lifetime of outstanding achievement, dedication to the community, and service to the nation. In 2008, he was conferred an honorary doctorate in science by Ryerson University and in 2011 he was named a Cascadia Fellow. In 2013, he was elevated to LEED® Fellow, a designation of the U.S. Green Building Council, which recognizes exceptional contributions to the green building community as well as significant achievements within a growing community of sustainable design professionals. Peter was the recipient of the 2014 RAIC Gold Medal, an honor that recognizes a significant and lasting contribution to Canadian architecture. He has over 200 design awards to his credit, including six Governor's General Awards, thirteen Lieutenant Governor's Awards, two AIA COTE awards, and many sustainable design, wood design, and innovation awards.

Peter Busby

Introduction

Busby Bridger Architects staff; ca. 1989

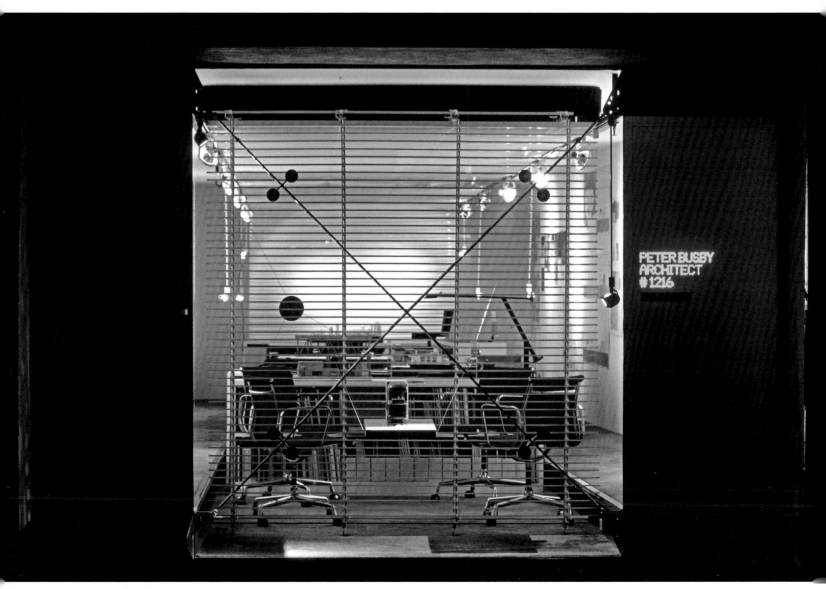

1216 Granville Street office, street view; Vancouver, BC; 1984

Exploration

Architects must aspire to do more than build. It is our job to invest passion into our work – passion for more than just the project or building. We need to care deeply about what the buildings we design are capable of being, of doing, of changing. Our work must incorporate environmental and social principles alongside the fundamentals of form and function. We must think not just about structures, but about systems, and how each design affects what surrounds it; the public spaces, the community, the watershed and the biosphere of our planet. All things in nature are interconnected, which means that our work is always much bigger than we are, and it ripples outward in so many ways.

For 30 years, I have thought about my mission to change the very structure of the practice of architecture. I have devoted my professional life to setting the bar higher, experimenting with new approaches and innovations, and raising questions about standards that establish new priorities. I do not claim to be alone in this effort – far from it – but I feel privileged to have practiced during a time of great change within the industry. Lucky timing on my part has allowed me to work alongside some of the individuals who will ultimately be credited with altering the course of architecture. Our collective efforts have helped establish a new mandate. Together, we have begun to redefine the edges of architecture.

This book will explore some of the ideas and areas of practice that stray from any traditional definition of architecture, and what we do as a profession. These "new edges" seem to be accelerating in importance and number every year. Largely, we will trace these ideas through the seminal projects of my career, many of which include what I believe to be the most important architectural trends of our time.

On Technology

It is impossible to explore modern-day accomplishments – mine or anyone else's – without acknowledging the role of technology, as technological advancements have had profound influences on anyone born in the past century.

I still recall the excitement and optimism I felt during Gus Grissom's short flight into space on July 21, 1961. Like the rest of the free world, this nine-year-old Canadian boy was riveted. Man could do anything. Man would go to the moon, Mars and then the stars! Science and technology had recently delivered us televisions, dishwashers and air conditioning, so what could we not do?

Machines would rid us of drudgery and allow us to live in comfort anywhere on the planet. Polio was cured and all other diseases would soon be eradicated as well. These things we grew up believing without a hint of irony or foreboding.

By the time man walked on the moon eight years later, I was standing at the side of the road in Tok Junction, Alaska with my thumb out on a journey to see the wild beauty of the Great North. I was taking a brief but intentional break from the urban world. As soon as I returned, however, I dived head-first into my education and, soon enough, into my career, both of which blossomed in tandem with developments in science and industry.

I pursued the British "high tech" movement in architecture, spending formative time in Norman Foster's office in London, where the joy of technology, innovation and discovery made that practice famous and successful beyond belief. By the time I opened my own practice in 1984, I was proud to brandish an IBM AT with 64K of Ram and AutoCAD V1.4 that cost me $25,000 – half my net worth at the time. Then came the amazing fax machine in 1987, my first cellphone in 1992, and my first instant email communication on a smartphone. (That email was sent in 2004 from the top floor of the Cairo Hilton to a mechanical engineer, Blair McCarry in Vancouver, with a reply back in seconds, something I found astonishing.) I often think of the comparison between my parents' home, which had one telephone for 30 years, and my current household, which has seven phones, one of which typically gets replaced for a newer model every six months.

I can still recall searching card catalogue drawers at university in 1971, looking for hours to find two or three relevant references for a paper. Contrast this with the fingertip information assembled by Google Earth Street View, and the amazing ability of search engines to find any information anywhere on Earth in a nano-second. I see no reason why graduates today should not be the most intelligent people ever, and why facts and truth should not overpower ignorance and lies in every corner of the globe.

We in architecture love technology and find joy in incorporating it into our designs. New materials, innovative and elegant detailing, functional expressionism, lightness and legibility define our work, all with the help of technological tools. Ruefully, in the process of embracing all of this progress, we learned one key new truth: technology cannot solve everything. Indeed, our dependence on it is contrib-uting to the destruction of all forms of life on earth. Consider asbestos, hailed as "the penicillin of the construction industry" when introduced in the late 1950s. We now know just how wrong that was.

In much of this book, the underlying theme is about how we can address the failings of our reliance on science and technology, and about our efforts to define and develop design solutions that offset the devastating impacts this dependence has had on all of nature and the fragile biosphere on which all life depends.

Underpinnings

At the University of Toronto, I began a program in political science that ended with the study of philosophy, all under the umbrella of an arts degree. From the great philosophical discourses of history, I studied 2000 years of deliberations around one core idea: what constitutes right and wrong? This fundamental question was often argued from the perspective of man's original "natural" state, uncorrupted by evil that manifested as greed and inequality brought on by social and human "progress" (the Industrial Revolution and all that came after). Searching for the answers as a student gave me an understanding of moral and ethical values and a foundation for a career and an architectural practice based on environmentalism and social equity. Quoting directly from a speech I gave on February 13, 1986:

District of North Vancouver Municipal Hall, entrance; North Vancouver, BC; 1995

"I studied ... great (philosophy) books and in return got a profound sense of values and the worth of attaining higher levels of thought and being through actions... My movement (from studying philosophy) to architecture was based on (its) activity, creativity, and the possibility of putting the main philosophical lessons into practice. You know that architects at the most universal edge of their discipline are supposed to give thought to the best ways for man to live — in balance with materialism, each other, and nature..."

I still believe that. To this day, the majority of my work continues to be public planning and design of communities and buildings that educate, aid human health and fitness, assist good government, and do so with convincing environmental accomplishments and promising contributions to the public urban realm.

Nicola Valley Institute of Technology; Merritt, BC; 2001

The fact that I came of age in the late 1960s and early 1970s also means that my practice has been influenced by the challenges to conventional beliefs being raised at the time. It was a period of vigorous debate between liberal and conservative ideas; questions raged about civil rights for the 10.5 percent of Americans with black skin, equality for women in society and the workplace, and freedom from tyranny and suffering the world over. The 1970s in North America were also defined by the Vietnam War, a conflict that had a bitter personal impact on me.

Music was everywhere and everything during those years. Lennon and Dylan sang of peace and love, not war. Soul music, antiwar music and songs about love, freedom and sexual liberation underpinned the rock 'n' roll movement that bound a generation together. We felt our beliefs deeply; they helped formulate our commitments for life.

These conversations and events shaped my convictions and instilled in me social democratic ideals and liberal values that continue to weave their way throughout my work. This book details projects that celebrate the social responsibility that I believe every designer is obligated to take seriously. Even in our early work, my colleagues and I established how critical these philosophies are to us.

1 http://www.infoplease.com/ipa/A0922246.html

District of North Vancouver Municipal Hall, atrium; North Vancouver, BC; 1995

Metro McNair Laboratory, atrium; Burnaby, BC; 1996

Right: Metro McNair Laboratory, overall; Burnaby, BC; 1996

Squamish Lil'wat Cultural Centre; Whistler, BC; 2006

- At the District of North Vancouver City Hall (1989-1995), we unwrapped the council chambers and enclosed them in glass facing the street as a way of inviting community members in to participate in the political process and the shaping of their future.
- At the Metro McNair Laboratory building in Burnaby, BC (1993-1996), the lab technicians (90 percent female) were given prime space and facilities, ahead of administration and management.
- Our work with First Nations reflects our commitment to honor the broader goals of society. Projects include a post-secondary institution for First Nations education at Nicola Valley Institute of Technology in Merritt, British Columbia (1999-2001) and The Squamish Lil'wat Cultural Centre (Waugh Busby Architects, 2003-2008).

Influences

No discussion about the influences on my work would be complete without direct reference to several designers who inspired me to be better, to do more and to make a bigger difference.

The first is Dr. Ray Cole, who came to the School of Architecture at the University of British Columbia (UBC) from the United Kingdom in 1976. Ray

Ray Cole as a young professor in 1976 when he joined the University of British Columbia School of Architecture

introduced me to the ideas around the precarious future of our planet, and railed to us in riveting lectures about how architects, engineers and builders were blissfully ignorant of their complicity and responsibilities. He showed us that we could do a lot of good through the environmental design of buildings; that we could make a difference! He introduced us to the basic concepts of environmental approaches to design. Although the ideas back then were simple and exploratory, they made a lot of sense to me.

Inspired by Ray, I devoured *The Autonomous House* (Brenda and Robert Vale, 1975), *The Limits to Growth* (a report for the Club of Rome's Project on the Predicament of Mankind by Donella H. Meadows, Dennis L. Meadows, Jorgen Randers and William W. Behrens III, 1972) and *Design with Nature* (Ian L. McHarg, 1969).

I was also researching built architecture at the same time. I had a grand plan to study every one of the great architects, one at a time in alphabetic order. Fortuitously, I ended up spending six months focusing exclusively on the first entry, Alvar Aalto, just absorbing and appreciating the subtleties of his approach to deeply environmental design.

The first "oil crunch" came at that time (conveniently for Ray, since it established the weakness of our dependence on fossil fuels). Gasoline, when you could get it, spiked to the shocking price of 39 cents per gallon, cementing my views then and now that we should and could soon be rid of our dependence on fossil fuels. Not so simple, as it turns out.

In the years since I was his student, Ray and I have had a career-long relationship that includes attending almost all of the Green Building Challenge series (1998-2007), founding the Canada Green Building Council (CaGBC), bringing the U.S. Green Building Council's (USGBC's) Leadership in Energy and Environmental Design (LEED®) to Canada, delivering dozens of joint lectures and panels in many countries, and enjoying many teaching and mentoring experiences together. In 1998, Ray authored a monograph, "Access to Architecture: Intentions + Product" that accompanied the first traveling exhibit of our work, which was read and seen by people in Vancouver, Toronto, Ottawa, Seattle and a number of other cities in Canada and the United States.

Perkins+Will's sponsorship of the Dr. Ray Cole Architecture Scholarship at UBC began in 2004 and honors his lasting influence on our work. Most recently, Ray and I coauthored (with others) an article titled, "A Regenerative Design Framework," published in 2012 by Building Research & Information (reprinted as Appendix 2).Ray has mentored a generation of West Coast architects interested in sustainable design, many of whom passed through or are still at our office, and he has had a profound influence on the entire profession in Canada and the United States.

My second mention should be of Norman Foster, not so much for the length of time we spent together (late 1979 - 1982), but for the powerful influence he had on my way of seeing buildings. The energy of this man – his perceptions of beauty, elegance, and simplicity; his commitment to systems thinking; his respect for history and urban design; his studio's embrace of the full scope of design from the industrial design of products to city-scale urban design; his collaborative skills and interest in detailing – all can be seen consistently in my work. In a very real way, working with Norman taught me architecture.

Norman was fun to work for, in a very exciting time. When I first joined his London office in 1979, the firm employed 25 people. By the time I left, it was 160 strong. At that point, we were well into the construction of the Hong Kong and Shanghai Bank head office in Hong Kong, a project that we won in an invited competition and one that has given me a lifetime of stories.

Norman Foster; circa 1979

"Access to Architecture," *traveling exhibit;* 1998

Climatrophis; Foster and Partners, drawing by Birkin Haward; 1980

It was from Norman that I got the idea that architecture should be "on the street." The office was then on Fitzroy Street, a beautiful sheet of glass exposing the work of the office to the world around. We felt we had new ideas to share and new ways of working, and that the world should look in. It meant that architecture was not an "art" practiced in some loft out of sight, but an act of engagement with society. As the only art form with significant social, urban and human impact because of its physical nature, architecture carries a responsibility to "do right," as Norman would say.

The process of design at Norman's Fitzroy Street office was also very different from any I had experienced before. Unlike, say, Jim Stirling, Norman was an editor as much as an author. He encouraged all of us to join the discussion around the table at "crit" time, and contribute ideas equally. He would always run with the best idea, not necessarily the one that was his or yours. For a young architect like me, the process was thrilling and empowering. It still shapes the way I work and, I hope, inspires those who work with me.

I worked on only two projects while at Foster Associates. Before the Hong Kong and Shanghai Bank, I helped design a house in Hampstead for Norman and Wendy Foster themselves. Designed with Tony Hunt, a pioneering British structural engineer, the house was conceived as a completely prefabricated, modular system of a "kit of parts" to be assembled on-site. Aluminum beams and columns formed an exoskeleton, supporting an envelope of modular wall and roof panels that were to be "zipped together" with rubber gaskets. The space was to be a singular volume, a nod to the home of Charles and Ray Eames in Pasadena.

Back in Vancouver, our first completed building, Ebco Aerospace, was designed for Helmut Eppich in 1986-1987, in Richmond, BC. We created an

EyeMasters, interior of retail space; Yorkdale Shopping Mall, Toronto, ON; 1990

exterior structure, suspended above a simple repetitive modular envelope that contained zipper gasketed windows. That building was also our first collaboration with Paul Fast of Fast + Epp, a deeply talented structural engineer. In the years since, we have collaborated on hundreds of projects with Paul and his team.

As mentioned above, we were fascinated with technology and innovation. At Foster Associates, we were leading the way at incorporating those ideas into architecture and building. Contrary to ideas being presented by the mainstream architectural press at the time – Adhocism (Charles Jencks) and Postmodernism (Venturi and Graves) – we were creating buildings that had originality and craft; something that we thought would be timeless, based on value, precision, and an understanding of industrial and manufacturing processes. All of these ideas can be traced throughout our work over the years. The prefabricated "kit of parts" approach was best illustrated in the series of five interiors designed and installed for EyeMasters in 1990.

Later, I incorporated Norman's idea of having an office "on the street" into my first office on Granville Street in Vancouver. In that context, the concept became a political statement as much as an aesthetic one. At that time, in 1984, Granville was mostly boarded up and home to many of Vancouver's prostitutes. Out of my shiny new shop in the midst of it all, I lobbied City Hall for new zoning for the street, and in 1985 I founded the Downtown Granville Business Association, which went on to become one of the first Business Improvement Districts (BIA) in Western Canada and helped convert the neighborhood into the entertainment zone that it is today.

We knew that Granville would only change if people came to shop and live, and we worked directly with the local residents to turn things around. With their

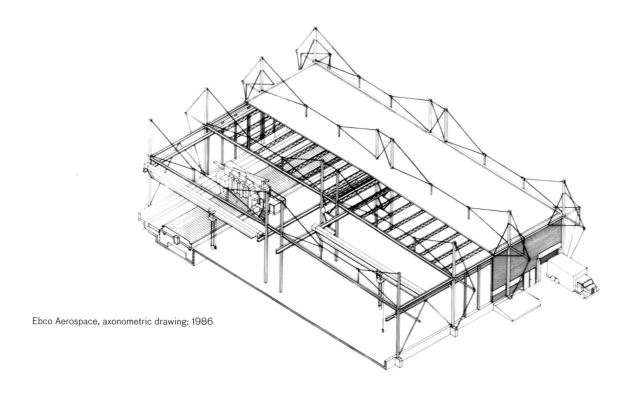

Ebco Aerospace, axonometric drawing; 1986

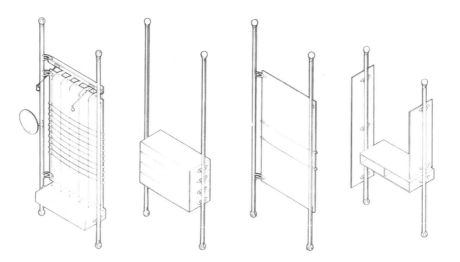

EyeMasters, axonometric view of kit of parts; 1990

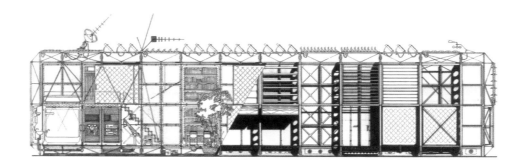

House for Norman Foster, section/elevation; drawing by Peter Busby; 1979

Ebco Table; 1988

help and support, we fought for, and won the rezoning of Downtown South, increasing density and inviting people to live downtown – an important idea at the time that seems self-evident now. The rezoning also included a battle to raise building height limits, spawning the small floor plate point towers that allow views and sunlight penetration that are now so characteristic of Vancouver architecture and urban design.

I have incorporated shopfronts and "architecture on the street" for every office location ever since.

While I was at the Foster practice, the originality of the firm's work drew the attention of some of the most creative designers interested in technology and innovation. We did an amazing collaboration for a theoretical project called Climatrophis with Buckminster Fuller. Climatrophis defined the workplace of the future designed with an open plan and multi-story interconnected spaces. It was based on Fuller's ideas of natural ventilation and air movement propelled by stratification, emerging from his work on geodesic domes, which he attributed to his study of ventilation in North American Natives' tents, a deeply environmental approach.

Other visitors to the Foster office included Charles and Ray Eames, who were there on several occasions around the time when they received the Royal Institute of British Architects (RIBA) Gold Medal in 1980. This time frame was while Jan Kaplický, Richard Horden and I were working with Norman and Wendy Foster on their house in Hampstead that contained many ideas discussed with Charles and Ray.

From my studies of the timeless and beautiful work of the Eames, I learned that design is a continuum, from the smallest detail of graphic design to the study of nature and the design of the universe. We have practiced industrial design in our firm ever since, enjoying the change of scale set against the continuity of our interest in design.

Luck also allowed me to sit in the Foster office with the obsessive Jan Kaplický, late of Future Systems, then a recent émigré from Czechoslovakia after the failure of the Prague Spring. He was working with Norman on a shop for Joseph in London that was so beautiful and original when completed in 1979, I have never forgotten it.

All of the ideas I collected from these inspiring and pioneering designers, underpinned by the environmentalism learned from Ray Cole and Buckminster

Image of Joseph Shop by Foster and Associates,
Sloane Square, London; 1980

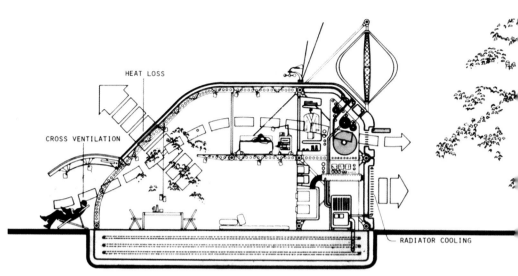

Peter Busby, "A House for the 1980s," *Canadian Architect,* October 1980: 20-23

Fuller, came together in a submission I made to a 1980 competition held by *The London Times* called "A House for the 1980s." Although I did not win the competition, my submission did get published in *The Sunday Times,* and later in *Canadian Architect*. At the time, it seemed that science and technology contained sophisticated solutions for a future defined by energy efficiency and mechanical systems, a view that today looks quite incomplete.

Upon returning to Canada in 1982, I belatedly took notice of Dr. David Suzuki, who was then well into his broadcasting career at the Canadian Broadcasting Corporation (CBC). As host of "Quirks and Quarks" and, later, "The Nature of Things" as well as author of dozens of topical books, he changed from a profoundly interesting scientist to a passionate and political environmentalist, warning of the perils of science and his fears for mankind.

I have heard David speak many times, and have never tired of his rants. From the beginning, I have taken them to heart, accepting his not-so-subtle implication that I personally had to be a part of fixing the problems he was defining.

In his broadcasts and presentations, David outlines the profound beauty to be found in nature. He is always with me when I am hiking – even when I was explaining the joys of the rainforest floor to my children on the Pacific Rim West Coast Trail, I could hear his voice in my own. On a recent trip to the Stein Valley, I could hear his voice again, echoing off the valley's great walls as I remembered the battle to "Save the Stein." Thankfully, it was saved.

My family has been to many vacation destinations that allow for enjoyment of unspoiled nature. We camped when our children were young, hiked, visited places like Costa Rica, Botswana and Tanzania, and most recently in 2013 toured the Gwaii Haanas National Park Reserve in Haida Gwaii, linking again with the ideas and efforts of Suzuki and the Haida to stop the logging on Lyell Island that led to the establishment of the preserve. Nature, when least disturbed by man, is astonishingly abundant and beautiful. As designers of buildings and communities for man, how can we reconcile these things?

When I did get David's personal attention in discussion, I argued that he should take the view that building design, done properly, offered solutions for the environmental issues about which he was campaigning. In 2007, he

Gwaii Haanas; 2013

responded by authoring the Introduction to our first publication, "Busby: Learning Sustainable Design," a contribution for which I am very grateful.

In 2009, David devoted an episode of "The Nature of Things" to sustainable building design, featuring our work at Dockside Green in Victoria. I attribute the time and effort I devote to constantly travelling and lecturing to the influence of Dr. Suzuki; he showed me that you have to give freely of your own time – for years – to convince others to do the right things if you hope to have any meaningful impact in life. At 75+, David Suzuki is still a profound public spokesman and advocate for environmental ideas, so we should be too.

—Peter Busby, Vancouver, BC, February 2015

1

Social Responsibility

Jones Street Neighborhood Nexus Community Art Day, San Francisco, CA; Perkins+Will, 2013

Architecture and the Public Interest

Green building is a relatively new phenomenon. As recently as the early 2000s, it was extremely unusual to find projects that incorporated green technologies or design. Today, approximately 60 percent of construction projects in the United States feature some environmental aspect.[1] In my opinion, architecture, more than any other profession, may be credited with driving this dramatic rise in responsible design and construction.

If one considers other market segments – transportation, manufacturing, law, and finance – none has changed its focus so dramatically in such a short amount of time as ours. (If they had, perhaps we would not be facing such a global environmental catastrophe today.) Responsible architects have adjusted and reprioritized design to accommodate urgent environmental needs in ways that many other sectors have yet to do.

The difference, I believe, lies in architects' ability to look forward; to think about the legacy our work will leave. If we do our job correctly, we will build structures that will last 50 to 100 years. We are not manufacturing widgets that will be packaged, sold, consumed and discarded in the short term; we are creating enduring interactive systems of buildings and communities involving people, technology and nature.

With this public face of architecture comes an enormous amount of social responsibility; an obligation to protect both the built and the natural environments. Architecture has become intertwined with social and human issues; it has evolved to incorporate not just the design of buildings, but also the study of how people live, work, move, interact with one another and relate to nature. The individuals who pursue and practice architecture in the 21st century are called to the craft in large part because we readily and enthusiastically accept this compelling challenge.

A Social Contract

Architecture is nothing less than the most public art. While one can choose to enter a museum to view the artwork housed inside, buildings on the street are unavoidable. When sculptors carve, when dancers dance, when painters paint, when musicians play, they – and their audiences – have choices about how private or public that art will be. Architecture is a form of art that carries an implicit trust; a social pact that we acknowledge the moment we enter design school and that lasts well beyond our lives.

Whatever the intended function of our work, generations of people expect us to do well by them. It is incumbent upon us to live up to those expectations. We can make healthy, productive, and safe environments; we can heal people and nature; we can nurture education; we can house the poor. We can add to, rather than waste the earth's resources. In short, we can enrich all facets of the public realm.

---

1. McGraw Hill Construction, *World Green Building Trends: Business Benefits Driving New and Retrofit Market Opportunities in over 60 Countries*, 2013.

This page: Princess Nora Bint Abdulrahman University; Riyadh, Kingdom of Saudi Arabia; 2011

All of this is our responsibility as architects, as we are agents of social change. We can only measure and respect great architecture if it does all of these things, well and at once.

We Are What We Build

Our work should combine aesthetic, emotional, cultural, social, and environmental missions. Rather than churning out drawings for office spaces that warehouse workers in chicken coop-style cubicle rows, why not challenge ourselves to create physical spaces that motivate people to do and be better? Instead of devoting our talents to lavish 25,000 square foot residences for wealthy individuals, why not focus on the more worthwhile endeavor of creating energy-efficient affordable housing? (Early in my career I spent a week getting a bathroom design "right" to the satisfaction of a rather fussy client. I decided then and there that for me, architecture was to involve higher goals that would have more meaningful impacts on society.)

Through the choices we make as architects, we have the opportunity to ennoble public life. Libraries, transit centers, airports, schools, hospitals, parks, and urban design influence and benefit the residents of the communities they serve. As designers, our job is to ensure that these are safe, healthy, inspirational places that support their occupants and encourage connections to the world beyond. Architecture, one might argue, is a form of public service.

The beauty of Victorian-era train stations reflects the grandeur of rail travel during the time when these magnificent spaces were designed and built. Even today, a visitor to Grand Central Station embarks on an emotional journey that begins well before boarding a train, all because its design fills one with an undeniable sense of excitement and wonder. Well-designed public spaces of any kind should achieve the same goal of connecting people and place, and seize opportunities to thrill and inspire.

As a firm we have focused much of our attention on buildings that have social purpose. Perkins+Will was founded on a strong K-12 practice in Chicago. The Crow Island Elementary School, Perkins+Will's first education project in 1940, established the firm as a leading edge and thoughtful design firm committed to

Crow Island School, Winnetka IL; 1940: Photograph copyright © Hedrich Blessing, Chicago History Museum

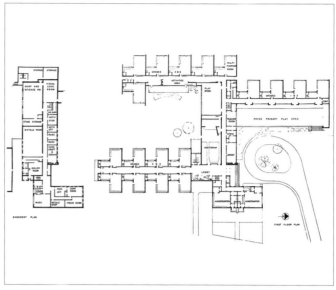

Crow Island School, Winnetka IL, 1940; Perkins+Will, Inc. with Eliel & Eero Saarinen

developing innovation as a core element of the design process. The project was (and still is) naturally ventilated, daylit throughout and features a creative plan for the school that supports educational teaching trends that are still considered progressive. Today, Perkins+Will is committed to a mission of "ideas and buildings that support the broader goals of society." We are strong nationally and internationally in the K-12 market, and are dominant in health care, higher education, and science and technology facilities. We publicly acknowledge that we do not design casinos or facilities for the incarceration of anyone. Our firm designs places with social purpose.

In one stunning project recently completed in the Kingdom of Saudi Arabia, Princess Noor University in Riyadh, the University opened to provide higher education opportunities to 40,000 women. The 20 million square foot facility involved 300 architects from six Perkins+Will offices working with Dar Al-Handasah and Partners to design and construct the facility in three and a half years. It is hard to imagine an architectural project that could do more to improve the social conditions and opportunities for women in the Kingdom.

More specifically, in our own work we have developed beautiful transit projects worldwide. We elevate the comfort and experience of transit ridership, bus systems and pedestrian pathways. Since 2004 we have worked in Riyadh for the Ariyadh Development Authority to develop the design for a massive transit infrastructure project that has grown to six underground lines, some 68 stations, a Bus Rapid Transit System (BRT), and shelters and signage for a bus system featuring thousands of stops serving all of the city's seven million residents. Currently under construction, the system will be the largest new transit system in the world, constructed for about $USD 30 billion.

Other work illustrated in this chapter includes overviews of our work designing libraries, community centers, daycare facilities and several types of affordable housing located on redevelopment sites in core areas of our cities — all building types that we feel have significant social purpose.

Advertisement, Turners Asbestos Cement Co. Ltd.; ca. 1940

We Are What We Specify

As architects, our social responsibilities extend into the technical aspects of our work. We have an obligation to incorporate safe, appropriate, environmentally friendly materials and technologies into our designs. Just consider how asbestos was widely promoted in North America as the "penicillin of the construction industry" until its harmful health effects were finally discovered and the U.S. Environmental Protection Agency (EPA) began to ban its use in the 1970s.[2] As a naturally occurring heat- and fire-resistant substance, asbestos offered the industry an inexpensive, seemingly safe, problem-solving building material. But it took decades for those who saw it for what it was to get their voices heard. Now, scattered throughout the world, we have thousands of buildings that are hazardous to occupy and even more hazardous to alter or tear down. What's more, the individuals who worked so hard to mine and process asbestos are dealing with terrifying health-related ramifications all these years later.

Architects are, in a very real sense, custodians of public health. It is no longer acceptable for us to blithely follow what our own industry establishes as standard, or what government agencies mandate as minimum levels of compliance (effectively, the least we can do without breaking the law) often years

2. http://www2.epa.gov/asbestos/us-federal-bans-asbestos

The beauty of Victorian-era train stations reflects the grandeur of rail travel during the time when these sacred spaces were designed and built. Even today, a visitor to Grand Central Station embarks on an emotional journey that begins well before boarding a train, all because its design fills one with an undeniable sense of excitement and wonder. Well-designed public spaces of any kind should achieve the same goal of connecting people and place, and seize opportunities to thrill and inspire.

after health effects become well-known. Just as we strive for beauty in our work, we must also strive to enhance our knowledge of the technical performance of what we specify. It is our responsibility to understand the sources, manufacturing processes, related health impacts and performance of all materials and technologies we put in place in and around our projects. We need to acknowledge the durability of materials as well as the potential long-term environmental impacts they will have on the waste stream.

At Perkins+Will, we have invested deeply in our commitment to safe materials and technologies. We work closely with clients and the manufacturing industry to specify products that we feel confident will protect the occupants of the buildings we design as well as the planet itself. Through our Sustainable Design Initiative (SDI), the firm has authored numerous public pieces that address the need for total industry-wide material transparency. We openly publish our Precautionary List (www.transparency.perkinswill.com) to coax the industry to consider these responsibilities and move forward. We are learning to demand Healthy Product Declarations (HPDs) of the manufacturers and suppliers of products in our projects. The goal is an audacious one, to be sure, but we want to demonstrate leadership in what is possible, to change the industry and ensure our survival!

Emotional and Social Content

Architecture never exists in a social vacuum. It has the power to define tyranny or terror; peace or hope. It can define and symbolize the rule of society, law and justice. It can even evoke society's fundamental rights of freedom and equality. These social and political attributes make architecture the most powerful of all the arts, as built structures can elicit emotion over the course of generations.

The social content of architecture, which is multidimensional and found at all scales, defines how it is inhabited and whom it houses. At the micro scale, we must cater to people's rights to universal accessibility. At the global scale, our responsibilities in the public realm reach as far as leaving a visual impact that can be seen from space. Either way, we must create a built environment that will leave a positive mark on history.

Adolf Hitler led rallies from the steps of the stark and imposing Zeppelinhaupttribune in Nuremburg precisely because it offered a backdrop of daunting, stony strength. At the other end of the spectrum, Toronto City Hall's welcoming design draws people in, as if to provide shelter for civil, productive public discourse. The United Nations uses its built campus to make noble statements about international diplomacy. These structures prove that architecture can produce more than buildings; architecture can nurture and present social values. As architects, we are entrusted to deliver a built environment worthy of those values.

Listen and Learn

There was a time when the architectural process was shaped by patron owners – corporations or other distant entities that were often far removed from the buildings themselves. Now, the wisdom of involving the occupants themselves in the design process is becoming exceedingly common. By giving individuals and communities a say in how the structures they inhabit will take shape, we infuse more meaning and life into the built environment.

The general public has gained increasing say as a stakeholder in this public art form we call architecture. At the beginning of my career, architects typically answered almost exclusively to owners. Today, we recognize that a broader

United Nations Secretariat Building, Wallace K. Harrison, Gaston Brunfaut, Julio Vilamajó, Le Corbusier, Nikolai D. Bassov, Oscar Niemeyer, Sir Howard Robertson, Ssu-Ch'eng Liang, Studio Ernest Cormier, Sven Markelius, Taylor, Soilleux & Overend; New York, NY, 1952.

audience has a say in how and what we build. The people who will live in, work in, pass by and reside near our designs have a right to weigh in. Architects have an obligation to listen to the public their work will serve. Public participation in the process is part of the new architectural order.

Even children can have a say, particularly in the creation of buildings designed to serve them directly. When we were asked to design the new Samuel Brighouse Elementary School in Richmond, BC, we got the students involved from the early stages. We hosted a charrette where we invited fourth to sixth graders to draw out their visions for their new school, making sure that these future occupants knew that their ideas would be heard and incorporated. They were, in all their glory, and they described a school bathed in sunshine and full of nature. The result is a school of beautiful, functional spaces where students are engaged and inspired in ubiquitous daylighting, and nature is visible and connected to every space.

We have had similar opportunities to incorporate students' input on many higher education projects as well. At the Nicola Valley Institute of Technology, a public post-secondary institute for First Nations in Merritt, BC, we had the distinct honor of bringing tribal elders to the site so they could offer their insights into the project's design. As we toured the grounds with these distinguished guests, they spoke of the historical occupation of the site (spanning several thousand years) and offered advice on the building's location and orientation for the front entry. We respected the advice. Imagine, for example when you are designing your next university building, involving several generations in urban

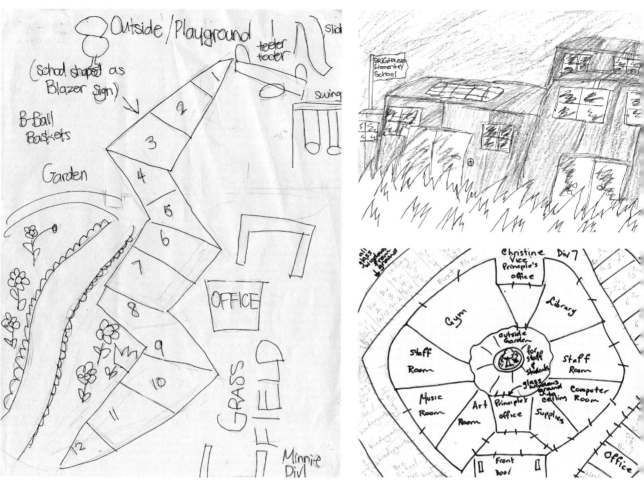

Sketches by Samuel Brighouse Elementary School students; 2009

discourse and having grandparents lend their expertise and perspective on the design of more public institutions. What better way to weave cultural threads into the fabric of education and our communities; to celebrate connections among land, place, history and people? Listening to the wisdom of the generations is one way architects can use their designs to link the past with the future.

Once we accept that architecture carries with it a serious social obligation, then we have no choice but to hold every practitioner accountable for his or her work in the field. Accepting our social responsibility is the same thing as committing to total transparency about our current and future intentions in the public realm. Choosing architecture as your profession means accepting those terms. We and the communities where we work are defined by what we build. We make contributions with our designs. We must ensure that those contributions serve the greater good. Schools over jails; libraries over casinos; sustainable materials over toxins. The choices, I believe, are clear.

Catalysts for Change

Architects are defined by what we design and build. Each of us has an opportunity to demonstrate a commitment to a sustainable future. Collectively, it is up to us to lead our industry and our communities on the path that will take us there.

Perkins+Will is committed to the Public Architecture's 1% Pro Bono Design Program, (http://www.publicarchitecture.org). We donate one percent of our gross revenues to pro bono work for the public good in our communities. We call

Samuel Brighouse Elementary School; Richmond, BC; 2011

Nicola Valley Institute of Technology; Merritt, BC; 2004

this effort, internally, our Social Responsibility Initiative (SRI). It is wildly popular among staff, who compete to work on these projects, and end up donating even more of their personal time to the projects, adding to the social contribution, and teaching them about other life views in the process.

I have often said that if every architectural professional in Canada contributed just one percent of his or her time in pro bono service, it would add up to approximately 160,000 hours annually – the equivalent of an 80-person firm working full time for the public good. The American figure would easily be ten times that, comprising one of the largest firms in the nation! Imagine the good we could do if every architect in North America made such a commitment.

Across the firm, we believe strongly that architects should engage in the community and reach out from their traditional roles by sitting in volunteer roles on boards and involving themselves in organizations in our communities. They promote sustainability and design as strong aspects of those organizations, but they also make a social contribution to the communities they engage. In this role, I have served on dozens of boards, including four years on the board of BC Hydro (as the first architect ever to sit on their board) where I had an influence on expanding and strengthening their Power Smart initiative through the reduction of energy consumption in buildings. All leadership levels of Perkins+Will are encouraged to engage in community organizations.

As individuals, we have a responsibility to look out for one another, for society, and for the environment. As architects, that responsibility spills into and emanates from our work. We can make a monumental difference to society and the people we affect with our work.

Nicola Valley Institute of Technology, elders; Merritt, BC; 2004

Tenderloin Museum
San Francisco, CA

Centrally located in downtown San Francisco, the Tenderloin neighborhood has a rich cultural history as a vibrant hub of activity for jazz, rock 'n' roll, theater, and activism. With 409 buildings listed in the National Register of Historic Places, the neighborhood's stunning architecture includes the world's largest collection of historic SROs (single room occupancy hotels). The Tenderloin has had its share of problems since the 1970s but is now on the rebound.

The new Uptown Tenderloin Museum aims to celebrate the area's history and strengthen pride of place for Tenderloin residents. The museum will be located in the ground floor and basement of the historic Cadillac Hotel, which now functions as an SRO. Perkins+Will's design for the museum showcases the historic architectural features of the hotel and includes state-of-the-art, interactive exhibitions designed by West Office Exhibition Design. The revitalized exterior will increase transparency to invite passersby into the museum. Once inside, a bright red sculptural window piece will become a wayfinding device, attracting patrons to the various museum functions. Perkins+Will's renderings and models were central to the project's fundraising efforts.

The list of current SRI projects in the firm follows, demonstrating the vast range and impact of this program.

- 41 East Hastings, Affordable Housing, Vancouver, BC
- 1220 Homer Street, Public Parklet, Vancouver, BC
- Bailey-Boushay House, Kitchen Remodel, Seattle, WA
- Arden Garden Public Marketplace, Master Plan for Affordable Farmer's Market, Sacramento, CA
- Atlanta Birth Center, New Building Programming and Conceptual Design, Atlanta, GA
- Benjamin Banneker Memorial, Site and Pedestrian Experience Enhancement Analysis, Washington, DC
- The Center for Victims of Torture, New Administrative Headquarters Design, Minneapolis, MN
- Clearbrook Commons, Community Room, Rolling Meadows, IL
- Clinton Commons, Affordable Housing, Oakland, CA
- College Summit, Interior Improvements, Washington, DC
- Community Coalition for Haiti (CCH), Mont Fleur School and Community Center, Mont Fleur, Haiti
- Community of Hope, Education Center, Washington, DC
- ENfold, Temporary Installation, Evans Way Park, Boston, MA
- Fraser, Revitalization and Renovations, Minneapolis, MN
- Ghana Musical Village, Conceptual Design of Music Studio and Central Pavilion, Ada, Ghana
- GiGi's Playhouse, Activity Center and Prototype Design, Hoffman Estates, Chicago, IL
- Girls Prep Lower East Side Middle School, Mary Mitchell Library, Redesign, New York, NY
- Gordon Neighborhood House, Revitalization, Vancouver, BC
- Jerusalem House, New Building Programming and Conceptual Design, Atlanta, GA
- Jones Street Neighborhood Nexus, Urban Study of Public Plaza and Community Art Day, San Francisco, CA
- La Bajada, Vision Plan for West Dallas, Dallas, TX
- Lifecycle Building Center, Adaptive Reuse, Atlanta, GA
- Lincoln Heights Jail Reinvention, River Revitalization Corporation (RRC), Los Angeles, CA
- Literacy Partners, Interior Workplace Upgrade, New York, NY
- Miami Children's Hospital, Radio Lollipop Control Room, Miami, FL
- The Mill City Renaissance, Neighborhood Development Planning, Dallas, TX
- The Nature Conservancy, Regional Office Design, Atlanta, GA
- New York City Department of Education, Hurricane Sandy – Damage Assessments, New York, NY
- Oak Park & River Forest Day Nursery, Revitalization, Oak Park, IL
- Olympia Hotel + Weldon Hotel Concept Designs, Affordable Housing, Skid Row Housing Trust, Los Angeles, CA
- Paws in the Panhandle, Pet Shelter Design, Lancaster County, PA
- People United Foundation, New Building Conceptual Design, Atlanta, GA
- Ponce De Leon Center, Building Renovation, Atlanta, GA
- Project HOOD, Community Center, Chicago, IL
- Rapidly Deployable Health Clinic (RDoC), Architecture + The City Festival, Resilient SF Competition Entry, San Francisco, CA
- Rogers Road Community Center, New Community Center Design, Chapel Hill, NC
- Sarah's Circle, Adaptive Reuse, Chicago, IL
- SEVA Food Bank, Sikhs Serving Canada, Food Bank and Community Hub, Mississauga, ON
- Sow Much Good Urban Farm, Farmstand, Office Space/Demonstration Kitchen, Chicken Coop/Storage Shed, Charlotte, NC
- Studio 89 Centre, Resource Centre Design, Mississauga, ON
- Tenderloin Museum, Design for Community Museum, San Francisco, CA
- The Work Place DC, Programming Study for Headquarters, Washington, DC
- Youthlink, Threads and Breads Renovation Project, Minneapolis, MN
- Woman's Global Education Project, Concept Master Plan, Kenya

More information on Perkins+Will's SRI program is available online: http://perkinswill.com/purpose/social-purpose

Tenderloin Museum; San Francisco, CA

Mount Pleasant Centre

Vancouver, BC

This unique facility has become the catalyst for urban renewal at the center of Vancouver's Mount Pleasant neighborhood. Its central location, multitude of uses, and proximity to transportation make it an ideal community facility accessible for all individuals. The 136,000 square foot (12,591 SM) facility houses a community center, fitness facilities, library, childcare center, retail, and parking in addition to 98 residential units.

Mount Pleasant Centre; Vancouver, BC; 2009

New Edge Innovations

Through building form and density, and multiple mixed-use functions linked closely to the community, this project demonstrates how expansive mixed-use and high density can be.

The building uses solar shading and daylight controls to reduce solar heat gain while maximizing natural daylighting. Integrated underground "earth tube" air intakes combined with a geoexchange system provide natural heating and cooling for the building and reduces its energy consumption by 57 percent compared to a similar building built to the Canadian Model National Energy Code.

Green roofs minimize water runoff while mitigating the urban heat island effect. Portions of the green roof are adjacent to the childcare center where a playground allows for learning and physical activity. The landscape is irrigated with water that is captured on-site and stored in a purpose-built cistern. To ensure the best use of materials the building underwent a Life Cycle Assessment to inform the design and selection of construction materials. An integrated design process involving the entire project team, users, and community groups helped the design team arrive at unique strategies to take the project beyond its original LEED Silver mandate to LEED Gold.

Beyond full design services, Perkins+Will was asked by the City's Director of Planning to conduct an urban design review of the surrounding Mount Pleasant district. Within the review, the firm was asked to provide recommendations for zoning enhancements, street edges, and building massing, height, and occupancy, many of which have been implemented into current zoning for the area.

PROJECT Mount Pleasant Centre
LOCATION Vancouver, BC
CLIENT City of Vancouver Corporate Services, Vancouver Park Board, Vancouver Public Library, City of Vancouver Social Planning Department
DESIGN 2003-2004
CONSTRUCTION 2004-2009
SIZE 135,528 sf / 12,591 sm
DESIGN TEAM Perkins+Will (formerly Busby + Associates Architects):
K. Abraham, R. Bens, J. Belisle, S. Brent, P. Busby, J. Doble, D. Dove, S. Mani, T. Maunu, G. Miu, D. Pepin, K. Robertson, S. Schou
STRUCTURAL ENGINEER CY Loh and Associates
MECHANICAL ENGINEER Keen Engineering
ELECTRICAL ENGINEER Schenke Bawol Engineers
CODE CONSULTANT Gage Babcock
TRAFFIC CONSULTANT Hamilton Associates
COST CONSULTANT Jim Bush & Associates
ENVELOPE CONSULTANT BC Building Science

LANDSCAPE ARCHITECT Durante Kreuk
GEOTECHNICAL ENGINEER Trow Associates, Inc.
ENVIRONMENTAL CONSULTANT Keystone Environmental, Ltd.
ACOUSTICAL CONSULTANT Brown Strachan Associates
COMMISSIONING AUTHORITY KD Engineering Co.
PHOTOGRAPHER Martin Tessler
AWARDS RECEIVED:
- Precast Concrete Architectural Recognition Firm Award Canadian Precast/Pre-stressed Concrete Institute, 2012
- Georgia Straight Best of Vancouver Awards, Best Community Centre, Second Place, 2010
- Sustainability Ratings LEED Gold
- Reference to Publications
- Jim Taggart, "Mount Pleasant Centre," SABMag, December 2010, 20-27.
- Claudia Kwan, "Centre directs community to its centre," Vancouver Sun, November 7, 2009.
- Cheryl Mah, "Serving a community," Design Quarterly, Summer 2009, 12-13.

Pioneer Pedestrian Bridge

Surrey, BC

An important part of the City of Surrey's Greenways Program, the Pioneer Pedestrian Bridge helps to create healthy communities by promoting physical activity and alternatives to vehicular transportation. Crossing Highway 99 in South Surrey, the Bridge connects neighborhoods on either side, eliminating a key missing link in the Pioneer Greenway, a multi-use pathway that will eventually connect Surrey to the Peace Arch border crossing. The Bridge also connects Grandview Heights to the Semiahmoo Trails and to a planned seawall walk along the shores of the Semiahmoo Peninsula.

Pioneer Pedestrian Bridge; Surrey, BC; 2011

The three-meter-wide and 73-meter-long steel arch pedestrian bridge utilizes the gentle slopes of the site's natural topography. It consists of a single-span steel-arch bridge with concrete foundations. The span was prefabricated to allow for installation in one night, reducing highway closure requirements to the absolute minimum.

New Edge Innovations

The Pioneer overpass is an important part of the City of Surrey's Greenways Program, which is working to create healthy communities by promoting physical activity and alternatives to vehicular transportation, which helps reduce greenhouse gas emissions.

Materials were selected for off-site prefabrication, to reduce highway closure to 10 hours on one night.

Creating a highly visible gateway for South Surrey, the bridge is enhanced through public art; colorful LED lighting illuminates the bridge at night, providing both visual delight and increased pedestrian safety. Lighting content is updated to suit seasonal changes and special occasions. Beyond its healthy transportation role, the Pioneer Pedestrian Bridge serves as a modern yet playful public art feature within the community.

PROJECT Pioneer Pedestrian Bridge
LOCATION Surrey, BC
CLIENT City of Surrey
DESIGN 2009-2010
CONSTRUCTION 2010-2011
DESIGN TEAM
Perkins+Will: P. Busby, R. Bremer, C. Phillips,
J. Huffman, A. Slawinski
PROJECT ENGINEER Associated Engineering
GEOTECHNICAL ENGINEER Thurber Engineering, Ltd.
LANDSCAPE ARCHITECT space2place
ARTISTIC LIGHTING EOS Light Media
PHOTOGRAPHER Perkins+Will
URLS https://www.youtube.com/
watch?v=ntVCwLgbEyY#t=107
https://www.youtube.com/watch?v=mG7lF55kGw8

St. Mary's Hospital
Sechelt, BC

Located on British Columbia's Sunshine Coast, St. Mary's Hospital serves the local Sechelt Indian Band as one of its primary patient groups. When faced with functional shortages at St. Mary's Hospital, Vancouver Coastal Health (VCH) turned to Perkins+Will for their trusted healthcare design expertise. In association with Farrow Partnership Architects, we worked in close collaboration with VCH to provide design solutions to accommodate the expanded needs of St. Mary's emergency, diagnostic imaging, ambulatory, and special care services. New areas were also designed to provide additional in-patient accommodation.

St. Mary's Hospital; Sechelt, BC; 2013

New Edge Innovations

Two new floors of single occupancy and same-handed patient rooms minimize the spread of infections and bacteria that often occur in shared inpatient rooms. Through additional consultation with hospital staff, parallel and separate circulation areas were designed to enhance privacy and isolate sensitive movements. The LEAN principles for healthcare were employed throughout the planning of the new addition.

Through the extensive input of the Native Band, the design became based on a traditional native bent wood box with a focus on nature. On-site respite gardens, a light-filled lobby, and large patient room windows maximize natural daylight and views and emphasize the Band's belief that a connection to nature is essential to healing. The facility contains a prayer room and accommodation for Elders.

Biophilic design features include views to nature in almost all internal working and recovery spaces. All staff workstations are daylit and have views outside. All patient rooms are naturally ventilated through operable glazing.

Beyond providing additional space and upgrades, the expansion and renovation of St. Mary's Hospital presented unique opportunities to push the envelope of sustainable healthcare design. St. Mary's Hospital, achieved LEED certification at the Gold level and was designed with the goal of becoming North America's first carbon-neutral hospital. In addition to a high-performance building envelope, the hospital includes a complex geo-exchange system which provides near net zero carbon heating and cooling for the building. Using the new mechanical system to replace aging infrastructure in the existing building significantly reduces the full facility's carbon footprint, bring about the net zero carbon designation.

LOCATION Sechelt, BC
CLIENT Vancouver Coastal Health
DESIGN 2008- 2010
CONSTRUCTION 2010- 2012
SIZE New addition 51,667 sf / 4,800 sm RENOVATED SPACE 16,146 sf / 1,500 sm
DESIGN TEAM Perkins+Will:
S. Bergen, P. Busby, B. Greig, E. Latreille, R. Maas, T. McAuley, K. Meissener, G. Miu
Joint Venture Architect Farrow Partnership
STRUCTURAL ENGINEER Fast + Epp
MECHANICAL ENGINEER Integral Group (formerly Cobalt Engineering)
ELECTRICAL / TECHNOLOGY Acumen Consulting Engineers
LANDSCAPE ENGINEER Sharp & Diamond
CIVIL ENGINEER Stantec
CODE CONSULTANT CFT Engineering
QUANTITY SURVEYOR Altus Group
AWARDS RECEIVED
- The Design & Health International Academy Awards, Award for Sustainable Design, 2014
- The Design & Health International Academy Awards, Award for Use of Art in the Patient Environment, 2014
- Sustainability Ratings LEED Gold
- Reference to Publications
- Kristen Avis, "Canada's Greenest Hospital," Design Build Source AU, May 16, 2013, online.
- Frances Bula, "Hospital uses power of architecture to promote healing," Globe and Mail, May 6, 2012, p. B10.
- "Island Hospital," Journal of Commerce, May 26, 2010.

Smart Development
Vancouver, BC

Conceived as a contemporary interpretation of the surrounding heritage buildings, Smart combines four units of street-level retail with seven stories of residential suites. Leading the revitalization of the eastern edge of Vancouver's Gastown, the project provides a contextually sensitive and an economically, socially, and environmentally responsible solution to a demanding site and neighborhood.

Water Efficient Landscaping

Shared Courtyards and Private Patios
Exterior Circulation
High Recycled Content Concrete
Recycling
Bicycle Storage
Fitness Room
Meeting Room
Natural Cross Ventilation
Low VOC Interior Finishes
Residential Lobby
Low Flow Plumbing Fixtures
Commercial Retail Units at Grade

Smart Development; Vancouver, BC; 2009

Prolonged aggressive growth in the Lower Mainland's housing market has made home ownership inaccessible to most residents. By capitalizing on low land costs, maximizing density, and controlling construction costs, Perkins+Will was able to bring the Smart Development to market at substantially lower selling prices than comparable Vancouver real estate at the time of listing.

New Edge Innovations
Arranged in a U-shape around a south-facing green courtyard, the building plan is designed to maximize livability and efficiency. Single-loaded exterior corridors allow for natural cross-ventilation and provide views of Gastown, the north shore, the industrial port, the downtown core and False Creek. Shared and private green spaces are provided on three different levels to create a variety of opportunities for

urban respite, while a landscaped lightwell separates the building from its neighbor to the west. Smart's public facing façade along Powell Street is divided into four textured masses of varied heights, providing seamless integration into the surrounding urban fabric.

Efficiency drives the functionality and energy consumption of each of Smart's 90 units. Linear kitchens open up to combined living and dining areas while translucent glass sliding partitions permit light to penetrate bedrooms when closed. Low-flow plumbing fixtures and energy efficient lighting further reduce environmental impact.

PROJECT Smart Development
LOCATION Vancouver, BC
CLIENT Concord Pacific
DESIGN 2005-2006
CONSTRUCTION 2007-2009
SIZE 124,000 sf / 11,520 sm

DESIGN TEAM
Perkins+Will: P. Busby, R. Drew, J. Gravenstein, J. Huffman, D. Kitazaki, H. Lai, T. Miller, A. Minard, K. Robertson, J. Skinner
STRUCTURAL ENGINEER Jones Kwong Kishi
MECHANICAL ENGINEER Yoneda & Associates
ELECTRICAL ENGINEER Nemetz S/A & Associates, Ltd.
LANDSCAPE ARCHITECT PWL Partnership
CONTRACTOR JRS Engineering
INTERIOR DESIGNER Perkins+Will
CODE CONSULTANT B.R. Thorson Consulting, Ltd.
ENVELOPE CONSULTANT JRS Engineering

Smart Development; Vancouver, BC; 2009

Smart Development, Courtyard; Vancouver, BC; 2009

2

VANCOUVER
SEATTLE
MINNEAPOLIS
OTTAWA
TORONTO
DUNDAS
BOSTON
CHICAGO
NEW YORK
PHILADELPHIA
WASHINGTON, DC
SAN FRANCISCO
RTP
CHARLOTTE
LOS ANGELES
ATLANTA
DALLAS
HOUSTON
ORLANDO
HONOLULU
MIAMI

SAO PAULO

Corporate Responsibility

SHANGHAI

DUBAI

A global project portfolio

The Business of Doing the Right Thing

Perkins+Will Sustainable Design Initiative Strategic Plan;
2007-2010

Perkins+Will Sustainable Design Initiative Strategic Plan;
2010-2015

Perkins+Will Transparency Website;
http://transparency.perkinswill.com/

Companies of every size, across all market segments and geographic regions, representing each point along the profitability spectrum have something very important in common; a growing sense of corporate social responsibility. With increasing frequency, we are seeing businesses looking outward – beyond their own interests and their own bottom lines – to do what is right by their employees, their customers, their communities and the environment.

In the context of architecture, accepting corporate social responsibility is a matter of focusing on what we can do within our firms to change our behavior, our products, and our influence with clients so that, collectively, we create an all-around healthier industry. In other words, it means considering the potential ecological and societal effects our work may have, and how we conduct our business.

At Perkins+Will, we are redefining the field by folding our corporate responsibility into every aspect of what we do. From business development to employee relations to design output, it is factored into each of our strategies. It helps us align our priorities while demonstrating to our internal and external audiences that we practice what we preach. We do not simply encourage our clients to embrace sustainable design; we live and work according to high environmental standards. We believe that all of us – senior principals, mid-level associates, junior staff, as well as the individuals and organizations we serve – are participants in a business with a socially and environmentally sustainable future. We have embedded sustainable design and social responsibility in the core values of the firm and in our vision of what we do. Balancing these two values with profitability, we measure the success of our business according to the "triple bottom line."

In the following pages, we will look at some of the things Perkins+Will has done to honor our responsibilities as an environmentally aware corporate citizen. In addition, the projects summarized in this chapter offer glimpses into three of our firm's own offices – in Vancouver, Atlanta and San Francisco – because we want our workplaces to speak of our values and we want our clients to find themselves there too. We cannot in good conscience exhort our clients to do things we would not do for ourselves.

Perkins+Will Sustainable Design Initiative

In 2004, under my leadership, Perkins+Will established the Sustainable Design Initiative (SDI), initially envisioned as a five-year plan to green the firm and its output. The SDI has been so powerful that it has been modified and renewed several times since its introduction and we are now well into our third plan. The SDI is structured around a firmwide leadership group and green team leaders (GTLs) in every office who act as advocates and a network for information dissemination. We also have researchers and resource experts for a number of our areas of practice. Green team leaders are our foot soldiers in this drive, so I would like to call out our 2014 team and thank the many dozens of others who have contributed to making Perkins+Will the industry leader in sustainable design:

Co-Chairs: Tony Layne, Paula McEvoy
Atlanta: Seth Crawford, Joe Jamgochian, Nadia Kulczycky
Boston: Yanel de Angel, Anthony Paprocki, Deborah Rivers
Chicago: Amina Halstern, Gokul Natarajan, Sarah Wood
Dallas: Mary Dickinson, Julie Frazier, Tony Schmitz
Dundas: Lauren Clack
Houston: LeaAnne Leatherwood, Mollie Silver
Los Angeles: Eric Brossy de Dios, Benjamin Welle
Miami: Alejandro Branger
Minneapolis: Russell Philstrom, Doug Pierce
New York: Breeze Glazer
North Carolina: Patric le Beau, Dennis Freeland, Rachel Myers
San Francisco: Suzanne Drake, Drake Hawthorne, Krista Raines, Jeff Till
Sao Paulo: Douglas Koji Enoki
Seattle: Cameron Hall, Devin Kleiner, Megan Magraw
Toronto: Gregory Beck Rubin, Devon Miller
Vancouver: Robert Drew, Rebecca Holt, Max Richter, Kathy Wardle,
Washington DC: David Cordell, Jon Penndorf, Ken Wilson

One of the program's original goals was to explore how well we were educating our own people with regard to state-of-the-art green technologies, so we set out to get all professional staff to LEED® Accredited Professional (AP) status, making training and webinars available to our employees in all offices. As of this writing, we have approximately 1000 LEED APs among our ranks, most of whom now support advanced credentials maintenance, and we have four LEED Fellows. Since 2004, we have made it an employment requirement that all professional staff members must be LEED APs (now with specialties) within six months of joining the firm.

As new techniques and data are introduced to the field, we set new goals for the firm by refashioning the SDI. We continue to add energy modelers, researchers and subject matter experts to our teams as local and firmwide resources. As this initiative has evolved, it has helped position us as an industry leader in sustainable design. Perkins+Will has been recognized as the number one sustainable design firm by *Architect* magazine three of the last six years, and very high on the list in all other years. Perkins+Will is the inaugural winner of the "Best Architecture Firm - Large" award as part of U.S. Green Building Council's (USGBC) Best in Building Awards. The Best of Building Awards celebrates the year's best products, projects, organizations and individuals making an impact in green building.

We know that we must continue to realign our internal strategies toward fresh challenges in sustainable design and education if we want to maintain that leadership role. In the closing chapter, I will outline details of our thoughts about where we will go in the future. To this end, we have recently refocused our efforts around five "task forces":

- Transparency and Material Health
- Climate Adaptation and Resiliency
- High-Performance, Net Zero, and Regenerative Design
- Sustainable Communities
- Benchmarking and Data Collection

Each task force is conducting research, gathering data, developing a "center of excellence" firmwide program of charrettes, then disseminating and educating

TOTAL POTABLE WATER USE

Many offices do not have individual access to water consumption and the values reported used are typically a pro-rated amount against the entire buildings' use.

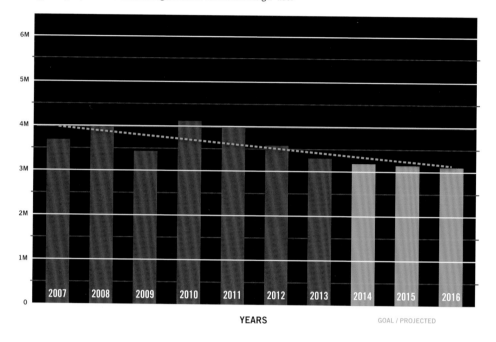

TREND LINE

GOAL

20%

reduction over 10 years based on trendline

ENERGY USE

Includes energy and heat usage. Note many offices do not control heat and the usage is estimated by area and included in their annual rent which is why there is a slight uptick.

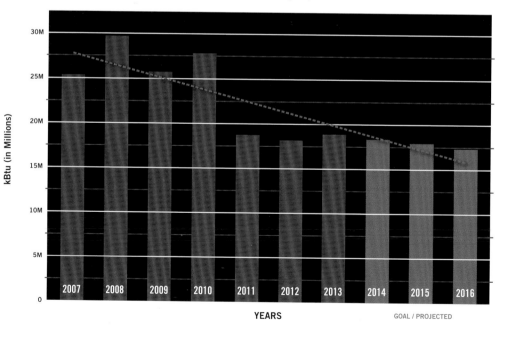

TREND LINE

GOAL

40%

reduction over 10 years based on trendline

colleagues throughout the company. We are maintaining our leadership in LEED and other design and compliance measures, but we are also turning ourselves into a research and information sharing organization.

The approach is fluid and transformational. As our SDI reshapes and evolves over the coming years, there is no question that it has been among the firm's most important internal innovations. It gets people excited; it generates enthusiasm; it engages the younger members of the organization. Based on those measures alone, we consider it overwhelmingly successful.

Perkins+Will Operations

In addition to greening our employee roster, the SDI mapped out operational strategies that would help us reduce our energy and water consumption in Perkins+Will offices, basically modifying our behavior, our habits, and our built environment at lease renewal points to achieve the same sustainable goals we are designing into our clients' projects. We have to walk the talk. We also examined waste streams in our operations and adjusted internal policies and procedures. For example, we looked carefully at procurement, asking: What goods do we purchase? Are they recyclable? Are they manufactured sustainably? How far do they travel to reach us? We examined our own patterns of waste production, seeking ways to cut down on how much we send to the landfill each week. Firmwide targets were set, and individual offices planned implementation strategies that worked for them. We have been benchmarking our own offices' performance and improving results.

The charts above show that our energy and water from operations are trending down, even despite the dip caused by the 2008 recession, and despite growth in our practices through acquisitions and mergers. The effort to improve our performance is ongoing. In 2004 we had no LEED-certified offices; today we have eight offices that are LEED Gold and five that are LEED Platinum. Every lease renewal is an opportunity to walk the walk.

Keeping Our Eyes On 2030

More recently, we have focused on the carbon footprint of our firm, as all businesses must do. Below is a chart of recently reported carbon impacts of the firm's operations and travel. As you can see, despite the ongoing growth of the firm and our increasingly international travel commitments, our carbon footprint is trending steadily down. We consider our firm carbon-neutral because, since 2007, we have purchased carbon offsets for the carbon we cause from our travel and operations. Perkins+Will is a net zero carbon emissions company, and proud of that achievement.

In 2007, our board formally committed to the 2030 Challenge, Ed Mazria's masterpiece (see sidebar). We were the first large-scale architecture firm to do so. We apply the concepts to our firm's operations and increasingly to everything we design. The 2030 Challenge also helps chart our progress, as it provides specific carbon neutrality targets for which we and all of our architectural colleagues can aim. We now look at all Perkins+Will projects (including the design and occupancy of our own offices) through the prism of the 2030 Challenge lens. We ask ourselves if we are adhering to 2030 guidelines and whether we are designing buildings that will meet short- and long-term 2030 goals for a carbon-neutral built environment.

The numbers show that in the first year of the 2030 program, approximately 36 percent of Perkins+Will's projects were successful based on Challenge

The 2030 Challenge

The 2030 Challenge was issued by Architecture 2030, a non-profit, non-partisan organization established in 2010 by architect Edward Mazria. It asks the global architecture and building community to adopt the following targets:

All new buildings, developments and major renovations shall be designed to meet a fossil fuel, GHG-emitting, energy consumption performance standard of 60 percent below the regional (or country) average/median for that building type.

At a minimum, an equal amount of existing building area shall be renovated annually to meet a fossil fuel, GHG-emitting, energy consumption performance standard of 60 percent of the regional (or country) average/median for that building type.

The fossil fuel reduction standard for all new buildings and major renovations shall be increased to:

- 70% in 2015
- 80% in 2020
- 90% in 2025
- Carbon-neutral in 2030 (using no fossil fuel GHG-emitting energy to operate)*

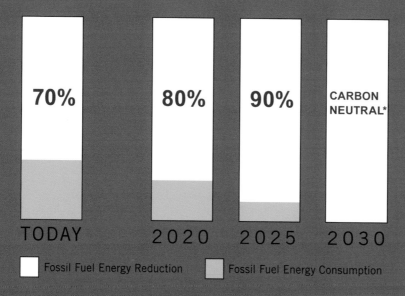

The 2030 Challenge

* http://architecture2030.org

TOTAL CARBON FOOTPRINT
Includes airline travel

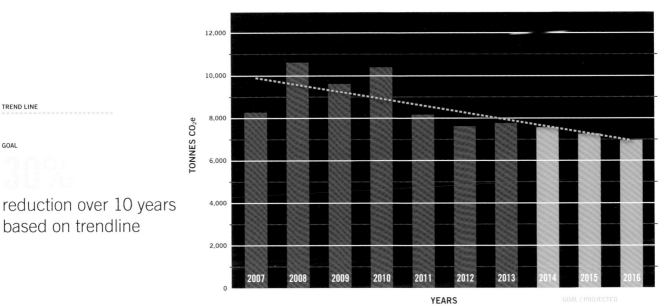

TREND LINE

GOAL

30%

reduction over 10 years
based on trendline

criteria. The following year, we were disappointed to learn that our success rate dropped to 18 percent. However, upon further reflection, we were not surprised that the numbers came down, as the adjusted level was actually much more realistic, reflecting improved design team knowledge of the measures necessary to meet the Challenge. We continue to gain knowledge about strategies to reach carbon neutrality and how to calculate and measure project performance.

It is a long-term goal, but we are confident that our volume of work will help us build a useable database that will allow us to reach the 2030 target net zero carbon goal. Indeed, in 2013, two completed projects (VanDusen and CIRS) met the 2030 Challenge ultimate goal of zero carbon. Dockside Green and the design for Blatchford Redevelopment in Edmonton also met the goal earlier. Indeed, if one considers the millions of square feet of space Perkins+Will designs across the globe annually, the success rate is a sizeable improvement in the built environment's carbon impact. It gives us solid, measureable evidence of progress. What we are doing is working to effect real and lasting change.

The 2030 Challenge

The 2030 Challenge was issued by Architecture 2030, a non-profit, non-partisan organization established in 2010 by architect Edward Mazria. It asks the global architecture and building community to adopt the following targets:
- All new buildings, developments and major renovations shall be designed to meet a fossil fuel, GHG-emitting, energy consumption performance standard of 60 percent below the regional (or country) average/median for that building type.
- At a minimum, an equal amount of existing building area shall be renovated annually to meet a fossil fuel, GHG-emitting, energy consumption performance standard of 60 percent of the regional (or country) average/median for that building type.

Perkins+Will Research Journal

- The fossil fuel reduction standard for all new buildings and major renovations shall be increased to:
  - 70% in 2015
  - 80% in 2020
  - 90% in 2025
  - Carbon-neutral in 2030 (using no fossil fuel GHG-emitting energy to operate)[1]

The Quantifiable Value Of Research

As the industry leader in many areas, we rely heavily on research, and year after year Perkins+Will devotes more of our internal resources to this important function. As of this writing, we have approximately 15 full-time researchers across the firm. Some focus their efforts on performance-based technologies, some on analytics for daylighting or energy performance, some on computational design tools, and others on charting the future of building design within different market sectors. Together, these professionals amass a body of information that proves invaluable to our designers. So valuable, in fact, that we produce a semi-annual research publication (Perkins+Will Research Journal) that we make available to internal and external audiences. All our published journals can be found on our website for public enjoyment at http://perkinswill.com/purpose/innovation.

Most recently, we have established AREA Research, a non-profit arm's length research entity that harnesses the research investments of Perkins+Will and other firms as a way of sharing knowledge about the built environment. We have done this to broaden the reach of research we initiate, as well as to make the publications and findings more accessible to the profession. AREA Research is committed to free public dissemination of all its findings. More details about AREA can be found at www.arearesearch.org.

It Is All Material

Transparency is key to our corporate culture at Perkins+Will. And key to our commitment to transparency is our practice of offering clients green and healthy alternatives to give them the opportunity to make informed decisions when it comes to construction supplies and materials.

Whether we are specifying a private residence, a neighborhood school, or a 400-bed teaching hospital, we are committed to avoiding the use of contaminants and toxins in our projects. We formalized this commitment to material health with the introduction of our Precautionary List in 2009. What began as a published list of items that had already been proven to have negative environmental and/or human health effects has gradually become a cornerstone of our practice. The Precautionary List is now available as a free download for any individual or professional – including our competitors – interested in avoiding toxins in the built environment.[2]

We took care not to present the Precautionary List as a strict list of items that professionals should avoid at any cost. Instead, we offer it up as an information source to concerned architects, engineers, and interior designers who want to take *precautions* to protect people's health. Once we assembled this important list, it would have been irresponsible of us not to share it.

---

1. http://architecture2030.org
2. http://transparency.perkinswill.com/Main

The list is categorized by substance name, category, health effect, and construction industry division. Links to published scientific studies established the database for inclusion of these chemicals. Additional information related to asthma triggers and flame retardants is also available on the site, as are supplemental resources and media reports on the topic. The other credible prohibition lists in the public space are the Cradle to Cradle Products Innovations Institute's (C2C) list and the International Living Future Institute's Red List. Watch for this subject area to explode in the near future. As a firm and in the person of Suzanne Drake of our San Francisco office, we are outspoken lobbyists for the reduction in the use of brominated flame retardants in home furnishings; useless toxic chemical additives (driven by the chemical industry) that are killing our firefighters, and likely toxic to all.

Change Built On Resiliency

It is also the architect's responsibility to design things that last; structures that stand up to the forces of man and nature. We will address the topic of resiliency in more detail in Chapter 6, in which we explore the future of cities, but it is important to mention it here as well.

At Perkins+Will, we believe it is one of our fundamental responsibilities to adjust our designs to accommodate the effects of global warming on the built environment. We have been focusing for years on designing buildings and communities to reduce the harmful impacts that cause climate change, and we must continue to do so. But Hurricanes Katrina and Sandy, increasing storm events, flooding, and rising sea levels affecting the communities where we live, work, and build have compelled us to understand that climate change is here,

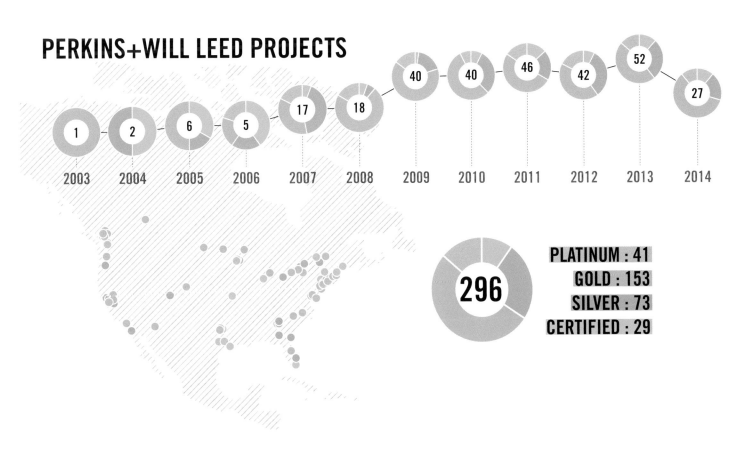

PERKINS+WILL LEED PROJECTS

2003	2004	2005	2006	2007	2008	2009	2010	2011	2012	2013	2014
1	2	6	5	17	18	40	40	46	42	52	27

296

PLATINUM : 41
GOLD : 153
SILVER : 73
CERTIFIED : 29

Pier 1, San Francisco, CA; 2002 AIA-COTE
Award Winner

and we have to design for climate adaptation and resiliency. We recognize that mechanical and electrical equipment should be taken out of basements and elevated higher into buildings to avoid risk of water damage. We know that site- and neighborhood-specific energy and water systems reduce risks to buildings (and their occupants) in emergency situations. We understand that building envelopes must be made stronger to withstand increased winds and flying storm debris. We have studied climate change's many potential consequences and will continue to gather data as more evidence is presented. These changes increasingly require our attention. Soon, resiliency will be a required element of every architectural design.

Exemplary Projects

There is no better proof of a firm's commitment to sustainability than its portfolio of work. At Perkins+Will, we are immensely proud of the projects we have completed and we continue to pursue any and all assignments that allow us to flex our sustainable muscles.

We are honored to have been involved with LEED Gold and Platinum structures throughout North America that serve the market sectors meeting society's most critical needs. We believe that designing green buildings for healthcare, education, science, technology and other essential community services is the best way to meet our obligations as a for-profit business. Simultaneously, the attention we get for doing greener work actually gives us a measurable competitive advantage over firms that have not stayed as nimble. The chart on the previous page illustrates the history of our LEED certified projects, since our first (White Rock Operations building, LEED Gold) in 2003. The dip in 2011-12 reflects the trailing impact of the recession.) Note the shift in certification types over time. Early projects were predominantly Silver; today almost all are Gold or Platinum. This is evidence of a shifting marketplace, client engagement in sustainable principles, and growing knowledge about the strategies, costs and benefits of sustainable design. It is irreversible.

Other measures of results exist. The AIA Committee on the Environment (COTE) awards are one measure, and Perkins+Will is pleased to have won five of these awards. Another is the Clinton Foundation's Clinton Climate Change Initiative (which targets community scale success), and we have had two projects selected for this honor.

We have also found that our shifting focus toward sustainable design has changed what our clients think about the types of buildings they should develop. In a way, it has become a form of friendly competition among businesses – almost a type of peer pressure – that has made the larger client population more open to sustainable approaches and guided them toward greener ways of thinking. In this regard, we like to think that our sense of corporate responsibility has rippled outward.

Synergy at Dockside Green; Victoria, BC; 2009 AIA-COTE Award Winner

White Rock Operations Centre; White Rock, BC; 2004 AIA-COTE Award Winner

1315 Peachtree Street, Perkins+Will Atlanta; Atlanta, GA; 2012 AIA-COTE Award Winner

Dockside Green; Victoria, BC; Clinton Climate Positive Development C40 Program Project

Treasure Island Development; San Francisco,
CA; Clinton Climate Positive Development C40
Program Project

Great River Energy Headquarters, Maple Grove,
MN; 2009 AIA-COTE Award Winner

A New Era Of Accountability

When the practice of sustainable design was in its infancy, architects and engineers focused on buildings' green features and predicted how we *expected* our buildings would behave. That was an important way to gain attention for the concept of sustainability, but our understanding has moved well past that point. Back then we did not take responsibility for our buildings after they were constructed, primarily because we were not capable of doing so. Now, we can and must measure what we are doing to track the *actual* performance of our buildings to ensure that they – and we – are doing all that is possible. Benchmarking is fundamental to redefining the edges of our responsibilities related to our architecture.

Benchmarking does more than just provide performance data. It helps us remain accountable. Across Perkins+Will, we tabulate the results of many of our projects' energy, water, and operational performance and enter the information into a rapidly growing database. These measurements inform every project that follows. The more we track, the better able we are to hone our designs to improve performance. Our database grows, we improve, our clients benefit and the built environment becomes healthier. Accountability serves every person, every place and every client involved.

Gathering more data over the years, we have found that there is one factor that undeniably affects a building's performance: its occupants. When we conduct post-occupancy reviews of our buildings to compare their predicted and actual performance, we discover that the distinguishing characteristic of a successful, high-performing building is usually occupant behavior. We are exceedingly pleased to observe that well-designed buildings actually teach people how to behave in a more environmentally responsible manner. When occupants are engaged and interested, they adapt to a green building's systems and modify their behavior to suit performance goals. People learn how to operate shading devices, get better at turning off lights, adjust to on-site water treatment processes and generally become more aware of how to live and work more responsibly.

In the last decade, as more buildings are incorporating sustainable design principles such as daylight, natural ventilation, views and natural materials, the study of the behavioral effects of green building design has just begun to emerge. A study completed in 2013 at the University of British Columbia found a connection between occupying a high-performance building and pro-environmental behavior related to recycling and waste disposal. The building at the center of the study, the Center for Interactive Research on Sustainability (CIRS), was designed to meet LEED Platinum and Living Building Challenge targets, and incorporates features such as a green wall, an exposed wood structure, photovoltaics, natural daylight and fresh air. The study found that users of a deep green building were more likely to choose the correct disposal bin (recycle, compost, or trash) than users of a similar building that was not focused on sustainable design principals. This research reinforces my conviction that sustainable design is a subtle but important tool to help encourage environmentally friendly beliefs and behaviors.

A Sustainable Building Promotes Pro-Environmental Behavior: An Observational Study on Food Disposal

ABSTRACT

In order to develop a more sustainable society, the wider public will need to increase engagement in pro-environmental behaviors. Psychological research on pro-environmental behaviors has thus far focused on identifying individual factors that promote such behavior, designing interventions based on these factors, and evaluating these interventions. Contextual factors that may also influence behavior at an aggregate level have been largely ignored. In the current study, we test a novel hypothesis – whether simply being in a sustainable building can elicit environmentally sustainable behavior. We find support for our hypothesis: people are significantly more likely to correctly choose the proper disposal bin (garbage, compost, recycling) in a building designed with sustainability in mind compared to a building that was not. Questionnaires reveal that these results are not due to self-selection biases. Our study provides empirical support that one's surroundings can have a profound and positive impact on behavior. It also suggests the opportunity for a new line of research that bridges psychology, design, and policy-making in an attempt to understand how the human environment can be designed and used as a subtle yet powerful tool to encourage and achieve aggregate pro-environmental behavior.

Citation: Wu DW, DiGiacomo A, Kingstone A (2013) A Sustainable Building Promotes Pro-Environmental Behavior: An Observational Study on Food Disposal. PLoS ONE 8(1): e53856. doi:10.1371/journal.pone.0053856
Published: January 9, 2013

PERCENTAGE OF PROPER WASTE DISPOSAL

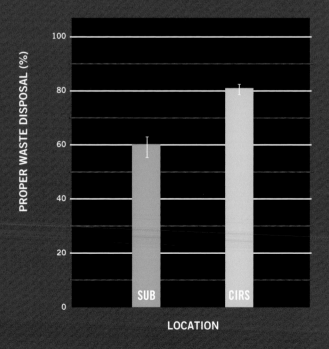

SELF-RATINGS OF ENVIRONMENTAL CONSCIOUSNESS

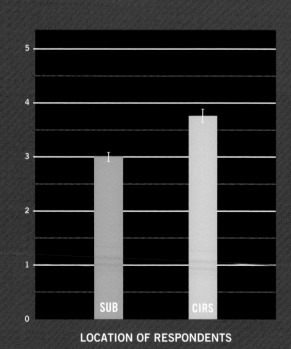

This research demonstrates that the architect can become an agent of change, capable of building things that guide others toward more responsible behavior. Through our work, we are capable of creating cultures of environmental sensitivity and responsibility, from the individual and building level all the way to the community level.

Elevating Architecture

We look forward to a future where we can offer a type of building performance "warranty" associated with annual "commissioning" reviews much like an automobile tune-up. We note that no one would buy a dishwasher without a warranty, so as an industry we have to find a path around insurance and liability issues to extend our services over time and ensure that our buildings perform as designed. We have conducted post-occupancy evaluations of five of our early green buildings, and the results were shocking. Problem performances were traced to lack of operator knowledge; exemplary performances were linked with stable user/occupant groups and knowledgeable "caring" by operations staff.

Some businesses will make good social and environmental choices for the sake of the bottom line; others for the public relations bump it brings. At Perkins+Will, our sense of social and environmental responsibility is inextricably tied to the core values of our practice. It defines us, it teaches us, and it makes us better at what we do. It attracts and retains the best talent and makes for a more focused and meaningful design philosophy. Our success is far from perfect, but we strive to raise the bar — for our own firm and for the industry at large. Taking care of the environment is a way of taking care of design, a practice we want to vigorously preserve, adapt, and enhance.

1220 Homer Street, Perkins+Will Vancouver

Vancouver, BC

Requiring additional office space, Perkins+Will's Vancouver office saw immediate revitalization potential in a 1946 warehouse situated in the heart of Yaletown, the city's historic warehouse zone and premiere live-work district. Originally a candy factory, the warehouse presented enormous opportunities for high efficiency by virtue of its high ceilings, exposed concrete mass, and open floor plan.

1220 Homer Street, Atrium and multi-level work space; Vancouver, BC; 2000

New Edge Innovations

To infuse natural ventilation into the space, two large openings were cut into the floor slabs creating atria at the front and center of the building, each sized for optimum levels of ventilation and daylighting. The central atrium serves as the organizing element for the office, providing visual connection among the three levels of workstations, while also directing natural light throughout the space via an operable skylight overhead.

Circulation spines run the office's length on each floor, providing separation between service and work areas. Workstations are organized to optimize flexibility in team sizes and maximize daylight and ventilation at each station. Custom designed by ourselves, the workstations are composed of an easily reconfigurable system of components, allowing for maximum flexibility in arrangement.

A large-scale interior living wall, with a recycled water hydroponic supply, cleans the air and adds biophilic design to the workplace. The main atrium features a 90-year-old handmade cedar strip canoe, one of the most beautiful and efficient transportation devices ever created by mankind that had no environmental impact from its creation or its decades of operation.

CLIENT Perkins+Will
DESIGN 2000
CONSTRUCTION 2000
SIZE 23,400 sf / 2,174 sm
DESIGN TEAM Perkins+Will (formerly Busby + Associates Architects): P.Busby, D.Dove, S.Gushe, S.Ockwell, A.Minard, S.Schou, R. Wu
STRUCTURAL ENGINEER Glotman Simpson
SKYLIGHT CONSULTANT Fast + Epp
ELECTRICAL ENGINEER Flagel Lewandowski
MECHANICAL ENGINEER Keen Engineering
PHOTOGRAPHER Nic Lehoux
AWARDS RECEIVED IIDA Lighting Design Awards, BC Section Award and Pacific Regional Section Award of Merit, 2002
SUSTAINABILITY RATINGS LEED Platinum
REFERENCE TO PUBLICATIONS
"1220 Homer Street," New Life Old Buildings, December 2009, p. 18-20

1220 Homer Street, Atrium with living wall; Vancouver, BC; 2000

1315 Peachtree Street, Perkins+Will Atlanta

Atlanta, GA

Perkins+Will designed the 78,000 GSF renovation of a 1970s office building. The location was chosen over other possible sites because of the demonstration design challenge to reuse an existing building. Located in the heart of Midtown across from the High Museum of Art, the mixed-use building shares space with the Peachtree Branch of the Atlanta-Fulton County Public Library and the Museum of Design Atlanta (MODA). The Perkins+Will office occupies the top four floors with space for 240 employees.

1315 Peachtree Street, Balcony; Atlanta, GA; 2010

A holistic approach to sustainability in the workplace focuses not only on the environment, but also the health and well-being of the building's occupants and the surrounding community. Perkins+Will's Atlanta office demonstrates how design can leverage the overlap between sustainability and well-being and fosters a strong sense of culture and community.

New Edge Innovations

The goals established for the project guided the design of the building systems. The goals included LEED Platinum certification, energy reductions meeting the 2030 Challenge, reductions in greenhouse gas (GHG) emissions of 60 percent, and application of systems supported by cost-benefit analyses.

Of the stated goals, the GHG reduction target of 60 percent had the largest influence on the system solutions. It was determined from concept phase analysis that to attain the desired reduction in GHG, partial energy source substitution was required. Since approximately 95 percent of the power sold by Georgia Power is generated by burning coal, utility power is very carbon-intensive. The energy substitution solution involved a cogeneration strategy using

natural gas-fired micro-turbines to provide power, hot water for heating, and cooling from a hot water driven adsorption chiller. This combined solution extracts the maximum amount of energy from the natural gas source at a much lower carbon intensity than coal.

An integrated design approach was followed to evaluate and maximize the energy reductions of the building. Solar studies and energy modeling efforts informed decisions regarding daylighting, glazing replacement, glazing materials, and shading systems. These studies, along with lighting analysis, were critical to inform the load calculations and sizing and selection of the HVAC systems. The resulting systems were chosen to maximize energy reductions as well as meet occupant requirements of quality of the workspace and flexibility of space layouts.

The HVAC system selected is the most efficient system available, offering a combination of radiant cooling and heating with displacement ventilation air. The radiant system, using water as the energy transmission source, is dramatically more efficient than air-based systems. The displacement ventilation system limits air distribution to only ventilation air

required by the occupants. This air is delivered at very low velocity to the space through a raised floor plenum which maximizes the effectiveness of the ventilation air delivery. The air supply incorporates energy recovery from the exhaust air stream to further enhance energy efficiency.

The power and lighting systems focused on reducing lighting energy and internal cooling loads as well as maximizing flexibility. The raised floor was used for power and data distribution. Floor boxes were used in lieu of wired furniture to facilitate relocation of workstations without requiring electrical modifications and to reduce the cost of the furniture. Lighting systems use efficient fluorescent indirect lighting sources with occupancy/daylighting controls. The ambient light levels provided by these fixtures were reduced to provide visual comfort for computer use. LED task lighting is added at workstations to provide increased light levels at the work surface for activities requiring higher visual acuity. The results of these lighting energy reduction efforts resulted in a lighting power density of 0.5 watts/square foot, approximately 50 percent of typical office area lighting power densities.

The water usage of the building was addressed by adding a greywater flushing system combined

1315 Peachtree Street, Atlanta, GA; 2010

with low flow fixtures. The roof drainage system was modified to allow collection of this water for treatment and use for toilet flushing.

PROJECT 1315 Peachtree Street (Atlanta Perkins+Will Office)
LOCATION Atlanta, GA
CLIENT Perkins+Will
DESIGN 2009
CONSTRUCTION 2009–2010
SIZE 78,000 sf / 7,246 sm
DESIGN TEAM Perkins+Will:
- ARCHITECTURE K. Chamness, K. Duckworth, M. Finn, S. McCauley, B. McEvoy, D. Reynolds
- BRANDED ENVIRONMENTS B. Erlinder, E. Maddox, B. Weatherford
- INTERIORS V. Logsdon, R. Miles, T. Moore, D. Sheehan,
- PLANNING AND STRATEGIES J. Barnes, K. Farley
- URBAN DESIGN AND LANDSCAPE J. Cooper, Z. Stewart
- SUSTAINABILITY CHARRETTES P. Busby, B. McCarry, P. McEvoy
STRUCTURAL Uzun & Case
MEP Integral Group
CONTRACTOR Brasfield & Gorrie
PHOTOGRAPHER Eduard Hueber

AWARDS RECEIVED
- Top Ten Green Projects, American Institute of Architects Committee on the
- Environment (COTE), 2012
- Development of Excellence Award, ULI-Atlanta, 2011
- Design Award, AIA-Georgia, 2011
- Development of Excellence Award, Atlanta Regional Commission and the
- Livable Communities Coalition, 2011
- Award of Excellence for Sustainability, Atlanta Urban Design Commission, 2011
- Golden Shoe Award, PEDS (Pedestrians Educating Drivers on Safety) For Pedestrian-friendly Site Redesign, 2011

REFERENCES TO PUBLICATIONSU
- Sheila Kim, "Perkins+Will Atlanta." Contract, September 18, 2012. http://www.contractdesign.com/contract/design/features/PerkinsWill-Atlanta-7742.shtml#
- "1315 Peachtree Street: 2012 AIA COTE Top Ten," Architect, August 23, 2012. http://www.architectmagazine.com/award-winners/2012-cote-1315-peachtree-street.aspx
- Emily Badger, "How to Green Southern Cities Built in the Age of Cars and Air Conditioning"

CityLab, April 18, 2012. http://www.citylab.com/design/2012/04/how-green-southern-cities-built-age-cars-and-ac/1619/
- Paula Vaughn and Grzegorz Kozmal, "Designing for Design: Perkins+Will Offers up Opportunities and Insights from designing its own LEED Platinum-Certified Spaces" ECOBuilding Pulse, June 3, 2011: http://www.ecobuildingpulse.com/commercial-projects/designing-for-design.aspx

2 Bryant Street, Perkins+Will San Francisco
San Francisco, CA

In June of 2014, the Perkins+Will San Francisco office moved into new premises at 2 Bryant on the Embarcadero. The space was designed to exhibit our workplace design skills, our sustainable design knowledge and commitment, and to be a great place to work. Perkins+Will occupies the entire third floor and a portion of the second floor of the building.

2 Bryant Street, Exterior with view to Bay Bridge; San Francisco, CA; 2015

2 Bryant Street, San Francisco, CA; 2015

New Edge Innovations
The net zero energy target renovation in an existing building in an urban setting was achieved through aggressive energy use reduction strategies, consumption culture change, and the lease of the rooftop to generate the annual energy needs on-site.

Demand reduction strategies include 100 percent daylighting, significant envelope improvements, and the addition of external and internal shading.

Complete daylighting of the entire space is achieved with the introduction of 12 skylights for the main office space that incorporate Sunbeamers (mini heliostats) to columnate and direct natural light down into the space. Custom designed reflectors add interest and beauty to the space while efficiently distributing the daylight onto ceilings, effectively eliminating glare and direct solar radiation in the workspace. Solar tubes are installed to daylight support spaces such as washrooms. Artificial illumination is provided exclusively with state-of-the-art LED fixtures.

The existing envelope's thermal performance has been upgraded through the creation of an internal "double envelope" by retrofitting high-performance wood windows behind existing exterior walls, enhancing thermal performance and improving the acoustic environment. Locally made out of low-cost poplar wood, the sliding windows are thermally broken, double glazed, and allow for continuous natural ventilation. Large internal fans provide enhanced air circulation. Exterior aluminum sunshades have been installed to achieve 100 percent solar shading coefficient. A pre-existing atrium skylight is shaded internally.

Designed for speed of construction, flexibility, future deconstruction, and waste minimization is achieved through the use of demountable DIRTT partitions throughout. The partitions include phase change materials that act as a thermal mass to absorb excess heat and re-release it into the space later when the space is cooler. Large demonstration Cross Laminated Timber (CLT) panels enhance some enclosures, to allow our clients to view and touch this revolutionary product.

As part of our healthy workplace demonstration, all selected materials are toxin-free, meeting the Perkins+Will Precautionary List commitment and the Living Building Challenge Red List requirements. Every occupant has access to natural ventilation, daylight, and a visual connection to nature, a biophilic design objective.

Almost all materials are locally sourced, reducing the carbon footprint of materials due to transportation to the site. Examples include utilization of salvaged and recycled 100-year-old Douglas fir pilings recently removed from the Transbay Transit Center excavation for all internal wood finishes and furnishings. Recycled furniture from previous offices has also been retrofitted with the same recycled wood to eliminate the majority of plastic laminates from the office. Ceramic tiles are not used; instead a locally sourced tile composed of cast recycled Cathode Ray Tubes (TVs before flat screens) pointing a way for future reuse of the mountains of discarded televisions.

The design incorporates a water efficient design that is set up to perform to Living Building Challenge standards in the future,

when we can build the storage capacity. Creative, enhanced energy monitoring and continuous communication of our performance will be used to engage occupants and help us reach our energy reduction goals through culture change.

The building is located within close proximity to multiple modes of public transportation. The design further discourages car use by incorporating showers, changing rooms, and secure bike storage on-site.

PROJECT 2 Bryant Street (San Francisco office of Perkins+Will)
LOCATION San Francisco, CA
IMAGE TBD- Project not completed
CLIENT Perkins+Will
DESIGN 2013-2014
CONSTRUCTION 2013-2014
SIZE 21,170 sf / 1,966 sm
DESIGN TEAM Perkins+Will: S. Andersen, P. Busby, T. Campbell, R. Clocker, D. Hawthorne, A. Hoffert, C. Leighton, Y. Matsushita, R. Muir, K. Raines, S. Schou, A. Wolfram
CONTRACTOR NOVO Construction
STRUCTURAL Holmes Culley
MEP Integral Group
PHOTOGRAPHER TBD-Project not completed
SUSTAINABILITY RATINGS Registered with the certification goal of LEED Platinum. Pursuing the Living Building Challenge (LBC) Petal Certification for Site, Energy, Health, Materials, Equity, and Beauty. We intend to achieve the Water Petal in the future. The project meets the 2030 Challenge at the 2030 level.

2 Bryant Street, Lobby; San Francisco, CA; 2015

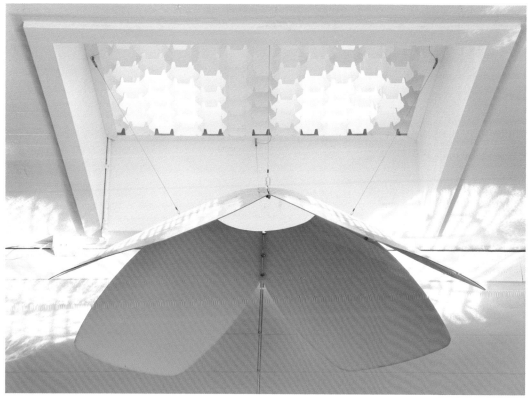

2 Bryant Street, Custom designed solar reflector; San Francisco, CA; 2015

Culture of Innovation

Fostering Ingenuity

In architecture, as with almost every field of endeavor, innovation is the most valuable ingredient for success over time. Fortunately for those firms that focus on sustainable design, the challenge has always been around innovation; there was never a pattern book or ready set of solutions. Our 25-year experience with sustainable design, during which we have always searched for better solutions and ideas from allied professions, educational institutions, research, nature, and a host of other sources, has compelled us to create design environments and processes that foster innovation across all corners of the practice. The first trick is to make enough space – literally and metaphorically – to allow people to think about new and better ways of doing things. A delicate balance of research and courage provides the underpinning for it all.

The heart of what we do is to get people to be creative. There are certain things we can do to provide an environment in which people think about being innovative. We set the stage with a lot of stimuli, interaction, and collaboration with others, a lot of outside influences that we bring in, as many examples that we can provide, and a lot of cross-pollination. Innovation results in mechanical systems, structural systems, envelopes, sustainable and environmental responses, and place design that are progressively changing and improving, across the full spectrum of what we do.

The next biggest challenge is to foster innovation in the face of company structures and processes without allowing profitability issues to get in the way. We must make enough room (and provide the necessary time) to let people think about different ways of doing things. We see that the successful firms are the ones that have a culture of innovation. They do it through the design of the places where they work, and in the ways that they work, allowing people time to research, time to chase new ideas, time for peer exchange. At Perkins+Will, we have had an "innovation incubator" for the last five years, an internally funded idea development program that nurtures young talent with interesting fresh ideas by giving them paid time to pursue their ideas. Recipients compete across the firm for the grants, and approximately 16 are awarded each year. Recipients develop their ideas with research and design into papers, proposals, and projects. We note the program is very popular, and a good screen for the "rising talent" in the firm.

When designing for clients, in every building we do now, whether it is a university facility or a workplace design, we allow innovation to be nurtured in many ways. Peer exchange opportunities abound, whether via wide landings with seating on stairs, standup coffee stations where people linger and talk about ideas, or a wall of white boards and writable glass so people can talk about and chase ideas whenever and wherever the mood catches them. These ideas apply to the spaces we design for the innovative institutions and companies we work for, and also to ourselves. If you have people in closed offices talking to themselves, you will not get much innovation. You may get brilliant minds chasing ideas, but true innovation comes when people collaborate, exchange ideas, and build things together.

I have always been interested in innovative architecture, structure, systems design, and product design. I visited the Pompidou Centre in the early 1970s, watched FROG design from their early days, and enjoyed the work of Jean Nouvelle, Renzo Piano, and Nicholas Grimshaw. I have always studied people, firms, and designers that are innovative. The one thing that ties these firms and individuals together as a catalyst for innovation is the time and resources spent on research. At Perkins+Will, we have a serious commitment to invest in research, as described in Chapter 2 (Corporate Responsibility) above.

This chapter on innovation is organized around three categories of ideas that we use to create a culture of innovation. The "Physical Innovations" section is about the physical things (structures, et cetera) we have been successful in innovating, through sustained development of incremental design ideas over time. But innovation also happens because of "Ideas" that back those designs; ideas such as whole systems design, urbanism, sustainable design, climate change, and more. Finally, we discuss processes we use to stimulate and ensure innovation in our ideas and physical design work. In the pages that follow, we will explore all three key types of innovation and examine a variety of projects that showcase the value of innovation in new approaches. The examples are drawn from the entire 30-year history of my involvement in the practice to illustrate the continuity of investment, research, and thinking in the pursuit of innovation. Fruitful innovation requires commitment, staying power, investment, and patience.

1. Physical Innovations

Architects and designers usually endeavor to have a resultant physical solution to their ideas. So, in looking for threads of innovation in the practice, it is useful to follow categories of physical ideas. What I hope stands out is that we and our engineering and design collaborators have never rested; we build on one idea after another, learning from experience and research. We have an explicit strategy to try to develop and deploy at least one, and hopefully more new ideas on every project.

1.1 Structural Exploration

When contemplating sustainable structural innovations, architects always bring engineers into the conversation. On our own, designers can come up with virtually any idea for new and different structures. But without well engineered performance systems, even the most spectacular visual expressions are worthless. That is not to say that it is unwise to dream up a crazy idea and give it to a great engineer to figure out. We have always preferred a more collaborative and creative approach that involves sitting together, discussing, learning from each other and, more often than not, finding cool new ideas to test and prove feasible as the design evolves. Together, architects and engineers can identify new approaches, material efficiencies, cost savings, and operational systems that allow our buildings to perform as well as or better than intended. I am very fond of saying that good engineering is good architecture. Good architecture takes many different physical forms.

Peter Busby Architect Office at 1216 Granville Street
VANCOUVER, BC, 1984
The point-fixed glazing and suspended structural wall assembly in our very first office reflected a daring tone of a startup firm committed to demonstrating and

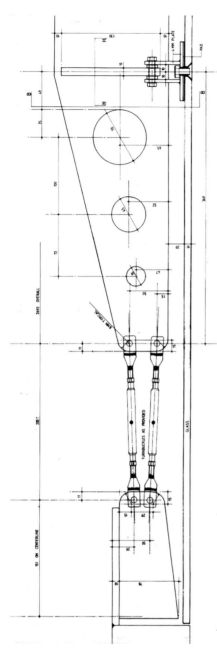

1216 Granville Street; structural detail; 1984

encouraging innovation in a street-front setting. "Architecture on the Street" engineer John Rockingham helped us create this then-revolutionary glazing system, which has since become commercially available. The project was a true design-build endeavor; starting out, I had no work or employees, so over five months I built every aspect of the office myself.

Ebco Aerospace
DELTA, BC, 1986–1987
Paul Fast of Fast + Epp Engineers worked with us to develop this beautiful clear span exterior suspended steel structure. Helmut Eppich, the client and owner of the building and business, was a strong innovator himself, encouraging us all the way. Other innovations in this project include zipper gasket glazing systems and greenhouse inflatable ventilation systems for internal mechanical system ducts. The building still stands, virtually intact.

Stanley Park Tropical Complex
VANCOUVER, BC, 1986–1987
The most striking aspect of this project, another John Rockingham collaboration, was a beautiful system of suspended cable structure enclosures for two types of primates at the Stanley Park Zoo. Other innovations included the extensive use of artificial crafted rockwork, new in 1986, now common in every zoo. Our unbuilt design was a collaborative effort with Cathy Simon of SMWM, who would become my partner at Perkins+Will 22 years later.

Metro McNair Clinical Laboratory and Office
BURNABY, BC, 1994–1996
With the help of Paul Fast we developed this beautiful glazed atrium roof using small fabricated steel triangles with pairs of splayed cables in tension to span the main arrival space. This was our first design-build project with Fast + Epp. Ledcor, the contractor (our first collaboration with them too), was comfortable letting us design, fabricate and supply our innovative structure to the project directly without resorting to a bid subcontractor who was unlikely to give us what we had dreamed up. Fast + Epp went on to found StructureCraft to take the same approach on many subsequent projects for us and many other architects.

One Wall Centre
VANCOUVER, BC, 1996–2001
This structural system was inspired by the design of a yacht mast, complete with outriggers and tension members that help stiffen the building. We were constrained by a narrow lateral footprint on the site for one axis of the building, so the engineers Glotman Simpson used tension columns and compression "spreaders" from the top to bottom, which enhanced the building's strength in its thinner cross dimension. A tuned mast damper composed of a 150,000 gallon U-shaped water tank at the top of the building doubles as seismic stability and a fire suppression head.

Nicola Valley Institute of Technology
MERRITT, BC, 1999–2001
Working with Equilibrium Consulting Engineers, we developed North America's first vertical wood structure supporting horizontal concrete. We used recycled timber from the site and custom iron castings to connect the wood to the concrete delicately in ways that reflected the surrounding environment.

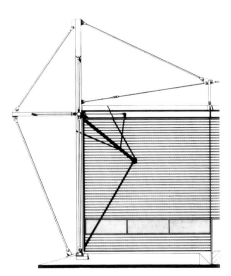

Ebco Aerospace; Delta, BC; 1987

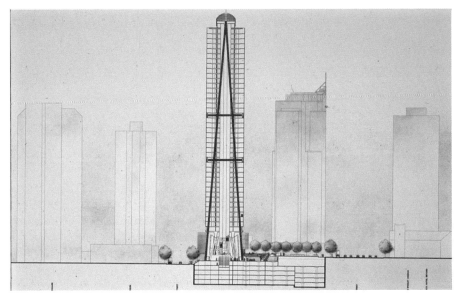

One Wall Centre; Vancouver, BC; 2001

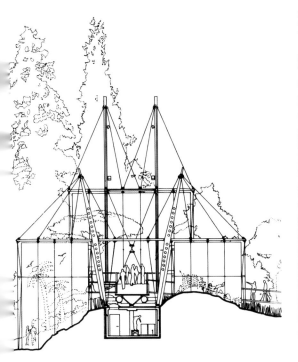

Stanley Park Tropical Complex; Vancouver, BC; 1987

Metro McNair Clinical Laboratory and Office, Atrium; Burnaby, BC

Nicola Valley Institute of Technology, Vertical wood structure supporting horizontal concrete;; Merritt, BC; 2001

Brentwood SkyTrain Station
BURNABY, BC, 1999–2002
Working with Fast + Epp, we created a distinct solution for this transit stop by combining steel and wood. Since steel has the highest strength in bending moments, it performs well and offers great durability at the base of the structure. In the span, we used curved glued laminated members (different lengths, but all from the same jig) to support a two-by-four-foot (used lumber) diaphragm roof (edge nailed in place) to give the building its graceful shape and structural seismic rigidity.

Riyadh Light Rail Transit Stations
RIYADH, SAUDI ARABIA, 2004–2016
Fast + Epp helped us fashion a structure from a single structural tube size with unevenly spaced members that reflect the bending moments necessary to support the overall assembly. This was also our first experience using photovoltaics (PV) on a large scale, projected at the time to be three megawatts. Now under construction with 68 stations in total, the PV installation will be 15 times that when completed in 2016. This was also our first opportunity to use Ecotect software to help understand the structure's shading requirements – crucial to reach an appropriate shading solution for the region.

Dubai International Financial Centre
DUBAI, UAE, 2006–2007
An unbuilt 90-story scheme for an office tower, residential and hotel complex at the heart of Dubai featured ultra-slender towers. By creating a vertical Vierendeel truss (with design by engineers from Magnusson Klemencic and Fast + Epp), forming cross-bridges that also serve as structural struts, we reduced the use of rebar in the project by 17 percent. Working with RWDI from Guelph, Ontario, we also shaped the towers to capture and accelerate prevailing winds through vertical axis windmills to generate 15 percent of the building's energy requirements.

Structural design fascinates us. We start all projects thinking about the structural requirements right up front. We collaborate with our engineers immediately, and have benefitted from wonderful and creative relationships with many gifted engineers over the years.

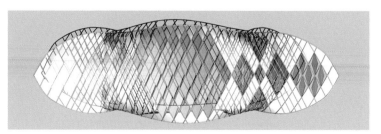

Riyadh Light Rail Transit Stations, Riyadh, Saudi Arabia; 2018 (projected)

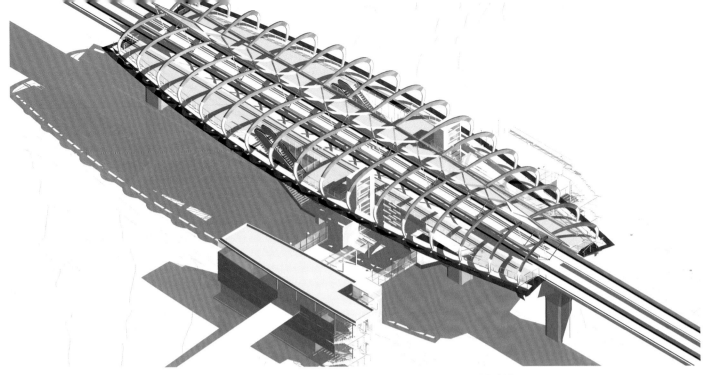

Brentwood SkyTrain Station, Structural diagram; Burnaby, BC; 2001

Dubai International Financial Centre; Dubai, UAE; 2008

CULTURE OF INNOVATION

75

1.2. Modular Approaches

Inspired by the work of Kiyoshi Kurokawa and other forward-thinking architects who examined prefabrication seriously in the 1970s and before, we have experimented with modular and prefabricated designs as a way of simultaneously achieving beauty, sustainability, and cost effectiveness. By investing in higher quality repetitive elements, we can accomplish more, aesthetically speaking, while minimizing environmental impacts and keeping overall project costs lower.

Pemberton Airport

PEMBERTON, BC, 1987–1989

Given this site's distance from Vancouver-based construction labor and materials, we designed a composite steel and wood structure that could be panelized and prefabricated off-site and delivered in the fewest possible shipments. Mechanical systems were engineered and ready to be shipped in a similar fashion. The unbuilt project also featured an undercroft and foundation for the building made of modular precast concrete culverts, post tensioned, which allowed for storage of equipment in the event that the valley flooded, which it does regularly.

Pemberton Airport; Pemberton, BC; 1989

EyeMasters Stores

VARIOUS LOCATIONS ACROSS CANADA, 1990–1992

We worked with this retail chain to create modular furniture, display systems, glazing, and wall systems made from prefabricated extrusions, castings, and wood parts that were built in Vancouver then shipped to stores throughout the country. This strategy provided the client with a consistent interior design brand across all locations, along with installation simplicity and cost savings. Six stores were built, most taking only two weeks to fit out.

Concord Pacific Presentation Centre

VANCOUVER, BC, 1993–2000

We created an entire building out of modular components so that it could be transported to any location where the company was building new towers, then relocated when sales for that neighborhood were complete. Built in three months using fabrications, extrusions, and castings all of our own design, it has been moved multiple times with no structural issues, and added to several times.

BC Rail Control Tower

NORTH VANCOUVER, BC, 1993–1995

Working with Fast + Epp again, designing this rail yard control tower, we used post tensioned precast sections for the vertical structure, which also housed the elevator and provided support for a cantilevered exit stair. We fabricated the main deck of the tower on the ground, where it was easiest to construct the curved dish form before lifting it into place as a single pre-cast element.

Revenue Canada Building

SURREY, BC, 1997–1998

For this building (another design build project with Ledcor), we implemented modular approaches throughout – for everything from underfloor air distribution and raised flooring to the building's prefabricated modules for mechanical, electric, and communication systems. We also built modularity into the solar shading systems and daylighting around the perimeter using curved glass supported in castings.

Revenue Canada Building, solar shading; Surrey, BC; 1998

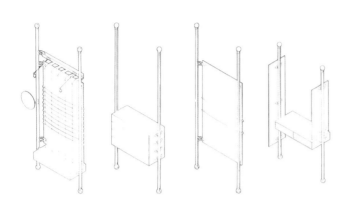

EyeMasters Stores, Kit of Parts; 1992

EyeMasters Stores; Various Locations Across Canada; 1992

BC Rail Control Tower; North Vancouver, BC; 1995

CULTURE OF INNOVATION

Sustainable Condo, Traveling Exhibit; 2004

Gilmore SkyTrain Station

BURNABY, BC, 1999–2001

For this modular roof design, we used single sheets of 8-by-16 foot TimberStrand along with pre-fabricated laser cut steel king posts to provide a self-supporting element that satisfied the needs for structural integrity, roof, and interior finish and came to the site with an installed waterproof membrane.

Sustainable Condo

VANCOUVER, BC, 2004

Designed as a flexible exhibition display for Globe 2004 to demonstrate innovative designs for sustainable condominiums aimed at a developer audience, we took a modular approach to the entire structure. Its six key components included floor systems, roof systems, ramps (our first use of ductal concrete from Lafarge) and furnishing elements throughout. The display had to be installed in 24 hours in each location where it was exhibited. It subsequently toured in North America and exhibited in many locations in six years of its life, including Greenbuild in 2006.

Canada Line SkyTrain Stations

RICHMOND, BC, 2007–2010

Building on the Gilmore Station experience, we implemented a hybrid modular approach to the roof systems for these stations, using steel and wood prefabricated units to reduce costs and improve quality of the finished product. The units were delivered with roof membranes and pre-wired electrical systems, and featured curved design in two dimensions.

VanDusen Botanical Garden Visitor Centre

VANCOUVER, BC, 2007–2012

For this project, we implemented a much more complex modular approach to the roof systems. These units all varied in size and shape (three-dimensional variations in every panel) and were delivered to the site with roof membrane, prewired electrical, plumbing, sprinkler, acoustic, and lighting systems as well as interior ceiling finishes.

We see unlimited opportunities to prebuild modular construction elements in all our future projects. These will include structures, floors, walls, roofs, washroom, and kitchen elements, as well as mechanical, electrical, and sprinkler systems. They offer great opportunities in the future for cost efficiencies on-site, improving the quality of construction and quality of the design and physical environments we are creating.

VanDusen Botanical Garden Visitor Centre, modular roof system, image courtesy Structurecraft; 2012

Gilmore SkyTrain Station; Burnaby, BC; 2001

Canada Line SkyTrain Station, Richmond, BC; 2009

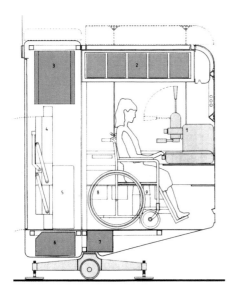
Urban Expresso Kiosk, Vancouver, BC; 1987

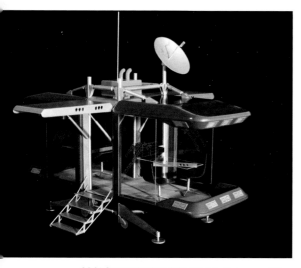
2001 Communications Sales Module, Vancouver, BC; 1984–1985

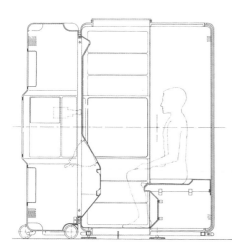
Videogram Kiosk, Vancouver, BC; 1989

1.3 A Design Studio that Includes Industrial Design

I was lucky enough to be exposed to industrial design as part of an architectural studio design while studying the works of Alvar Aalto, Buckminster Fuller, Jean Prouvé, and later working with Norman Foster. I have always believed that architects should be as equally interested in the detailed elements of their projects as they are with the large-scale aspects of buildings. Understanding and practicing industrial design affords us the opportunity to inject innovation into every aspect of our work. I taught an industrial design studio at Emily Carr University of Art and Design for four years, co-founded the British Columbia Industrial Design Association, and served as board member and/or chair for six years, all in the early 1990s, in an effort to bring industrial design into the mainstream in British Columbia. What follows are a few highlights of our pursuits in this arena, many of which emerged from our dedicated product design and fabrication companies, Designlines, Ltd. (1987-2004, now closed) and Componance, Inc. (2001-2011, since sold).

Urban Expresso Kiosk
VANCOUVER, BC, 1985–1987
These retail kiosks for my first paying client were designed to be self-contained for power, water, and waste. They were fabricated of fiberglass, steel, and acrylic components. Designed around the abilities of paraplegics to allow them to be fully functional servers of coffee and treats in the public realm by themselves, the project was a joint venture between an entrepreneur and the Canadian Paraplegic Association. The kiosks contained hoists to facilitate the independent function of their employee-operators. Four were constructed, and all have since been lost.

2001 Communications Sales Module
VANCOUVER, BC, 1984–1985
These unbuilt retail kiosks were designed for a company to market cable television services at exhibitions. The design featured modular mirrored fiberglass fabrications fixed to a mobile steel frame.

Royal Academy Kiosk
LONDON, UK, 1986
This mobile observation kiosk was designed as part of a competition entry to redesign the use and space of the courtyard in front of the Royal Academy in London.

EBCO Table
RICHMOND, BC, 1988
EBCO Aerospace was one of our first buildings. We designed these table structures to use repurposed aluminum waste cut from milling machines testing and calibrating for the manufacture of aircraft components. We created an AutoCAD profile for this table's structural elements that was fed into the CNC machines to mill the components directly, a direct CAD to manufacture process that was unique at the time. In all, ten tables were constructed.

Videogram Kiosk
VANCOUVER, BC, 1987–1989
This kiosk was designed to allow the recording of a short video (using VHS tape) as an update to the ubiquitous photo booth in shopping malls. Primary materials were light steel and fiberglass. We designed and constructed one prototype for testing.

Giraf Table; 1998

District of North Vancouver Municipal Hall

NORTH VANCOUVER, BC, 1989–1995

Throughout this building, there is early evidence of what has since evolved into a continuous commitment to utilize industrial design in support of architecture. There are many small industrial design components throughout the building, utilizing laser cuttings, extrusions, and castings that provide stair, handrail, and other details, finishes, structure, and sunshading. The industrial design contributes to the larger design impact of the building as a whole. The project set the stage for the future of our industrial design efforts, generally focusing on support of our architecture.

L-01 Gill Wall Sconce

VANCOUVER, BC, 1991

We obtained Canadian Standards Association (CSA) approval for the distinct design of these lights, which are made of castings. Hundreds were sold.

Giraf Table

VANCOUVER, BC, 1998

Simplicity and structural integrity meet a modern design aesthetic in this table made of laminated wood elements, which is essentially the wood counterpart to the aluminum Ebco Table, above.

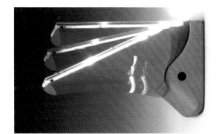

L-01 `Gill' Wall Sconce; 1991

Designlines, Ltd.

VANCOUVER, BC, 1987–2004

Between 1987 and 2004, we set up a separate product design company called Designlines. At one point employing seven industrial designers, we designed furnishing and fittings for our buildings, fabrications, and even developed a line of telephones for Nortel in 1988.

Componance, Inc.

VANCOUVER, BC, 2001–2010

For nine years, we ran this industrial design and fabrication company. Componance, Inc. allowed us to focus on product innovations for architecture – the "jewelry" that decorates our buildings – and sell our goods into our projects and to other architects via a dedicated website. The firm specialized in extrusions and castings, glazing, and handrail support systems.

Street Furnishings -Vancouver

VANCOUVER, BC, 2000–2002

We designed a complete suite of street furniture for Pattison Outdoor in support of their bid to obtain the street furniture concession from the City of Vancouver. Designs included waste receptacles, bicycle racks, seating and bus shelters. Subsequent bids were successful in other cities in British Columbia including Langley, Delta/Tsawwassen, and Surrey, where our designs were constructed.

Componance, Telephone Design

Street Furnishings; Vancouver, BC; 2002

Componance, detail of stair at Telus Building, Vancouver, BC; 2001

Urban Expresso Kiosk, Vancouver, BC; 1987

Profile X F1 Podium
VANCOUVER, BC, 1999–2000
Our most sophisticated mobile kiosk design to date, this project involved the design of a mobile self-sustaining stage that would be shipped worldwide in three containers, then could be deployed in three minutes at the end of an F1 Grand Prix to display the winning car and driver to gathering fans in the pit area. No prototypes were built. The design and evolution of the project can be seen on YouTube.

Industrial design has always been an important part of our practice. Industrial design expertise teaches all our designers to think about how things are and could be made. We still retain an industrial designer on staff (the exceptionally talented Sören Schou has been a collaborator on almost all our projects for over 15 years), so that custom pieces will continue to make our architecture interesting and beautiful at a reasonable cost.

1.4 Innovation in The Use of Materials

We have always tested the use of alternative material choices in our projects. This discussion could be very extensive, as we usually have several material innovations on every project, but the following illustrations show our consistent approach to discovering and using new and different materials in the work we have undertaken over decades.

Urban Expresso Kiosk
VANCOUVER, BC, 1985–1987
These innovative retail kiosks were constructed of fiberglass, steel, and acrylic components and fortified by moldings, castings extrusions and laser-cut elements. We studied and learned fiberglass manufacturing methods and borrowed industrial design inspiration from Ferrari. We received an NRCan research grant to develop the fabrication method for the three-dimensional acrylic enclosures.

District of North Vancouver Municipal Hall, North Vancouver, BC; 1995

Materials Testing Facility, Vancouver, BC; 1999

District of North Vancouver Municipal Hall

NORTH VANCOUVER, BC, 1989–1995

The building includes our first cast handrail brackets, our first water jet fabrications (the brackets at the entry glazing) and our only (so far) use of curved glass. The extruded window mullion sunshades on the south façade have since become industry standards, after Kawneer helped us with this glazing innovation. This project was also our first use of aluminum extrusions for repetitive stair elements. Frits de Vries Architects collaborated on the interiors.

Materials Testing Facility

VANCOUVER, BC, 1997–1999

This project pioneered our knowledge about the use of salvaged materials. Eighty percent of the material content of this building – including mechanical equipment, electrical equipment, toilets, doors, glazing elements, flooring, and structural systems – was from salvaged and recycled elements from a factory that had previously occupied the site and from local demolition yards' waste streams. The project's wooden "curtain wall," an idea we borrowed from a mid-century modern building in Vancouver, was fabricated from used lumber and has performed perfectly for 15 years.

Telus Office Building; Vancouver, BC; 2001

Energy. Environment. Experiential Learning, University of Calgary, Calgary, AB; 2011

MacMillan Bloedel Research Laboratories; Burnaby, BC; 1989

TELUS Office Building
VANCOUVER, BC, 1998–2007

This project included our first building-integrated photovoltaic (BIPV) system, installed near the top of the ventilated façade (double envelope) surrounding the building. The unique envelope was installed as part of a renovation and was the first of its kind in North America. Frit patterns that vary by elevation provide shading of the internal glazing. The four-sided silicone glazing system is a suspended curtain wall system that uses compression and tension members to support the walls.

Energy. Environment. Experiential Learning Building (EEEL)
CALGARY, AB, 2008–2011

This project, designed in association with Dialogue, features a unique skin made of superform aluminum panels. Molded by the automobile industry at the nadir of the Great Recession, the panels differ on each elevation to direct (by reflection) low winter solar illumination to public spaces around the building at grade, areas that would otherwise be in shade most of the winter. Other innovations include motorized external shutters, three long underground earth tubes, and the largest "sun scoop" we have designed to date at the top of the internal atrium. The building is nearly 100 percent illuminated with daylight, despite a very deep floor plan.

1.5 Wood: The Original Building System

We have been interested in incorporating wood elements into our buildings since our practice began 30 years ago, and we anticipate always using it in new and innovative ways as we move forward. Aside from its appealing natural appearance and textures, wood is an inherently sustainable design choice, because it is usually locally grown and manufactured in most parts of the world. When used for structural purposes, it helps us avoid the use of steel or concrete, both with significantly higher carbon footprints from manufacture and transportation. Wood is an ideal component of regenerative design as it is the only building material made by the sun. During its life it creates oxygen and sequesters carbon, becoming two-thirds carbon by weight when dried and used in buildings. When wood is harvested responsibly (FSC certification required), fewer logs fall to the forest floor, where they would decompose, generate methane, and contribute much more significantly to global warming. Even the combustion of waste wood is considered a renewable energy strategy, because the methane produced through decomposition has 17 times the climate change impact than the carbon produced from combustion.

MacMillan Bloedel Research Laboratories
BURNABY, BC, 1987–1989

This was our first project to incorporate Parallam®, a fabricated product made from waste wood and resin. We showcased Parallam in this building, which housed the researchers who developed it, manufactured then only by MacMillan Bloedel. We were challenged to use the material at its full manufactured length of sixty feet, which we utilized as columns supporting a dramatic open stairway that shines light on the beauty, strength, and utility of wood. This project also featured the use of prefabricated fiberglass window surrounds with integral sunshading eyebrows.

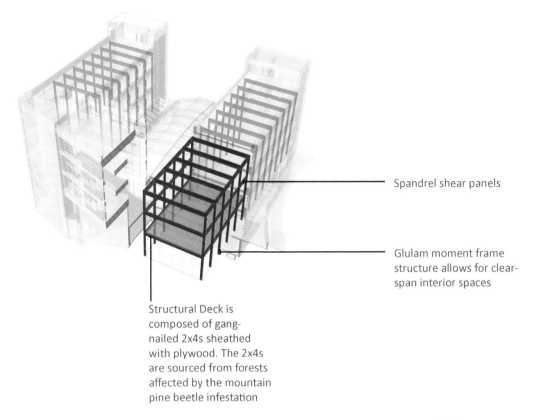

Spandrel shear panels

Glulam moment frame structure allows for clear-span interior spaces

Structural Deck is composed of gang-nailed 2x4s sheathed with plywood. The 2x4s are sourced from forests affected by the mountain pine beetle infestation

Centre for Interactive Research on Sustainability, University of British Columbia; Vancouver, BC; 2011

District of North Vancouver Municipal Hall, North Vancouver, BC; 1995

District of North Vancouver Municipal Hall

NORTH VANCOUVER, BC, 1989–1995

Working again with Paul Fast, we created a composite steel and wood roof over the atrium in the heart of the project. Steel tension rods and castings connected to a grid of Parallam to form a three-way truss system over the main space. The roof is "base isolated" for seismic performance, fixed to the new structure but sliding on Teflon glides over the older existing structure. Glazing above is frit with 60 percent coverage, designed to allow daylighting, sightlines to the clouds and mountains, yet still provide a reasonable shading coefficient.

Centre for Interactive Research on Sustainability at UBC

VANCOUVER, BC, 2008–2011

We maximized the potential use of wood throughout the design of this building. The structural system is comprised of vertical Vierendeel trusses of glue-laminated wood members to provide seismic braces through the building. Flooring systems are prefabricated, laminated, modular wooden diaphragms of common lumber. Topped with poured concrete, these diaphragms provide support for underfloor air systems and the raised floor. In this building we first became aware of the issues around carbon content in buildings, looking for ways to create carbon-neutral structures in the design of the fabric of the buildings themselves. Our initial estimates based on wood content of building (wood is 60 percent carbon by weight), we estimate that the building is close to carbon-neutral. The sequestered carbon in the wood structure and finishes of the building (about 600 tons) balance the carbon used in fabrication and transportation of all the other elements in the building, including glazing, extrusions, concrete, and other finishes.

The Vale Living With Lakes Centre, Laurentian
University, Sudbury, ON; 2011

Living With Lakes Centre at Laurentian University
SUDBURY, ON, 2006–2011
Relying heavily on wood, this project was designed to perform well in current conditions and future-proofed to adapt to a 2050 climate. In this regard, wood's functionality contributes to the building's longevity while its inspirational beauty enhances occupant productivity. Exterior wood is laid up horizontally, but shingle style to control staining.

Ottawa Confederation Line; Ottawa, ON; 2017
(projected)

Ottawa Confederation Line
OTTAWA, ON, 2010–2012 (DESIGN ONLY)
For this series of seven transit stations spread out across the city, we developed expressive prefabricated laminated wood and steel structures using computational tools that allowed us to create a distinct design for each location, incorporating a direct approach to climate responsiveness. The project was bid as a public private partnership (P3) and the stations under construction differ significantly from our design.

VanDusen Botanical Garden Visitor Centre
VANCOUVER, BC, 2007–2011
This dramatic project gave us our first opportunity to use the Rhino® design platform, which helped us create three-dimensional variations in the prefabricated, laminated structural wood diaphragms that shape the building. All panels were fabricated off-site and each is unique.

Samuel Brighouse Elementary School
RICHMOND, BC, 2009–2011
At this school, we also used laminated wood roof elements, in this case comprised of two-by-three-inch lumber laminated into prefabricated panels in eight-foot widths. The joy comes from the gentle undulations of the roof, and the delicate kingpost and cable supports that occur every few feet along the entire roof, obviating the need for any secondary structure.

Earth Sciences Building at UBC
VANCOUVER, BC, 2009–2012
This project utilized our most sophisticated floor assembly to date, designed by Equilibrium engineering. The floor is composite wood and concrete, but a proprietary Austrian invention: a perforated metal clip angle allows both

Earth Sciences Building at UBC
Vancouver, BC; 2009–2012

Samuel Brighouse Elementary School; Richmond, BC; 2011

materials to act together, the wood acting as a tension as a bottom chord and the concrete in compression, and also as flooring. The elegant cantilevered wood stair at the entry is also a composite structure, with steel plates scarfed into the stringers. This is also our first use of cross-laminated timber (CLT) diaphragms, a new product in the North American market, which form the structure, roof, and soffits to the rain protection canopy around the building, adding a warm and graceful public feature to the pedestrian space.

Wood has been used by mankind for structures since the beginning of time. Some of the most beautiful and enduring structures, halls, and temples around the globe are built of wood, many hundreds of years old. The advent of steel, concrete, and high-rise construction along with the development of restrictive fire codes limited the use of wood in larger construction since the mid-19th century. Now we are redeploying wood in our structures, driven by the push to innovate in the face of the carbon imperative.

Going forward, we see opportunities to use wood in a wide variety of building types. We have proposed wood structures for hospitals, and we are working on a 14-story office building in wood and a major employee center in the Bay Area made out of wood. In the future, we foresee multi-story high-rise wood residential and office building construction, as the technology and systems improve and outdated building codes are replaced.

We note the tremendous support we have had from the wood industry as we pioneer the penetration of innovative wood structures into all areas of building. Wood is a carbon sequestration strategy but also an important step forward in regenerative design. Harvested responsibly, it overcomes a significant cause of global warming. The "new edge," of course, is the idea that all material choices must be seen through the lens of climate impact, our responsibility at all times.

Association of Professional Engineers and Geoscientists of British Columbia (APEGBC), Vancouver, BC; 1995

District of North Vancouver Municipal Hall, North Vancouver, BC; 1995

Revenue Canada; Surrey, BC; 1998

2. Ideas as a Framework for Innovation

Innovation is often driven by the pursuit of an idea. Sustainable design, whole systems thinking, urbanism and climate-specific design are four ideas that have driven us over the years to think continuously of innovations so that we might do better work every time. Following these threads, innovation becomes an organic process, building on what is there already, growing, changing, and improving over time.

2.1 Sustainable Design

Sustainability permeates every building we work on – affecting how we create the design, how we think of the performance and how we strategize the operations. In our first published book (*Busby: Learning Sustainable Design*), we outlined how sustainable design was a learned process, always changing and improving with every project. Selecting sustainable design ideas for inclusion in this book is difficult, so a few of the notable earlier innovations are listed below:

Cape Roger Curtis
BOWEN ISLAND, BC 1989–1992
Following patterns established by Ian McHarg in *Design with Nature*, we created a plan to develop this beautiful piece of land using overlay mapping to minimize the impact on the ecosystems. It was the first time we fully incorporated considerations about flora and fauna into a design. The plan included strategies for 77 percent of the native forest to be set aside and preserved, and the project would have its own water and sewage treatment systems. Island politics are often unique. After decades of discussion, eventually the entire site was subdivided into 55 acreages, and the promise of a comprehensive solution lost, along with a steep price paid by nature and ecosystems. Bowen Island NIMBYs be ashamed.

District of North Vancouver Municipal Hall
NORTH VANCOUVER, BC 1989–1995
This was our first foray into exterior shading as a way of accomplishing deep daylighting goals, without solar heat gain. These strategies have been a constant part of our design vocabulary since.

Association of Professional Engineers and Geoscientists of British Columbia (APEGBC)
VANCOUVER, BC 1994–1995
In this, our first completed geoexchange system, we achieved high levels of energy efficiency through a variety of physical and mechanical methods, ending at 10 percent better than ASHRAE 90.1 – which was also the first time we measured that statistic. We utilized exterior glass fabrications for shading and to reflect light deep into the space to create a 100 percent daylit interior, and inside Lycra sails to soften, extend and shape daylighting effects. This is the first project where we removed all ceiling finishes, accessing thermal mass potential from the roof deck. We considered these appropriate innovations for the headquarters of the Association of Professional Engineers and Geoscientists of British Columbia.

Revenue Canada Building
SURREY, BC 1997–1998
We created our first underfloor displacement air distribution system and again removed ceilings in this building to expose its concrete structure as a more

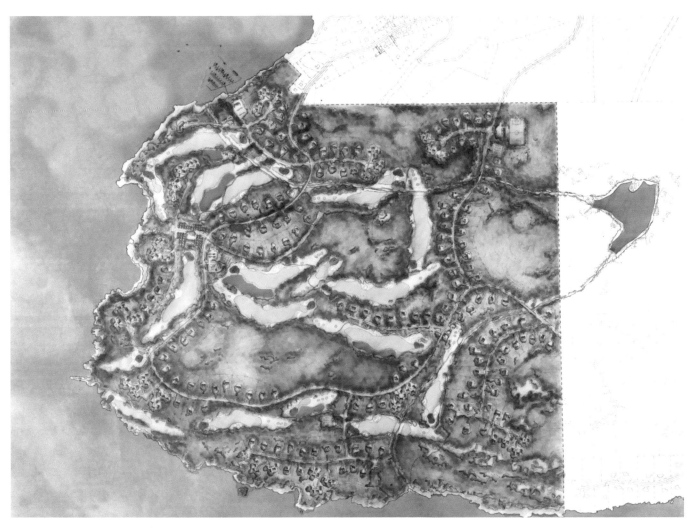

Cape Roger Curtis; Bowen Island, BC; 1992

efficient way of using it for thermal mass energy storage. We also pioneered the use of interior light shelves and exterior shading devices for maximum daylighting and energy efficiency. Operable windows were deployed throughout for the first time, a fact that seems unbelievable today, but clients and engineers were conservative during those years, and we had to fight for each and every innovation.

York University Computer Science Building
Toronto, ON, 1998-2001

Stack ventilation and stratification provides all of this building's ventilation energy and fresh air. The atrium is an energy sink during summer and winter peaks. We daylit all spaces using atrium and perimeter glazing. The building has beautiful insulated shutters in the classroom block that open and close to facilitate daylighting as well as temperature control and energy savings. The project includes underground tunnels to temper winter and summer intake air. All four façades are distinctly different to facilitate daylighting, ventilation and solar shading. A pivotal collaboration with Van Nostrand Di Castri Architects (now Architects Alliance) and Keen Engineering (now Stantec), and a first in the large market of Toronto, this project received a great deal of publicity and brought sustainable design to the attention of most Canadian architects and engineers.

Architectural Institute of British Columbia; Vancouver, BC; 1998

White Rock Operations Centre; White Rock, BC; 2003

Normand Maurice Building; Montreal, QC; 2006

Architectural Institute of British Columbia
VANCOUVER, BC, 1997–1998
This project was our first use of heat pump systems to distribute and reuse energy in various zones of a building simultaneously.

TELUS House Revitalization/William Farrell Building
VANCOUVER, BC, 1998–2001
Our first use of an innovative double envelope design which effectively creates a greenhouse that surrounds the southeast and southwest faces of the building and forms a ventilated façade that conditions the internal spaces.

White Rock Operations Building
WHITE ROCK, BC 2001–2003
Our first LEED building (and Canada's first LEED Gold new building) featured photovoltaic and solar hot water systems. LEED showed us how to incorporate many site design strategies (native landscaping, permeable paving, efficient site lighting) and to think about interior comfort, views, recycled building and furniture content. Water conservation and reuse was a new area of focus, and this project contains our first greywater used for toilet flushing. A reused underground sewage tank filled with community stormwater is used as a heat sink for heating and cooling. This was a revolutionary project for us, as LEED broadened our horizons to think about larger environmental issues. (Earlier projects were built largely around energy efficiency and operations costs.) This strategy of thinking about broader impacts eventually resulted in whole systems thinking and regenerative design, which we now incorporate into everything we do.

Normand Maurice Building
MONTREAL, QC 2002–2006
For this, the first LEED Platinum building in Quebec, we employed more refined daylighting strategies. Working with Montreal-based ABCP Architects and Beauchamp Bourbeau Architects, we studied optimal conditions for daylighting and solar shading and designed rooftop light scoops that send daylight deep into the building, even in winter. Also, a distinctive 45-degree extruded shading screen for the southwest façade allows 100 percent solar shading in summer and 80 percent solar penetration in winter – all while using substantially less material content. We have employed this strategy in several buildings since, most recently EEEL in Calgary in 2012. Inside, winter sun falls on a Trombe wall comprised of salvaged bricks that line the circulation corridors behind the southwest façade.

Dubai International Financial Centre
DUBAI, UAE, 2006–2007
Computational fluid dynamic (CFD) software allowed us to study velocity changes to winds traveling over the building surfaces and compressed between the two shafts of this building. Using CFD data, we were able to capture accelerated air for use in the vertical axis windmills designed to provide 15 percent of the power needed to operate the building.

Student Center, University of Texas, Dallas
DALLAS, TX, 2008–2010
We continued our interest in experimenting with new exterior shading devices in this project, using prefabricated ceramics to provide the beautiful exterior shading envelope that protects three of the structure's elevations. This project

Student Center, University of Texas, Dallas; Dallas, TX; 2011

Dubai International Financial Centre, Wind Turbines; Dubai, UAE; 2008

York University Computer Science Building; Toronto, ON; 2001

Husky Union Building (HUB), Wood Shutters, University of Washington; Seattle, WA; 2013

also featured our first large scale "light scoop" installed over the central atrium to provide year-round daylighting without solar gain.

York University Computer Science Building
TORONTO, ON, 1998–2001
Shutters have been used for energy efficiency reasons on buildings for thousands of years, and are ubiquitous to cultures around the world, yet they are hardly used at all today. This building has beautiful insulated shutters in the south facing lecture hall that open and close to facilitate daylighting as well as temperature control and energy savings.

Husky Union Building (HUB), University of Washington
SEATTLE, WA, 2008–2013
The south west facing glazing in the multipurpose hall has motorized perforated wood shutters that insulate, control daylight, reduce energy consumption and provide acoustic sound control, all very beautifully.

There are many other sustainable design innovations that could be included in this section, including unique aspects of almost every project. Many are described in other chapters in this book in more detail, particularly more recent projects. Today, our goal is to infuse each new project with regenerative design properties, getting buildings as close as possible to net zero energy, carbon, waste, and water.

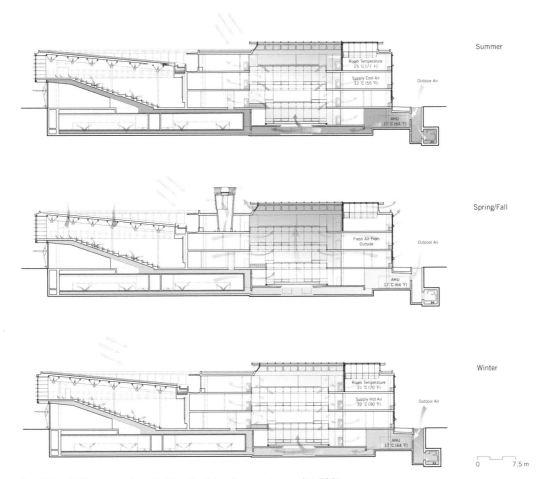

Summer

Room Temperature
25 °C (77 °F)

Supply Cool Air
12 °C (55 °F)

Outdoor Air

AHU
17 °C (64 °F)

Spring/Fall

Fresh Air From
Outside

Outdoor Air

AHU
17 °C (64 °F)

Winter

Room Temperature
21 °C (70 °F)

Supply Hot Air
32 °C (90 °F)

Outdoor Air

AHU
17 °C (64 °F)

0   7.5 m

York University Computer Science Building, Ventilation Diagram; Toronto, ON; 2001

Husky Union Building (HUB), University of Washington; Seattle, WA; 2013

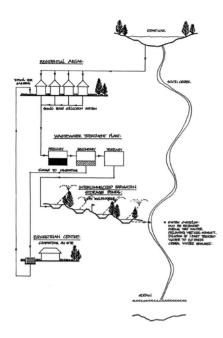

Cape Roger Curtis; Bowen Island, BC; 1992

2.2 Whole Systems Thinking

Sustainable design has matured away from a singular focus on high-performance buildings – an important developmental stage, but one whose benefits were typically limited to site-specific. We now know that decisions we make about buildings need to be paired with a more thorough understanding of all the contextual, environmental and climatic impacts of all aspects of related flows of water, waste, energy, and carbon associated with our projects. A comprehensive understanding of all related impacts of our lives, habits, and constructions on the environment and biosphere would seem daunting at first. But as can be seen in the projects below, they can be assessed and impacts can be mitigated. With experience and wisdom, we now design with consideration toward impacts that we know of, increasingly gaining understanding of how they interact with one another and the surrounding environment, present and future. We call this process "whole systems thinking." (A more extensive discussion about this approach occurs in Chapter 4.)

Cape Roger Curtis

BOWEN ISLAND, BC, 1989–1992

The plan for this project included strategies for self-sufficiency of its own water and sewage treatment systems. The illustration above dating from 1989 shows water collection and storage (behind a dam), then sewage collection in small bore pipes and treatment to primary, secondary and tertiary levels. Effluent is then filtered through four levels of natural ponds before being released to the stream and ocean.

Dockside Green

VICTORIA, BC, 2004–2009

Sustainability was factored into every aspect of this 26-building, 130,000 square meter development. Working with Keen Engineering and the landscape architects at PWL Studio, we created designs and systems that served individual buildings as well as the entire site. We incorporated sustainable design solutions for energy, water, and waste that previously had been the sole concern of mechanical and civil engineers.

Initial concepts for the competitive proposal featured carbon-neutral operations and on-site wastewater treatment as the team did not want any part of the regional sewage system that did not include treatment.

Tertiary wastewater treatment produces reclaimed water that is used for toilet flushing, irrigation, and central stream makeup and discharge to the ocean. An integrated design process brought the concepts of handling of stormwater without the normal underground storm drainage pipes with the discharge of excess reclaimed water. Bioswales were used for an additional pre-filter for the reclaimed water and all water discharged to the ocean went through another bioswale for final cleaning. Some of the reclaimed water is sold to a nearby concrete plant as part of its industrial process.

The carbon-neutral building operations goal posed a special challenge for the team as we had not done a carbon-neutral project before. Significant research of alternatives led to a biomass gasification system to provide district heating to the project. Clean waste wood from local sources would be fuel. For an economic installation, the peak heating loads, that do not occur frequently, would be handled by a peaking gas-fired boiler. This small use of peak load gas energy and the small emissions related to the clean electricity grid did provide some residual carbon emissions from the site. To more than offset this emission, the district heating system was extended off-site to a nearby hotel. Carbon-neutral heat sold to the hotel displaced their gas use and more than offset these residual emissions to result in carbon-neutral operations.

As an example of the synergies among systems, the sludge produced as a by-product of the sewage treatment system has a significant amount of the moisture removed and is blended with the biomass fuel to produce some district heating energy. This process effectively eliminated the operating cost of the disposal of the sludge.

Once these systems were up and running, we began to assess them and think of them as whole systems design. This is thinking that permeates the design of all larger scale community and urban design projects since.

Point Wells

SNOHOMISH COUNTY, WA, 2009–2020 (PROJECTED)

We developed a stormwater and wastewater treatment system for this 3000-unit community (still in the permitting process) that was modeled largely after the strategies successfully implemented at Dockside Green. The district energy system that meets all of the community's heating and cooling needs is fed by biomass of agriculture waste product delivered by rail.

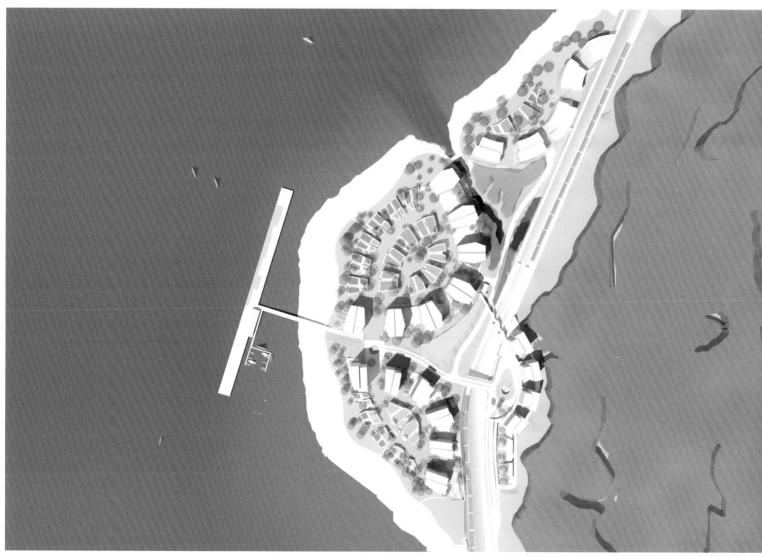

Point Wells, Site Plan; Snohomish County, WA; 2020 (projected)

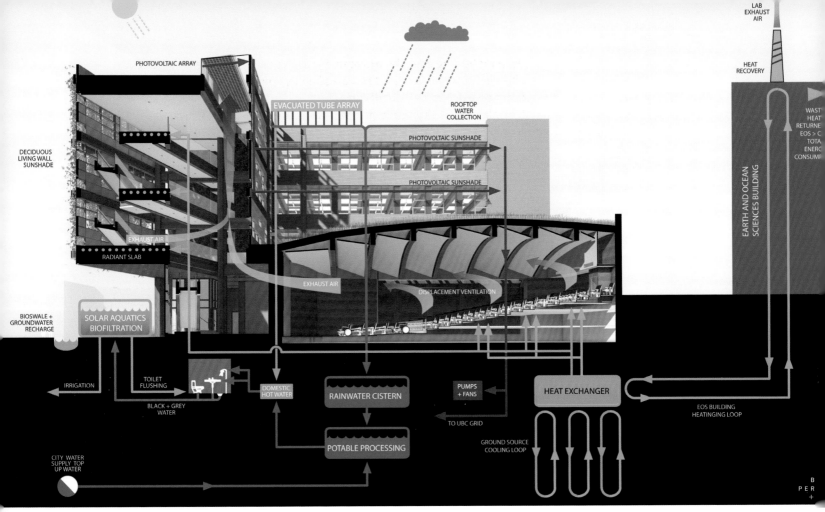

Centre for Interactive Research on Sustainable Design, University of British Columbia; Vancouver, BC; 2011

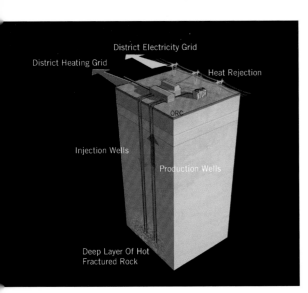

Blatchford Redevelopment; Edmonton, AB; 2013

Blatchford Redevelopment

EDMONTON, AB, 2011–13 (DESIGN)

For this land redevelopment plan, we began with a whole systems approach then expanded it to include true geothermal energy. Extracting thermal energy from 3000 meters below ground to steam turbines will generate the bulk of the community's required electricity and all necessary heat to the buildings. Agricultural waste is also used in bioreactors to generate electricity and heat energy. The municipality is planning to channel waste sludge and biomass from municipal collection and treatment systems in the planned development. Stormwater collection and treatment by natural means in this project is resolved by a major water feature in the 76-acre park, the functional part of which has five levels of water storage as part of a public amenity that defines the heart of the project.

As part of infrastructure for the project, we planned for the development of urban agriculture at several scales, supporting public markets and services.

The competition brief for the Blatchford Redevelopment Master Plan called for carbon-neutral operation of a new community for 30,000 people in a region with a coal-fired electrical grid. The project would have to generate both electrical and heating energy for the development. A biomass, combined heat and power system fueled by industrial waste wood, would be developed in stages to provide the energy needs for the development and have heat available for an expansion of a heating grid to nearby facilities. With research funding, deep geothermal energy at six kilometers deep for power generation or 3.5 kilometers deep for heating could be explored. Further research into the waste opportunities in Edmonton revealed some additional opportunities: clean waste wood could be used as fuel, dried sludge from existing ponds could provide additional fuel, cleaned sewage gas that is currently flared could be used for on-site cooking facilities and also fuels some of the transit buses serving the site.

A central series of lakes were developed as an amenity in the park and these lakes served to collect site stormwater for reuse in toilet flushing and site irrigation. Excavation material from the lakes and the building foundations would be used to create a hill at the northern edge to provide protection from the winter winds.

The UBC Centre for Interactive Research on Sustainability
VANCOUVER, BC, 2008–2011

A more sophisticated approach to whole systems thinking is evident in this project and is behind all of the mechanics that support this building. Rainwater collection, treatment, and storage cisterns are used for non-potable sources in the building. The bioswale for final greywater cleaning is located at the entrance of the building. (One must literally step over it.) Surplus stormwater is directed to actively recharge an aquifer located under the campus. Thermal energy is extracted from waste energy through heat recovery coils located in the manifold of fume hoods in the adjacent Earth Sciences Building. The energy extracted from this source provides all heat necessary for the CIRS building itself and more, the additional energy being returned to the adjacent Earth Sciences Building, offsetting fossil fuel consumption in that building. Strategies at CIRS for water, waste, and energy result in the building being net zero energy annually as well as net zero carbon in the operation of the building. The building contains a solar aquatics sewage treatment system, also near the front door. In summer months, when student activity significantly decreases, sewage is imported from a main on the campus to sustain the biological activity of the solar aquatics filtration system. Whole systems thinking has a beneficial effect on several buildings around it, and on the campus aquifer, a precursor to regenerative design.

Vancouver View Studies; Vancouver, BC; 1989

2.3 Urbanism

As a practice, we have always worked and designed in urban cores, as suburban development connected by highways and business parks is simply unsustainable. Ultimately, the carbon footprint of our cities is defined by the buildings in them, the fuel sources that feed them and the transportation required to make them work. Our goal is to promote and enhance livable, workable, enjoyable, beautiful cities with low carbon impacts. As architects, it is our responsibility to strengthen the fabric of great, sustainable urban places. Examples of a wide variety of urban solutions and innovations that we have authored follow.

City of Vancouver View Studies
VANCOUVER, BC, 1988–1989
With this early implementation of AutoCAD 3D modeling, we helped the City of Vancouver develop its public view protection policy, for which we analyzed and projected a 3D model to predict the city's future form and maintain sightlines to its most beautiful physical (mountain) features from 33 key public places. In the decades since, the project has informed all projects in the city as well as Vancouver's development permitting procedures, and has protected the public right to treasured views from key open spaces. The views protection policies have been updated twice since, and we have been involved both times. Our efforts have shaped the city.

Great Northern Way Business Park
VANCOUVER, BC, 1998–1999
Relying again on 3D modeling, this was our first urban design project that took into account the need to share solar access. An ideal combination of density and height was determined that could serve the present and future needs of the built environment, anticipating and enshrining solar access in the design of the project, and in property rights for the owners. In some European cities and in China, access to sunlight laws have existed for years, where the rights to solar access defines the spacing of buildings. In Russia and other northern countries, the cause is absence of sun in the wintertime. In China, spacing, building, and heights are defined by access to sun into living spaces. In the future, solar access rights will be a feature of planning law in every city.

Abu Dhabi Plan 2030
ABU DHABI, UAE, 2005–2007
The chance to apply urban design ideas on a larger scale came when we were asked to plan the future of Abu Dhabi and its anticipated population boom. Working with a comprehensive team that included Larry Beasley of Beasley and Associates, CIVITAS Urban Design & Planning, and many others, we examined the region's natural aspects and its infrastructure, ultimately developing criteria that would protect the environment while supporting residential, commercial and recreational development. Published as Abu Dhabi Plan 2030, notable aspects included a plan to densify the city and to add a million residents to it. It resulted in mixed-use densification of the downtown core, new transportation infrastructure, roadway transit and access networks, development of a secondary core for the city (which would become the capital district), new parks and open space policies and retail districts. We also examined natural aspects of the waterfront and created a planning policy that led to the protection of desert wildlife refuges and marine conservation areas. In four years of work, we took ideas of urbanism, pedestrian orientation, transit dependency, mixed-use

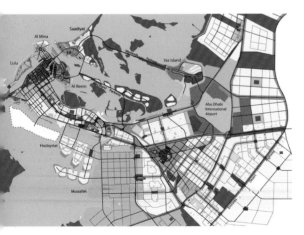

Cross Roads; Vancouver, BC; 2009

Plan Abu Dhabi 2030; Abu Dhabi, UAE; 2007

Marine Gateway, Vancouver, BC, 2015 (projected)

Point Wells; Snohomish County, WA; 2015 (projected)

Blatchford Redevelopment; Edmonton, AB

approaches to densification and developed a template for developing cities around the world.

Cross Roads

VANCOUVER, BC, 2004–2009

This mixed-use urban project contains equal parts retail, residential and commercial space and is built according to a model of shared assets. Energy systems in the project are engineered to circulate necessary resources throughout the daily cycle for maximum efficiency and utility, for both public and private occupants.

Marine Gateway

VANCOUVER, BC, 2005–2015

We helped rezone and densify this site to turn it into a world-class transit-oriented community that allows residents, customers and employees to walk or travel by transit. Built to high sustainability standards, the project includes significant investment in infrastructure for on-site water treatment and energy systems. Now under construction, this project epitomizes transit-oriented development (TOD), an idea with a strong future as we move away from automobile-driven development patterns.

Point Wells

SHORELINE, WA, 2009–2017

The heights and arrangements of all buildings on this site are determined by sun angle, access to views and ease of pedestrian circulation. Mixed-use elements ensure that the community provides vibrant residential, retail, and recreational opportunities – all within easy access to public transportation and supported by environmentally friendly systems, and a district energy plant.

Blatchford Redevelopment

EDMONTON, AB, 2011–2013

This planned development is intended to serve 30,000 residents on 500 acres of prime vacant land near the center of Alberta's capital. The advanced urban design includes density driven by access to transit, a commitment to nature in the design, innovation in stormwater systems, and a full development of urban farming.

2.4 Climate-Specific Design

By and large, the development of western architecture as a global phenomenon in the last 40 years has been irrespective of climate and location. Generally, office towers in Edmonton and London and New York and Riyadh and Sydney all look the same. As a practice concerned with environmental solutions, it seems to us that the consideration of climate should create much more differentiation among building solutions in varying climate conditions. Climate-specific solutions must inform envelope performance, shading strategies, material selection and aesthetic choices to reflect the appropriate historical and cultural influences in the region.

OltreMare

RICCIONE, ITALY, 1999–2003

Our first opportunity to design buildings in climates other than our own came in 1999 when we designed this entertainment venue, whose attractions included a dolphinarium, indoor and outdoor exhibits celebrating the region's natural flora and fauna. As part of the design process we studied the context of the local climate. Solutions that were implemented involved subterranean development to reduce heat absorption and to tap the naturally cooling effect of the ground, extensive natural ventilation, and heavy structural systems that provided both radiant cooling and thermal absorption, depending on time of day and year.

The Vale Living With Lakes Centre for Applied Research in Environmental Restoration and Sustainability

SUDBURY, ON 2006–2011

Wintertime temperatures can drop below minus 40°C in Sudbury, but global warming will gradually lessen the chill on the region. We designed a building envelope and an energy system strategy that will steadily adapt the building performance as climate conditions change over the course of 40 years.

The Vale Living With Lakes Centre, Laurentian University; Sudbury, ON; 2011

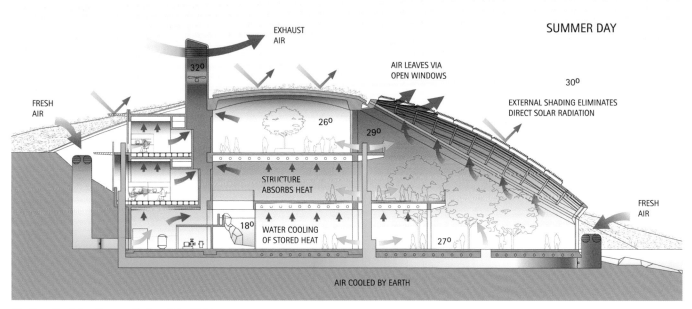

OltreMare, Ventilation Diagram; Riccione, Italy; 2004

Student Center, University of Texas, Dallas
DALLAS, TX 2008–2010

Solar analysis showed us that the ideal strategy for this building would incorporate full shading on its east, west and south façades. We added a large, indirectly illuminated atrium and a ceramic shading screen suspended around the perimeter, which provides a high percentage of effective solar protection while maintaining sightlines to the exterior.

King Abdullah Financial District Mixed-Use Tower
RIYADH, SAUDI ARABIA, 2007–2015 (PROJECTED)

Harsh climate conditions must be designed around, whether temperatures are tremendously hot or cold. For this project, we borrowed strategies employed in Northern Canada (where the extremes are reversed, but the necessity of a superior envelope is similar), incorporating extensive insulation properties in the envelope and full exterior louver solar shading on all elevations. Large shading structures are also provided over the public and semi-public spaces on the entire site. We also considered sandstorms and the effect of environmental storms (dust and dirt accumulation), and selected finishes (materials and colors) that are derived from historical precedents, the limestone and adobe buildings that were indigenous to the region.

All our buildings demonstrate climate-specific solutions. We research the climate and environment conditions in detail at the outset, and we develop physical planning, envelope performance, shading requirements, and material selection based on historical and indigenous examples interpreted in a modern way. Indigenous materials always have the lowest transportation carbon impact. All solutions vary dramatically from one another as one should expect when working with the climate and regional context. All our buildings look unique. Digital tools that help us predict how our buildings need to perform always drive the "look" of the project from start to finish. To do otherwise is environmentally irresponsible.

Student Center, University of Texas, Dallas; Dallas, TX; 2011

King Abdullah Financial District Mixed-Use Tower; Riyadh, Saudi Arabia; 2015

3. Exploration in Form

Like most firms just starting out, we began our practice cautiously, delivering simple, repetitive (mostly orthogonal), and economical designs for clients who were most often focused on cost issues. As we grow and developed a more expansive client roster, we were afforded more opportunities to experiment with the form-giving aspects of architecture. The real art of the discipline comes when we can combine adventurous formal solutions with sustainability and simplicity in design.

Ebco Aerospace
DELTA, BC, 1986–1987
This simple exterior suspended steel structure is repeated in 12 identical bays around a central spine. The economies of scale and repetitive features helped keep the costs of this industrial building close to those of standard tilt-up designs that were common at the time.

Nicola Valley Institute of Technology
MERRITT, BC, 1999–2001
This project marked our first non-orthogonal design. We were introduced to the idea that in designing a building for the First Nations community, the importance of circular design had significant cultural relevance. In the indigenous culture, the summertime nomadic tent structures and the wintertime pit house designs were circular in nature to afford the most efficient use of materials and resources for the largest volume of space. The location and orientation for the winter pit houses as a defense against climatic conditions were most important and compelled the openness of these structures to passive solar gain, facing due south. Developing a solution with the five Okanagan bands, we also learned the importance of the cardinal points. To the east

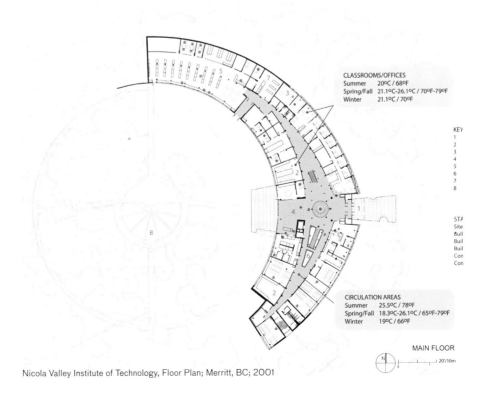

CLASSROOMS/OFFICES
Summer   20ºC / 68ºF
Spring/Fall 21.1ºC-26.1ºC / 70ºF-79ºF
Winter   21.1ºC / 70ºF

CIRCULATION AREAS
Summer   25.5ºC / 78ºF
Spring/Fall 18.3ºC-26.1ºC / 65ºF-79ºF
Winter   19ºC / 66ºF

MAIN FLOOR

Nicola Valley Institute of Technology, Floor Plan; Merritt, BC; 2001 (awakening/entry/beginning) would be the front door; the south would capture warmth and openness to land/views/food; the west would honor the evening/ enclosure/community; and the north would celebrate connections to nature/ hillside/resources and access to/learning from nature. All four of these cardinal points at NVIT became important elements of the building design, deliberately semi-embedded in the hillside like the indigenous pit houses. The structure itself, our first non-orthogonal structure, evolved into a thick flat-slab concrete design for thermal mass reasons, supported by vertical prefabricated timber elements made from recycled pine found in the area.

Brentwood SkyTrain Station
BURNABY, BC, 1999–2002

The Burnaby station is highly visible on the elevated tracks and, as such, its design is intentionally sculptural. The use of a wood roof diaphragm composed of recycled two-by-fours laminated together on-site allowed for a curvaceous form. The curves included shingle style glazing to protect from wind exposure. The center of the platforms is the widest point of the design, affording passengers space and comfort, yielding a design that has a sensuous form.

Brentwood SkyTrain Station; Burnaby, BC; 2001

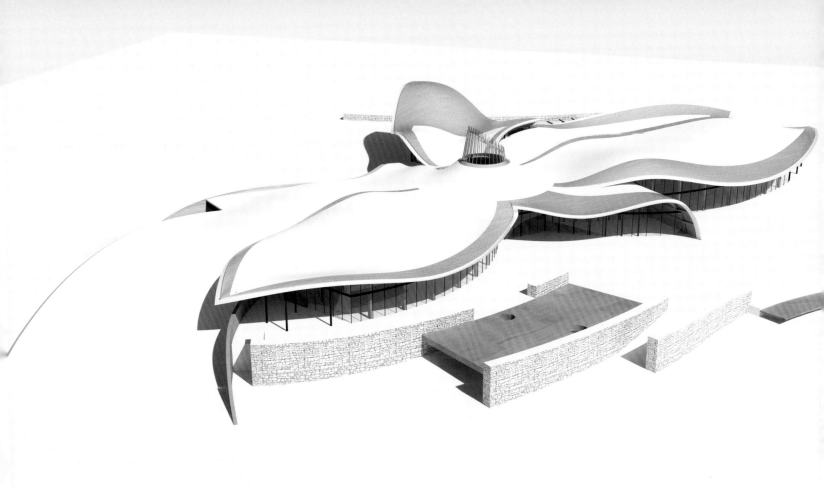

VanDusen Botanical Garden Visitor Centre; rendering in Rhino, Vancouver, BC; 2012

Ottawa Confederation Line; Ottawa, ON; 2017 (projected)

CULTURE OF INNOVATION

Kingsway Pedestrian Bridge; Burnaby, BC; 2008

Riyadh Light Rail Transit Station

RIYADH, SAUDI ARABIA, 2004–2019 (ESTIMATED)

By creating a strong "iconic" physical profile for these stations, we increased system legibility and recognition within the clutter of a crowded urban environment. The complexity of this form was possible only with the help of new 3D design software, which continues to help us experiment ever more dramatically with form.

Kingsway Pedestrian Bridge

BURNABY, BC, 2007–2008

Striking architectural form meets material efficiency here, as wood and steel are combined to achieve structural integrity and beauty. The result is a public amenity that contributes artistry and functionality to the urban landscape.

Ottawa Confederation Line Stations

OTTAWA, ON, 2010–2017 (PROJECTED)

Computational design tools helped us create a vocabulary of panelized wood and steel curved members that protect travelers from the elements while delivering structural and operational performance. By applying this basic strategy across a series of stations as a "kit of parts," we could create design distinctions for each station while maintaining overall material and economic efficiencies.

VanDusen Botanical Garden Visitor Centre

VANCOUVER, BC, 2007–2011

In our most complex form to date, made possible by the new software, Rhino, we combined lessons learned from previous projects incorporating laminated, modular designs. This expressive and iconic structure echoes the simple shape of the native orchid found in the local forests. The building's abstract expression suited the client's interest in organic forms while meeting the administrative purposes of the structure itself. More information on VanDusen may be found in Chapter 5, Regenerative Design.

3.1 Digital Developments Shape What and How We Design

As can be seen from the discussion above, drawing technology is literally reshaping the edges of our architecture. The practice began with drafting Maylines and AutoCAD V1.4 that led us to simple forms and orthogonal solutions. Now, with the emergence of 3d Studio Max, Rhino, Grasshopper, and other more powerful digital modelling tools, we are able to experiment more dramatically with form. The parallel development of computer driven manufacturing capability where a series of building components that are all unique but now no longer add significant construction premiums, as a result of the elimination of drawings in the construction process, gives us further freedom to experiment with form. This is the real breakthrough. A future of unfettered manufacturing capability driven by computational models we create looks very exciting, with unlimited future new "edges."

4. Evolving Design Processes

The process of designing projects has changed dramatically over the last 20 years – for the better. Most profoundly, members of the public (as well as the users and occupants of the buildings being designed) are increasingly involved in virtually every stage of project development. Engaging all parties in the process of how a building takes shape keeps architects and engineers accountable to the people and communities for whom we really work. Architecture has become a very public art, often the subject of political debate. All that is good!

4.1 Consultation and Engagement

It used to be that a developer would buy property, assemble a plan for how to use it, hire an architect who would obtain the approval from the city and the project would get built. Today, getting the go-ahead for any building – whether it is a public or private facility – requires extensive public consultation. Projects are shaped by policies as well as increasingly widening circles of stakeholder input. Twenty years ago, rezonings in Vancouver were rare. Today, 50 percent of all projects go through rezoning. Approval processes lengthen, from "10-12 weeks" (the mantra in the 1990s at Vancouver City Hall) to two-plus years now, the same length of time for a Master Use Permit (MUP) in Seattle, both dwarfed by the four or more year process in San Francisco. City planning departments have grown in size and power, which means that planning policies that were once advisory are now mandatory. In addition, community groups have a justifiable interest in voicing their opinion about how designs take shape. These shifts simply mean that architects must remain innovative as we engage with our many audiences.

We use design charrettes now to design all of our projects. Charrettes are not a solitary sketch process in an artist loft; they involve the stakeholders, experts, client representatives, and full design teams and can extend to three or four days at several intervals during the schematic design and development phases. They often involve the wider community, too, as they also have a stake in what we do. That involvement requires bravery on our part, letting the public dialogue shape the solutions, whether you think the results are right or wrong. We have to accept that the public will is not wrong, as we shape a very public art.

Samuel Brighouse, Elementary School;
Student Charrette; 2009

Samuel Brighouse Elementary School

RICHMOND, BC, 2009–2011

For what is arguably one of the most rewarding projects in our portfolio, we invited fourth to sixth grade students to participate actively in the design of their own school. The children formed a design committee, created a project blog and hosted workshops that enhanced our own professional efforts. Their drawings were sensational! Interestingly, they focused on introducing "sun" and "nature" into the building, perhaps a response to the desperately cheap and institutional existing school. The result is a spectacularly enjoyable sustainable school facility with which students feel an unbreakable connection.

Nicola Valley Institute of Technology

MERRITT, BC, 1999–2001

We collaborated closely with the Okanagan Band and other local First Nations communities while planning for, designing, and building this structure. Tribal elders helped shape the project early on by taking us to the site and offering design and orientation input based on historical and spiritual precedents. Even

Nicola Valley Institute of Technology; Merritt, BC; 2001

Mount Pleasant Community Centre, Charrette; 2009

the precise location of the front door was determined in accordance with their preferences. Imagine the grandmothers of students at other universities determining the front door locations for new capital projects!

Mount Pleasant Community Centre, #1 Kingsway
BURNABY, BC, 2003–2009
Whether we are designing a complex university building, a commercial project or a public community center, we want to honor the many people who will have something to say about the project. For this community center at #1 Kingsway in Vancouver, members of the local community were encouraged to attend and participate in the charrettes to ensure that they felt involved in the project's evolution. These boisterous evening meetings involved as many as 100 people from the public participating in developing design schemes for the project. As a result, the facility has been widely embraced by the community and, by attendance, is the most popular community center in Vancouver.

Vale Living With Lakes Centre for Applied Research in Environmental Restoration and Sustainability
SUDBURY, ON, 2006–2011
Beginning with this project, we learned the importance of folding ecologists into the project team to grow our understanding of ecological systems. The design of this project was driven by our conversation with them, and our newly gained understanding of ecological systems and the frail health of nature around us. The project is discussed in more detail in Chapter 5, but it has profoundly affected how we design. We continue to broaden the range of expert consultants who have expertise in various aspects of sustainability, whole systems design and resource efficiency as we strive to make a difference with new "edges" to our work.

4.2 Continuous Education

It would be impossible for us to innovate if we were not fully committed to an ongoing quest for professional knowledge. The education of architects, engineers, and planners never ceases. We have internal research initiatives mentioned in Chapter 2, Corporate Responsibility, that empower us to be more knowledgeable about our subjects and develop ideas that are more innovative in all of our projects. We have systems of organizing research and information internally within the company (such as the SDI or the Design Leadership Forum) where educational subjects are developed and disseminated from teams to the wider firm or within offices and projects.

We have also developed a number of externally facing programs for educating ourselves and others. In 2001, we began a Sustainable Design for Canadian Buildings program (SDCB) with the Royal Architectural Institute of Canada, a program that continues today with other architects providing content. During our involvement in the first three years of the program, we taught sustainable design to more than 1700 architects and engineers in full-day courses across the country.

Sustainable Condo; Traveling Exhibit; 2004

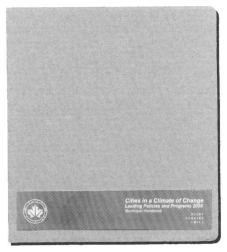

Canadian Cities in a Climate of Change, Throughout Canada; 2008

1650 West 2nd Avenue; Vancouver, BC; 1995

At Perkins+Will, our internal research and education initiatives empower us to develop innovative ideas and approaches that we are encouraged to apply to all of our projects and that we happily share with the industry as a whole, educating others in the process.

Sustainable Condo
VANCOUVER, BC, 2004
This educational exhibit proved to be very popular when first presented at Globe 2004 in Vancouver. It featured physical examples of sustainable design, equipment, and furnishing opportunities for "typical" condominiums, an area of design that was sorely lacking as compared to much more progressive sustainable design approaches for public and institutional buildings. The Sustainable Condo was featured at Greenbuild in 2006 in Atlanta, and then was exhibited in many venues in Ontario and other locations to serve as a traveling classroom for the public and developers.

Canadian Cities in a Climate of Change
ACROSS CANADA, 2007–2008
We developed a program and related documentation around policy alternatives for sustainable design that we took on tour to most of Canada's large cities. To prepare the tour's materials, we surveyed the sustainable design strategies in the major "green" cities in North America, choosing the best policies from each to showcase what was possible. Outstanding examples were obtained from New York City, San Francisco, Portland, Seattle, and Vancouver and incorporated into the presentations. The idea was to infect city politicians and planners with ideas gleaned from best practices elsewhere. The program was very successful.

We conducted other programs and developed content to educate our developer clients, offering the first "LEED for Developers 101" in 2008, version 201 in 2009 and 301 in 2010. We presented this information to developers in Toronto, Calgary, and on many different occasions, affecting and aiding the transformation of the marketplace.

Working with Dr. Ray Cole at the UBC (and a significant financial donation from Perkins+Will) we developed the first version of a Regenerative Design Framework, a tool for the design and evaluation of regenerative design. We published and presented the proposed standard on numerous occasions. (Discussed in more detail in Chapter 5.)

We have developed documentation and presented material around the subject of "Universities in a climate of change" to over 15 academic institutions across the country beginning in 2009. In these presentations, we discussed opportunities for high-performance building architecture but also whole systems sustainable design and sustainable design education at the universities.

In-house, Perkins+Will has developed education programs around the Precautionary List as well as the 2030 calculator, as discussed in Chapter 2.

We share all information and research across our industry through our website and public presentations. We have recently set up a not-for-profit (AREA) to further the dissemination of our innovation, research, and knowledge throughout the industry and beyond to a wider audience.

1050 Homer Street; Vancouver, BC; 1998

1220 Homer Street; Vancouver, BC; 2000

1220 Homer Street; Vancouver, BC; 2000

1650 West 1st Avenue; Vancouver, BC; 1992

4.3 The Office as Innovation Test Bed

We have always believed that our work environment was critical for many reasons. Whether new (all but one of our offices have been renovations) or renovated, our spaces have all been designed to attract and retain the best employees, to demonstrate to our clients and visitors that we are accomplished designers, and to model our understanding of the linkage between workplace and creativity. Our values must be "on display" to stimulate our thought processes and discussions with our clients. A necessary part of every office has been the inclusion of innovative materials and technologies. In chronological order, all our premises over the last 30 years:

1216 Granville Street
VANCOUVER, BC, 1984, EXPANSION 1987

In this office, we had a freestanding washroom pedestal made of molded fiberglass supporting a cantilevered toilet on one side, and sink, mirror and Vola taps on the other. The main shop front elevation was a single sheet of point supported glass, backed by a welded steel cross frame held in tension by eight turnbuckles. An illuminated door sign was made of green LEDs hand soldered (by myself) into a "dot matrix" pattern, that being state-of-the art printing technology at the time. (It was a while ago!) Inside the four-seat office (three were empty on opening day) hummed an IBM 360 computer with 64 K Ram driving AutoCAD V1.4, which, at a combined cost of $25,000 was half my start-off budget. The shop front remained until 2011.

1650 West 2nd Avenue
VANCOUVER, BC, 1990

In our new, much larger office (a converted warehouse), the "architecture on the street" concept compelled us to design a shop front glazing that was again unique. Vertical tension cables held custom cast aluminum "spreaders" that connected to waterjet cut steel flats that supported the glass. Outside wing-like canopies were created from shrink-wrapped plastic on milled spars. Inside, a two-story space featured the suspended tail assembly of a beautiful riveted aluminum 1950s-era aircraft. The building has since been converted into a sound studio by the musician Sarah McLachlan.

1650 West 1st Avenue
VANCOUVER, BC, 1995

Our only newbuild office so far, this project was an ambitious rezoning for a four-story mixed-use building on an inner city lot. Innovations included distributed mechanical towers in the four corners of the plan to allow for tenant controls, exterior shading structures, operable glazing, and a fully green roof. Five of the 11 townhouses on the roof were converted into a private residence for an art collector. The building remains largely unchanged today.

1050 Homer Street
VANCOUVER, BC, 1998

Our first office in a heritage wood building saw us develop our own modular furniture system based on wood fabrications and aluminum extrusions, as we concentrated on workplace innovation.

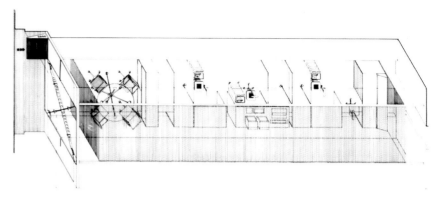

1216 Granville Street; Vancouver, BC; 1984

1220 Homer Street

VANCOUVER, BC, 2000

Just three blocks from our first office, this is still the home of our Vancouver practice. Located in Yaletown, it is within walking, transit, and bike distance for almost every employee. The five-story space is carved out of a 1950s concrete warehouse that was a candy factory at the time we leased it. A central atrium has a composite wood and glass skylight with operable glazing taken from the greenhouse industry. Operable windows front and back provide cross ventilation that obviates the need for air conditioning. Heating is primarily from recaptured thermal energy created by lights, equipment, and people, making the energy requirements ultra-low. Flooring is recycled rubber from tires. The modular furniture pioneered at 1050 Homer has been expanded and more completely detailed. Everything in the office, except chairs and lights, has been designed in-house. In the washrooms, we returned to the theme established in our first office: modular self-supporting washroom furniture. A graceful 90 year old handcrafted cedarstrip canoe is suspended in the main space. Recently a 25-foot high "living wall" has been installed to clean and refresh the air and remind us all of the importance of biophilia in design. A new curved stair reaches the recently inhabited basement. It is comprised of precast modular treads made of thin, strong, lightweight and elegant ductal concrete. All the values of the firm are on display at every turn.

2 Bryant Street

SAN FRANCISCO, CA, 2013–2014

The recent completion of our new premises in San Francisco includes many innovations. (A detailed project description is included in Chapter 2.) Workplace design for creativity and innovation includes the utilization of full mobile computing and audio visual support. Project rooms support ever-changing team structures. All partitions are fully demountable DIRTT system. Social space is highly supported to foster peer exchange and alternative workplace location and comfort. The office is 100 percent daylit with ten new skylights driving 40 Suncentral Sunbeamers, tracking the sun to create indirect daylighting everywhere. Reclaimed wood is used to create an interior rolling glazing system, a mini interior version of the Telus ventilated façade that improves envelope performance dramatically. Power systems include a long-term roof lease that will allow for the future installation of solar panels that will make us net zero for energy and carbon free in operations, a first for Perkins+Will. Interior material choices are based on the Living Building Challenge Red List and our own Precautionary List, intended to demonstrate the healthiest workplace environment possible.

4.4 Fostering a Design Culture

Almost all architects love design. Most importantly, we believe design needs to be nurtured and cultivated to flourish. Creating a culture of design is imperative. Thirty years of awards hang on the Perkins+Will walls in Vancouver and San Francisco. Thirty years of models have pride of place on the floor and walls. A wall of more than 25 magazine covers with our work hangs in Vancouver. Physical artifacts from past projects abound. Newer employees are treated to a "firm history" lecture that establishes recurrent design themes and expectations. Both offices are quite different (tuned to exhibit values to different clientele), but they exude design and care for details. All of these in-house displays help us foster collaboration and peer exchange. Some structural and organizational ideas and practices also support design excellence.

Internal Design Critiques
VARIOUS, 1984–PRESENT
The design process in our offices has evolved to include regular internal critiques. What began as Friday design sessions in our Vancouver office now extends to all offices across the firm at regular intervals.

Firmwide Peer Design Reviews
VARIOUS, 2008–PRESENT
The design process in our firm now includes comprehensive peer design reviews across the firm at regular intervals involving all major projects. In many instances, we take advantage of cross-office expertise, reaching out to leading authors around the company who are asked to weigh in on designs. At Perkins+Will, all significant work in the firm is reviewed annually, at both the design and construction completion phases, for design excellence and sustainability criteria in the forum of Design Excellence Annual Reviews (DEAR), chaired by our own dear Ed Feiner.

Design Leadership Forum (DLF)
VARIOUS, 2006–PRESENT
The key design leaders in Perkins+Will join the DLF and connect on a regular basis through calls and face-to-face meetings. Research, ideas, software, materials, innovations, and precedents are studied and discussed. Attendees return invigorated and stimulated by the discussion of design as a priority.

   The culture of our firm continues to change, which feeds our innovative spirit. The rich diversity of our staff provides us with a growing bank of ideas that originate from all corners of the earth. Our talented pool of professionals bring expertise about design solutions, sustainable design practices, and climate-responsive strategies that broaden our skills. A combination of sheer bench strength and a global presence allows us to develop numerous innovative ideas and put them into practice throughout the world.

Changing the Discipline Takes Discipline

It is the culture of designing in larger groups with more information and more interactive ways that has made our work more creative and richer over the years. The most important of these aspects has to do with an interactive design process that engages experts, planners, public, clients, contractors, manufacturers, consultants, engineers, and other experts and specialists to create more complete and more exciting architecture.

Technologies, materials, processes, environmental and climate data will continue to propel us toward architectural innovation. In the past three decades, our practice has evolved and grown continuously. We have moved from simple orthogonal buildings to crafting flowing prefabricated structures that emerge from the natural beauty that surrounds them. We have addressed the challenges of climate and technological change. None of this exploration would be possible without constantly challenging the norm, pushing standards, and changing the game. Innovation makes us question; it makes us experiment; it makes us better. It creates architecture's new edges.

University of Texas
Dallas Student Center, Dallas, TX

The University of Texas at Dallas had a clear goal for the Student Services Building: provide a destination that serves as a "one-stop shop" for all vital student services.

Student Center, University of Texas, Dallas; Dallas, TX; 2011

The project integrates student-facing departments such as Bursar, Registrar, Enrollment, Financial Aid, Health Services, Counseling, Career Services Center, and other student groups all under one roof. The design provides a gateway building and a new identity to the campus. Located at the southern end of a new pedestrian allée, the building contrasts the existing heavy, precast concrete vernacular with a new lightness and transparency, fitting for a student services building.

The four-story building is organized around a central atrium, providing natural daylight to internal functions, with two internal "bars" of functional uses that separate the atrium from a perimeter zone of offices. A three-story lobby is adjacent to the allée, engaging campus pedestrian movement. Formal and informal meeting spaces have been located adjacent to public gathering spaces to encourage chance meetings and encourage greater collaboration.

New Edge Innovations
As the first LEED Platinum building in the University of Texas system (and in all of Texas), numerous sustainable strategies were used, including cooling load reduction, daylighting, stormwater management, regional material use, wastewater management, and efficient mechanical systems. The

atrium is daylit with a large sun scoop, designed to capture indirect solar light to illuminate the core of the building, without attracting direct solar heat gain. The distinctive custom terra-cotta louver exterior shading system was designed to reduce heat gain and maximize shading as appropriate for each solar exposure. On the east façade this system is extended to create an interpretation of the Texan "porch" that provides respite from the hot sun.

LOCATION Dallas, TX
CLIENT University of Texas System
DESIGN 2008
CONSTRUCTION 2008-2011
SIZE 74,343 sf / 6,907 sm
DESIGN TEAM Perkins+Will: R. Bragg, D. Burns, P. Busby, L. Cavallin, B. Cay, P. Cowcher, S. Curry, D. Day, H. Kao, E. Latreille, R. Miller, S. Schou, A. Toney
STRUCTURAL ENGINEER Jaster Quintanilla & Associates
MECHANICAL ENGINEER Infrastructure Associates
ELECTRICAL ENGINEER Infrastructure Associates
CIVIL ENGINEER URS
LANDSCAPE ARCHITECT Kendall Landscape Architecture
CODE CONSULTANT Schirmer Engineering Corporation
Quantity Surveyor / Cost Consultant Halford Busby

PHOTOGRAPHER Charles Davis Smith
AWARDS RECEIVED
USGBC Central Texas Board Chapter Green School Design Awards, School of the Year Award (Higher Education), 2011
Association for the Advancement of Sustainability in Higher Education/USGBC Innovation in Green Building Award, Inaugural Award, 2011
Accessibility Professionals Association / Texas Governor's Committee on People with Disabilities, Accessibility Award, 2011
Green Project Award of Merit (ENR Texas & Louisiana magazine, 2011
College Planning & Management Magazine, Judge's Choice Award - Education Design Showcase, The Sustainability & Innovation Award, 2011
Dallas Business Journal Best Real Estate Deals, Best Green Project - Public Award, 2011
University of Texas System, Outstanding HUB Participation Award, 2010
SUSTAINABILITY RATINGS LEED Platinum
REFERENCE TO PUBLICATIONS
• Candice Carlisle, "University of Dallas at Texas Student Services Center," Dallas Business Journal, February 25, 2011, p. B42.

University of Washington

Husky Union Building, Seattle, WA

The Husky Union Building has been the "heart and soul" of the University of Washington for over 60 years—a much-loved building and the keeper of many traditions and memories.

Husky Union Building (HUB), University of Washington; Seattle, WA; 2013

In planning for the future, it was important that the design paid tribute to past generations. The original building constructed in 1949, and its subsequent five expansions between 1952 and 1975, had been cobbled together in piecemeal fashion. The HUB renovation and expansion project knits these elements together to create a single, unified center for the University community.

Major program elements in the new HUB include offices and meeting spaces for student activities and student government; enhanced student lounges and gathering spaces; conference and meeting rooms; auditorium/performance spaces; food service; banquet rooms; bookstore and retail; bike shop; a bowling alley and billiards; and an active outdoor area for food and vendors. The new design introduces new transparent contemporary façades on three sides of the building and fully glazed entry pavilions that mark the new three-story atrium space that is now the heart of the HUB.

New Edge Innovations

The University of Washington is committed to achieving a high level of sustainable design. Students were involved in the project from the beginning—in town-style meetings—and saw the new design as an opportunity to pass on a legacy of environmental stewardship to future generations of students. The renovation retains as much of the existing structure as possible. Energy usage throughout the building is significantly reduced by harvesting daylight, using natural ventilation systems, recovering heat from the campus chilled water loop, and incorporating motorized blinds and sun shades. Many of these systems are controlled by an Automated Building System that reacts to changes in the environment. In addition to energy reduction, the project utilizes water conserving fixtures to reduce overall water use by an estimated 36 percent. The project restores the existing open space known as HUB yard, provides new roof garden open space, and introduces a bioretention garden that collects and filters stormwater runoff. Of note is the multi-purpose room, with hybrid wood and steel structure, and operable wood shutters to the glazing.

PROJECT University of Washington, Husky Union Building (HUB)
LOCATION Seattle, WA
CLIENT University of Washington
DESIGN 2008-2010
CONSTRUCTION 2011-2013
DESIGN TEAM Perkins+Will: P. Busby, R. Bussard, S. Chan, A. DeEulio, J. Geringer, A. Gianopoulos, L. Leland, F. Long, J. Stebar, A. Wu
CONTRACTOR Skanska Construction
STRUCTURAL/CIVIL ENGINEER Coughlin Porter Lundeen
MECHANICAL ENGINEER AEI
ELECTRICAL ENGINEER AEI
LANDSCAPE Gustafson Guthrie Nichol
PHOTOGRAPHER Lara Swimmer; Ben Benschneider
AWARDS RECEIVED
Association of College Unions International (ACUI) 2014 Facility Design Award of Excellence, 2014
AIA Washington Council, Civic Design Awards, Honor Award, 2013,
Architectural Woodwork Institute, Award of Excellence, 2013
SUSTAINABILITY RATINGS LEED Gold
REFERENCE TO PUBLICATIONS
- "Civic Design Awards Interview with Ryan Bussard, AIA, Perkins+Will," *AIA Washington Council,* February 10, 2014   http //aiawa. org/2014/02/10/civic-design-awards-interview-ryan-bussard-aia-perkinswill/

Earth Sciences Building (ESB)

University of British Columbia, Vancouver, BC

Located at the University of British Columbia (UBC), the Earth Sciences Building (ESB) provides a dynamic home for multi-disciplinary collaboration and shared learning across three of the university's science departments – Earth, Ocean and Atmospheric Science; Statistics; and the Pacific Institute of the Mathematical Sciences – as well as the Faculty of Science's Office of the Dean.

Earth Sciences Building (ESB), University of British Columbia; Vancouver, BC; 2011

Driven by the goal to put "science on display," the ESB showcases a state-of-the-art mix of teaching, laboratory, and lecture spaces.

The building is also located directly across the street from the Beaty Biodiversity Museum, presenting an opportunity for the UBC to develop a "museum precinct" in this area of campus, contributing to and reinforcing the public realm along Main Mall, the campus's primary axis.

New Edge Innovations

Organized into two wings, the building surrounds a five-story open-concept atrium. Designed to enhance links between each department, the ESB provides valuable opportunities for shared learning and collaboration throughout the building. Acting as a front door for each of the departments, the fully glazed central atrium serves as a conduit for interaction. The incorporation of stone into the exterior curtain wall of the lecture theaters provides opportunities for formal and informal outdoor teaching. Additional informal learning opportunities are scattered throughout the building, while the generous landings on the cantilevered wood stair serve as catalyst for serendipitous interactions.

The building envelope has sophisticated, beautifully detailed shading strategies on all façades.

Wood features as the primary structural material throughout the academic wing, creating an inviting environment for faculty and students while reducing the building's environmental impact through carbon sequestration. Combining solid, cross-laminated, and concentrated composite panels, ESB is the largest wood panelized structure in North America and raises the bar for wood use in large-scale, high-performance projects. ESB incorporates over 1,300 cubic meters of wood, sequestering roughly 1,000 tons of CO_2, the equivalent of taking 415 cars off the road for a year. The central atrium features a dramatic free-floating cantilevered solid timber staircase, a first of its kind in the world. The stair's clean and elegant lines present a visual demonstration of the aesthetic and structural capabilities of modern engineered timber.

LOCATION Vancouver, BC
CLIENT UBC Properties Trust
DESIGN 2009-2010
CONSTRUCTION 2010-2011
SIZE 170,005 sf / 15,794 sm
DESIGN TEAM Perkins+Will: S. Bergen, P. Busby, A. Chmiel, J. Deutscher, J. Gravenstein, J. Foit, H. Kao, S. Schou, E. Stedman
Construction Manager Bird Construction
Civil Consultant Core Group Consultants
STRUCTURAL CONSULTANT Equilibrium Consulting
MECHANICAL CONSULTANT Stantec Consulting
ELECTRICAL CONSULTANT Acumen Engineering
PLUMBING CONSULTANT Stantec Consulting
LANDSCAPE CONSULTANT Eckford + Associates
GEOTECHNICAL CONSULTANT Geo Pacific
BUILDING CODE CONSULTANT GHL Consultants, Ltd.
ACOUSTICS CONSULTANT Brown Strachan
BUILDING ENVELOPE CONSULTANT JRS Engineering
AUDIO VISUAL CONSULTANT Mc Squared System Design Group
LABORATORY DESIGN Maples Argo Architects
COMMISSIONING AUTHORITY Airmec Systems, Ltd.
HAZARDOUS MATERIALS ABATEMENT ACM Environmental Corp.
PHOTOGRAPHER Martin Tessler
AWARDS RECEIVED:
- AIBC Innovation Award, 2013
- AIA-CAE / SCUP Merit Award, Excellence in Architecture for a New Building, 2013
- Wood WORKS! BC Wood Design Awards, Institutional Wood Design – Large, 2013
- Forest Products Society / American Wood Council, Wood Innovation Engineering Award, 2012
SUSTAINABILITY RATINGS LEED Gold
REFERENCE TO PUBLICATIONS
- "Earth Sciences Building," Arch Daily, March 16, 2013 http://www.archdaily.com/343465/earth-sciences-building-perkins-will/
- James Gauer, "Earth Sciences Building," GreenSource, March/April 2013, p. 44-49
- "New Earth Sciences Building Opens at UBC," Canadian Architect, February 9, 2013.
- URLs https://www.youtube.com/watch?v=z5beJygbTKOBest Green Project - Public Award, 2011
- University of Texas System, Outstanding HUB Participation Award, 2010
- SUSTAINABILITY RATINGS LEED Platinum
- REFERENCE TO PUBLICATIONS Candice Carlisle, "University of Dallas at Texas Student Services Center," Dallas Business Journal, February 25, 2011, p. B42.

Energy. Environment. Experiential Learning (EEEL)

University of Calgary, AB

Located at the University of Calgary, the Energy. Environment. Experiential Learning (EEEL) building is a five-story undergraduate teaching facility that allows students to learn in an experiential hands-on environment.

Energy. Environment. Experiential Learning (EEEL), University of Calgary; Calgary, AB; 2011

Placing a large emphasis on informal learning, the building centers on a "social stair" that facilitates interaction and interdisciplinary collaboration. In keeping with the goals of the project to put "science on display," EEEL includes undergraduate classrooms and labs that are fully glazed to the corridor beyond to encourage curiosity and engage passersby.

New Edge Innovations

The LEED Platinum project incorporates a number of solar control strategies such as solar shutters which actively track the sun to provide fully daylit interior spaces. The main atrium space has the largest "light scoop" we have ever designed, providing 100 percent daylighting to the interiors. Sculpted aluminum exterior spandrel panels are shaped and positioned to address individual façade conditions and act as effective solar light "redirectors" creating pools of daylight and sunshine at entry points in the periods of low winter sun. Additional environmental strategies include the use of thermal mass, an efficient envelope, natural ventilation, low-energy systems, native landscaping, and stormwater collection, reuse, and filtration. A large earth tube system warms/cools outdoor air with ground effect thermal mass during winter and summer. As a means to record building performance and lower operating costs, a Building Management System (BMS) collects all energy-related metrics of the building.

Designed with Dialog, EEEL contains approximately 75,350 square feet of teaching laboratories and 26,910 square feet of classroom and seminar space and up to 33,000 square feet of research lab space. The structural module and arrangement of the building systems allows the university long-term flexibility to convert spaces efficiently from one use to another. True to its "science on display" commitment, all building systems are visible and legible.

PROJECT ENERGY. ENVIRONMENT. EXPERIENTIAL LEARNING (EEEL), University of Calgary
LOCATION Calgary, AB
CLIENT University of Calgary
DESIGN 2008-2010
CONSTRUCTION 2010-2011
SIZE 264,050 sf / 24,531 sm
DESIGN TEAM Perkins+Will: P. Busby, A. Chmiel, A. McCumber, R. Piccolo, S. Schou, E. Stedman
DESIGN PARTNER DIALOG
CONSTRUCTION MANAGEMENT Ellis Don Construction
PROJECT MANAGERS Duke Evans, Inc.
STRUCTURAL ENGINEER RJC Engineers and DIALOG
MECHANICAL ENGINEER DIALOG
ELECTRICAL ENGINEER Stebnicki + Partners
LANDSCAPE ARCHITECT O2 Planning + Design
CIVIL ENGINEER AECOM
BUILDING ENVELOPE Building Envelope Engineering
CODE CONSULTANT Senez Reed Calder
ACOUSTIC CONSULTANT FFA
QUANTITY SURVEYOR Spiegel Skillen
PHOTOGRAPHER Tom Arban
AWARDS RECEIVED:
- The City of Calgary Mayors Urban Design Award, Civic Design Projects Category, 2013
- AIBC Special Jury Award For Animating the Program, 2013

- AIA-CAE/SCUP, Excellence in Architecture for a New Building, Honor Award, 2012
- The Alberta Association of Architects, The Saskatchewan Association of Architects and The Manitoba Association of Architects, Prairie Design Award of Merit, 2012
- Consulting Engineers of Alberta, Award of Excellence–Building Engineering Category, 2012
SUSTAINABILITY RATINGS LEED Platinum
REFERENCE TO PUBLICATIONS
- Alexandra McIntosh, "Bedazzled Box - A shiny addition to the University of Calgary provides a vibrant meeting place for students while achieving ambitious sustainability goals," *Canadian Architect*, October 2013.
- "Energy Environment Experiential Learning / Perkins+Will + DIALOG," ArchDaily, April 9, 2013. http://www.archdaily.com/356805/energy-environment-experiential-learning-perkins-will/?utm_source=dlvr.it&utm_medium=twitter
- Edward Keegan, "Energy.Environment. Experiential Learning," Architect, March 2012, p. 92-98.

Samuel Brighouse Elementary School
Richmond, BC

The Samuel Brighouse Elementary School had an impact on its community before it even opened its doors. Planned with the input of the community and the creative imaginations of students, this replacement elementary school is designed to adapt to a variety of needs.

Samuel Brighouse Elementary School; Richmond, BC; 2011

Including classrooms, administration space, library, community space, and renovated gymnasium, Samuel Brighouse School accommodates an enrollment of up to 500 students. The result of a collaborative design process that emphasized student and faculty involvement, the design supports the school's goals of transparency, collaborative learning, and connecting to nature and the community.

Creating flexible learning environments, the school includes indoor collaborative project areas located between classrooms, secure outdoor courtyards that serve as classroom extensions, low "peek" windows that connect even the youngest students to nature, and a garden that fosters connections with the community. A Neighborhood Learning Centre—housing community-based organizations offering during- and after-school care programs and adult literacy courses—is integrated into the design, extending the school's operating hours.

New Edge Innovations
Identified by the school district as an opportunity to demonstrate its environmental stewardship policy, the building was designed to become a tool to teach students about sustainability. The design pursued both passive and active strategies, including natural ventilation, daylight harvesting, material salvaged from the existing school, and the inclusion of triple-glazed windows, low-VOC materials, green roofs, and low-maintenance vegetation. Through geoexchange, carefully managed daylighting,

and solar hot water collectors, the school has operated without the use of fossil fuels on a number of occasions and expects an overall 57 percent reduction in energy use.

The primary structural system utilizes a laminated 2x3 diaphragm structure for the main roof, prefabricated and delivered to site complete with the custom king post supports.

LOCATION Richmond, BC
CLIENT Richmond School District No. 38
DESIGN 2009-2010
CONSTRUCTION 2010-2011
SIZE 50,590 sf / 4,700 sm
DESIGN TEAM Perkins+Will: E. Brossy de Dios, P. Busby, R. Drew, R. Maas, J. Rudd, A. Shum, W. Vaughn, J. Verville, C. Waight, C. Wang, L. Woofter
STRUCTURAL ENGINEER Fast + Epp
MECHANICAL ENGINEER Integral Group (formerly Cobalt Engineering)
ELECTRICAL ENGINEER Acumen Consulting Engineers
TECHNOLOGY CONSULTANT Acumen Consulting Engineers
LANDSCAPE ARCHITECT Durante Kreuk, Ltd.
CIVIL ENGINEER Hub Engineering
ECOLOGIST Raincoast Applied Ecology
BUILDING ENVELOPE CONSULTANT Morrison Hershfield
ACOUSTICAL CONSULTANT BKL Consultants
GEOTECHNICAL CONSULTANT Trow Associates
TRANSPORTATION CONSULTANT Bunt & Associates
SURVEYOR Matson Peck & Topliss

COST CONSULTANT Jim Bush & Associates
CODE CONSULTANT CFT Engineering
CONSTRUCTION MANAGER EllisDon Corporation
PHOTOGRAPHER Nic Lehoux; Latreille Delage Photography
AWARDS RECEIVED
- Wood Design Awards, Canadian Wood Council Wood WORKS! BC, Honorable Mention, 2014
- Vancouver Regional Construction Association, Silver Award in the category of Sustainable Construction, Gold Award in the category of General Contractor up to $15 million
- AIA Pasadena & Foothill Chapter Honor Award, Institutional / Educational, 2012,
- Lieutenant-Governor of British Columbia Merit Recipient, 2012
- BC Hydro Power Smart Excellence Awards, New Construction Category, Finalist, 2012
- Wood Design Awards Canadian Wood Council Wood WORKS! BC Engineering Category, 2012
- Vancouver Regional Construction Association, Gold Award in the category of General Contractor up to $15 Million, 2013
- Vancouver Regional Construction Association Silver Award in the category of Sustainable Construction, 2013
SUSTAINABILITY RATINGS LEED Gold
REFERENCE TO PUBLICATIONS
- Linda C. Lentz, "Schools of the 21st Century," Architectural Record, January 3, 2012, http://archrecord.construction.com/features/schools/
- Brian Salgado, "Learning Curve," Building & Construction, Fall 2010, p. 115-116

Samuel Brighouse Elementary School; Richmond, BC; 2011

Samuel Brighouse Elementary School; Richmond, BC; 2011

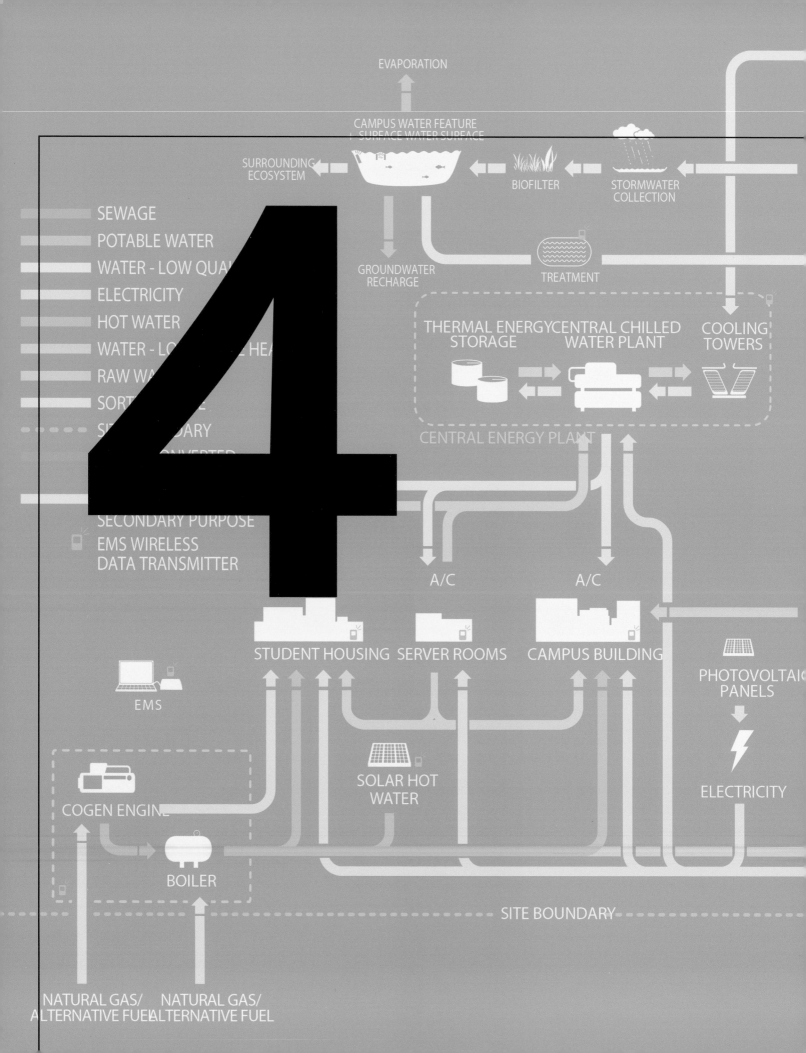

EVAPORATION

CAMPUS WATER FEATURE
SURFACE WATER SURFACE

SURROUNDING
ECOSYSTEM

BIOFILTER

STORMWATER
COLLECTION

SEWAGE

POTABLE WATER

WATER - LOW QUA

ELECTRICITY

HOT WATER

WATER - LO   HE

RAW WA

SORT

SE   DARY

NVERTED

SECONDARY PURPOSE

EMS WIRELESS
DATA TRANSMITTER

4

GROUNDWATER
RECHARGE

TREATMENT

THERMAL ENERGY CENTRAL CHILLED
STORAGE   WATER PLANT

COOLING
TOWERS

CENTRAL ENERGY PLANT

A/C

A/C

EMS

STUDENT HOUSING   SERVER ROOMS   CAMPUS BUILDING

PHOTOVOLTAIC
PANELS

COGEN ENGINE

SOLAR HOT
WATER

ELECTRICITY

BOILER

SITE BOUNDARY

NATURAL GAS/
ALTERNATIVE FUEL

NATURAL GAS/
ALTERNATIVE FUEL

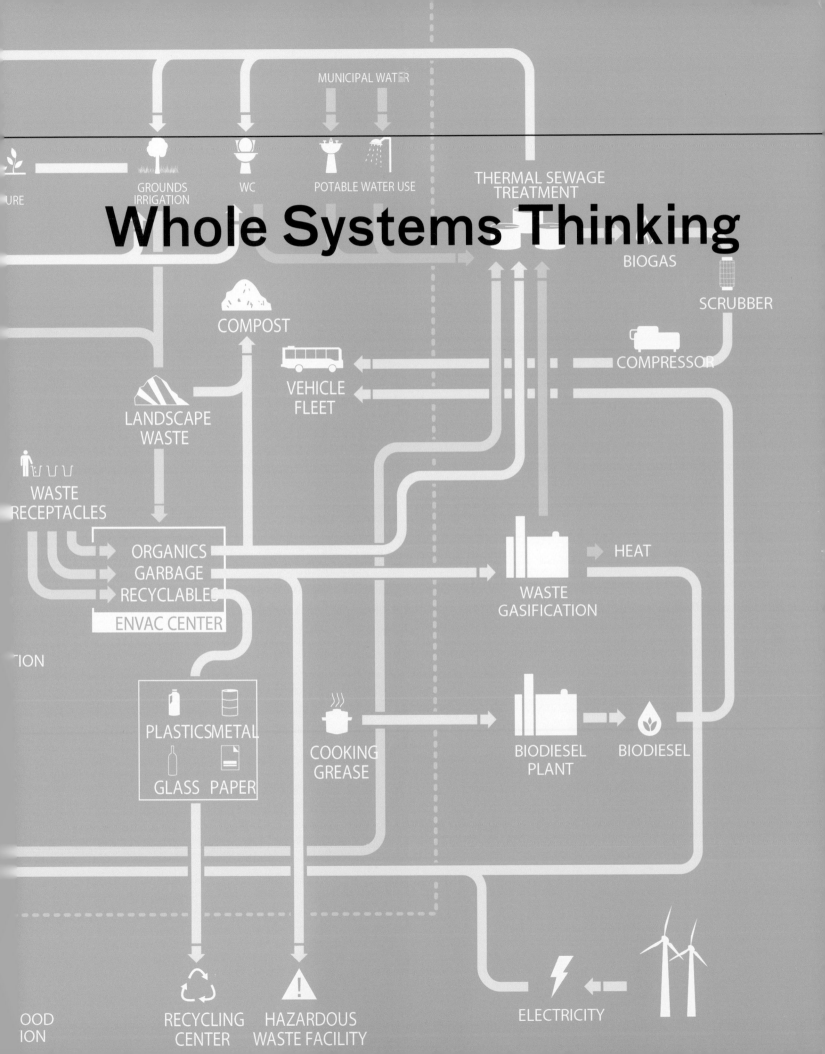

Whole Systems Thinking

MUNICIPAL WATER

GROUNDS IRRIGATION

WC

POTABLE WATER USE

THERMAL SEWAGE TREATMENT

BIOGAS

SCRUBBER

COMPRESSOR

COMPOST

VEHICLE FLEET

LANDSCAPE WASTE

WASTE RECEPTACLES

URE

ORGANICS
GARBAGE
RECYCLABLES
ENVAC CENTER

HEAT

WASTE GASIFICATION

ION

PLASTICS METAL

GLASS PAPER

COOKING GREASE

BIODIESEL PLANT

BIODIESEL

OOD
ION

RECYCLING CENTER

HAZARDOUS WASTE FACILITY

ELECTRICITY

Interconnected, as in Nature

Until relatively recently, architects usually practiced their craft independently, almost in creative silos. They drew their plans then handed them to engineers who would layer on the necessary systems. Only in the last decade has the field embraced more holistic systems-oriented approaches to building and community design.

When I first entered the profession, there was little to no mention of building systems beyond the basics: structural, mechanical, lighting, and electrical. Nobody worried very much about waste, water, garbage, or power systems because there was virtually nothing to discuss. Toilets were flushed, sewage disappeared into pipes, civil engineers made sure those pipes were connected to municipal lines, and the city would take care of the rest. Potable water was delivered to taps from pipes that drew from city sources flowing up through each building's basement. Garbage was disposed of in a bin in the lane or at a loading bay, where one or more times each week it would get picked up and taken away. Power arrived via an electrical transformer specified by the engineer and hooked to the building. Everything was fairly formulaic; there was no perceived need to stray beyond the tried-and-true solutions because it was assumed that everything would be alright.

Then, as we began to look beyond the footprints of individual buildings for answers to questions related to environmental responsibility, we started to examine the systems that enable buildings to operate. We started to think about where water and power comes from; where waste and runoff go. Were there better ways of creating and connecting these systems that would serve our projects as well as the environment? Of course there were. At the same time, design became a much more collaborative effort. Mechanical engineers worried about energy efficiency and thought architects could help. Similarly, civil, structural, and electrical engineers, plumbers, landscape architects, and others were searching for sustainable design results, all looking over each other's shoulders. The sustainable design charrette was born. We all realized we could help each other; it was up to us all to seek collaborative solutions to reach the next level of sustainable design.

European practitioners offered some valuable examples of systems thinking to those of us who were willing and able to study them. In my travels, I visited Scandinavia to see for myself some of the approaches that were getting international attention when the topic of sustainable community design was gaining traction. Sweden, for example, had made a commitment after the first oil crunch in the 1970s to wean itself off fossil fuels. From 1975 on, the Swedes began taking ownership of all of their waste, building district energy systems, and waste-to-energy plants to create environmental efficiencies for their cities. I was intrigued by this model of turning waste streams into energy opportunities, and have implemented variations on these ideas in all large projects since.

Designing deep green buildings as discrete entities began to seem incomplete. As my colleagues and I further experimented with systems interconnectedness, deliberately studying synergies among our buildings' operational areas, it became increasing clear that *whole systems thinking* is fundamental to the more successful strategies of sustainable design. Waste can provide energy, water can be repurposed on-site, and landscapes can serve plumbing functions. In short, all of life's support systems can and should benefit one another. Of course this is what happens in nature, where there is no waste and where all life depends on interconnected systems. We realized that architects could, and should, take ownership of systems that had previously been exclusively reserved for other professions. Even budget allocations began to adjust as dollars earmarked for energy, water, and waste infrastructure drifted into the architect's column as systems design became increasingly interwoven with building and community design. Coordinating our efforts with those of our engineering and landscape counterparts made the projects we collaborated on much more sustainable. *Whole systems thinking* was a breakthrough concept that radically affected our approach to design and unquestionably expanded its edges.

Dockside Green: An Early Implementation

One of the first projects for which we seriously considered and incorporated whole systems thinking was Dockside Green, a 15 hectare, 26-building, 130,000 square meter mixed-use community to be constructed on a brownfield former industrial site in Victoria, BC. In a developer led competition with two other proposals, we won the contract with Windmill Development Group to design a deep green, zero carbon project whose interconnected systems would enhance its short- and long-term environmental and market impact. We took this early opportunity to create a revolutionary project very seriously.

In 2005, we completed the master plan for the mixed-use Dockside Green development, which includes live/work, hotel, retail, office, and light industrial uses, as well as numerous public amenities. With a LEED Platinum target for each building on-site, it is a global showcase for large-scale sustainable development. In 2008, we completed Dockside Green Residential Phase I or "Synergy," which reached LEED Platinum at 63 points, making it the highest-scoring LEED Platinum project in the world at the time. Synergy includes four detached buildings constructed over a common underground parking structure, including a nine-story residential tower with commercial units at grade; a two-story townhouse; a six-story condo building with commercial units at grade; and a four-story residential building.

Dockside Green employs an integrated energy system that includes a biomass gasification plant that converts locally-sourced wood waste into a clean burning syngas to produce heat and hot water. The biomass gasification system, along with selling the extra biomass heat to a neighboring hotel, has rendered the project carbon-neutral on a net annual basis without the purchase of green power certificates. The development's many other sustainable features include: on-site wastewater treatment that will save more than 200 million liters of water annually at build out (Synergy alone is calculated to save more than eight million liters of water annually); rooftop gardens; a car co-op with Smart Cars; and additional energy-saving features including Energy Star appliances, heat-recovery ventilations units, low-E double-glazed windows and operable exterior blinds on the west and south faces of each building. A series of ponds spread throughout Dockside's central greenway also assist in on-site stormwater storage while the greenway itself provides significant public amenity space.

Unbelievably for a Western urban center, the City of Victoria has never had a sewage treatment plant; the municipality pipes all of its untreated human waste directly into the Strait of Juan de Fuca. So Dockside Green gave us a special

Dockside Green, Balance; Victoria, BC; 2009

opportunity to demonstrate cleaner, sustainable, scalable, on-site sewage treatment solutions. And an overall property-wide reduction in water consumption was key to the waste treatment strategies that followed. Senior engineer Blair McCarry supervised design of a district sewage treatment plant and captured stormwater system that repurposed both throughout the site. Stormwater is collected on multiple green roofs and sent to an artificial stream that cleans the overflow with flora and natural processes before the water flows to the harbor, delivering dramatically cleaner stormwater output to the open waters that surround the region.

Greywater and blackwater from washrooms and sinks is collected and treated in a membrane bioreactor plant on-site. Reclaimed water from the plant is treated to tertiary treatment level for on-site use and the excess is discharged to the stormwater stream for natural polishing in the bioswales before flowing into the ocean. Reclaimed water is also piped for use in toilets and irrigation throughout the project. Some of the excess reclaimed water is sold to a nearby concrete plant for its use in industrial processes.

Although similar water systems are used more commonly today, the integrated Dockside Green water strategy, which supported the project's performance efficiencies, was groundbreaking at the time it was designed.

Energy and Carbon

Fundamental to the Dockside Green vision and energy strategy was creating a net zero carbon project. We were lucky to have the unwavering support of Windmill's Joe Van Belleghem, who spearheaded the concept of a district energy system. Working closely with BC Hydro and others, we explored various options that would give us what we needed to provide energy to this ambitious project. Eventually, we selected a biomass gasifier that was sized and custom-built to serve the majority of the heating requirements of the site. A gas boiler provided backup and peak load capacity. The district heating system is connected to an adjacent hotel, where it replaces much of the fossil fuels being used to heat that property, more than offsetting the site emissions related to the peak gas heating and electricity used. This approach confirms the success in the project reaching the overall net zero carbon emissions goal. During the early phases of the project, smaller boilers were used to meet the site's energy needs, and they have since been incorporated into the complete district-wide system as peaking units, a capital efficiency strategy. The gasifier converts the wood waste in a hot, limited oxygen environment, turning it into syngas that is oxidized and sent to the boilers providing hydronic heat for the district energy loop, connected to all buildings on-site.

Originally, the gasifier was fueled by waste lumber contracted from a local demolition company, which diverted wood from landfills and prevented its conversion to methane – known to have a significantly more severe impact (17 times) on climate change than CO_2. Initially, we ran into difficulties with the waste lumber, as nails and other contaminants compromised the performance of the bioreactor, at one point shutting down the system for approximately three months. We eventually replaced the waste wood source with wood pellets obtained from the local lumber industry. (Wood pellets are pressed wood waste from the sawmill industry. Interestingly, wood pellets from British Columbia are shipped to Sweden to power some of that country's district energy systems.) Dockside Green was the first district energy system in Western Canada to be powered by this fuel source, which has breathed new life into the local wood pellet industry as more systems of this kind are appearing around the region. The sludge produced by the on-site sewage treatment system is dried and added to the biomass fuel for the gasifier. This produces additional heating energy and eliminates the cost of disposing of the sludge.

Initial designs for Dockside Green wove composted materials into the energy strategies. The idea was to collect kitchen, garden, and restaurant waste from around the site, dry it using waste heat from the bioreactor, and turn it into an additional fuel source. Although this particular strategy was not implemented, it was yet another innovation that this pioneering project inspired us to sketch out, and became a strategy that we have implemented in subsequent projects.

Since Dockside Green was a pilot program for BC Hydro and its district energy system was the first of its kind in North America, it was originally uneconomical. The federal and provincial governments believed so strongly in the value of this demonstration project that they supplemented its costs as a way of showing what was possible with regard to renewable district energy systems in North America. Since that time, the price of every piece of equipment has come down to the point where similar systems are now cost-effective. The demonstration subsidy proved worthwhile.

Dockside Green has had an extremely powerful influence on the design and building industries, with effects that continue to ripple across North America. Windmill's Joe Van Belleghem, Blair McCarry, and I enthusiastically spoke individually and together about this revolutionary project, delivering hundreds of presentations to public and professional audiences in the years since it was first designed. Following the development of the Dockside Green district energy system, we have seen dozens of similar systems patterned after our plans. We are particularly proud of the fact that Dockside Green was recognized in 2010 as one of 16 international projects that met the Clinton Climate Change C40 Standards. As of this writing, Dockside is approximately 50 percent complete, with a ten-year build-out horizon.

Dockside Green, Wastewater Treatment Plant; Victoria, BC; 2009

Dockside Green, Inspiration and Balance; Victoria, BC; 2009

Dockside Green, Site Plan; Victoria, BC; 2009

Nexterra's Gasifier Technology – How it Works

1. Fuel In-Feed
Locally sourced wood waste (including recycled clean wood construction and municipal tree trimmings) is loaded into the fuel bin and conveyed to a metering bin near the gasifier.

2. Gasifier
Fuel enters the gasifier and goes through several stages including drying, pyrolysis (chemical change brought about by heat), and gasification. The wood is converted into synthetic "syngas" that can be used like natural gas.

3. Oxidizer
The syngas is conveyed into the oxidizer where it is combusted, with the resulting flue gas directed through a boiler.

4. Boiler
Hot water from the boiler is transported by an underground pipe to provide heat and hot water for Dockside buildings. The cold water then returns to the boiler to start the heating process again.

5. ESP
After exiting the boiler, the flue gas is cleaned in an electrostatic precipitator (ESP) that filters out virtually all of the remaining particulate matter.

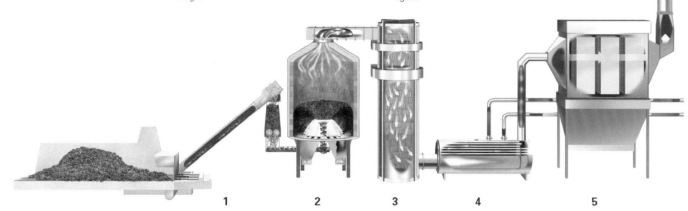

Used with permission of Nexterra Systems Corp.

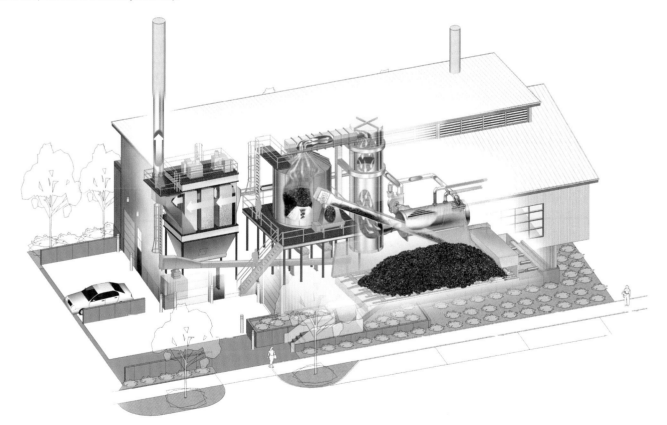

Used with permission of Nexterra Systems Corp.

Point Wells: A Vision for the Future

The Point Wells development will allow us to apply some second-generation expertise to whole systems thinking. We have helped develop design concepts to redevelop this 61-acre waterfront site in Snohomish County, Washington, converting it from an environmentally compromised industrial site (an oil storage depot) to a sustainable mixed-use community containing 3000 residential units. The developer tapped us for the project in part because of the systems approach we applied at Dockside Green. It is still in the approvals processing phase (lengthy in a litigious local environment), although rezoning has been approved. Interestingly, the project includes the design and construction of a rail transit station, a conscious strategy to reduce transportation impacts and emissions from the project.

There are two ephemeral streams that naturally flow through the existing site, so we did not need to design an artificial stream into the project's water plan. Since a major municipal sewage treatment plant is located nearby, we opted not to construct a site-specific treatment process for Point Wells. Water strategies focus on rainwater capture and greywater reuse. The streams are enhanced to provide biofiltration functions. The landscape architect, Peter Walker, has been a fantastic design collaborator.

With a rail line already in place within the perimeter of the project, we incorporated this ready-made delivery system into our overall energy strategies. We sited the project's district energy plant directly adjacent to the rail line, allowing agricultural biowaste to be brought in by rail from local farms and used as fuel for the bioreactor. Learning from Dockside Green, where the district energy plant was located in a separate industrial building on the property, we designed the Point Wells plant into the basement of the project's community center so the development's energy systems became a component of the public infrastructure and experience. The current emissions from the site are 25,000 tons of CO_2 per year. When the project is complete, we estimate that total emissions on-site will drop to 1,100 tons per year, a 96 percent decrease.

A Confidential Project Expands Whole Systems Thinking Horizons

Perkins+Will was retained in 2011 to provide whole systems thinking for a large mixed-use and entertainment property whose owner prefers that the project not be publicized by name until the project is complete. As of this writing, the project is under construction, and nearing completion.

A member of the developer's leadership team had seen me give a presentation about Dockside Green and was eager to bring a design team on board to apply the same types of innovative systems-oriented strategies to this new endeavor. The owner, a Fortune 500 company, is committed to reducing its carbon footprint, leading it to create a deeply green property where visitors and occupants can rely on clean sources of water, power, fuel, and other inputs. When we were retained, we were told that the project was part of a larger set of goals established by the corporation, which aimed for all of its developed properties to reach common green goals: net zero energy by 2030, zero waste across all tiers of the organization, minimal water use, and 20 percent renewable energy by 2020.

Energy
The first step in designing the project's energy system was to look for opportunities to reduce the energy use requirements. More efficient buildings and systems were

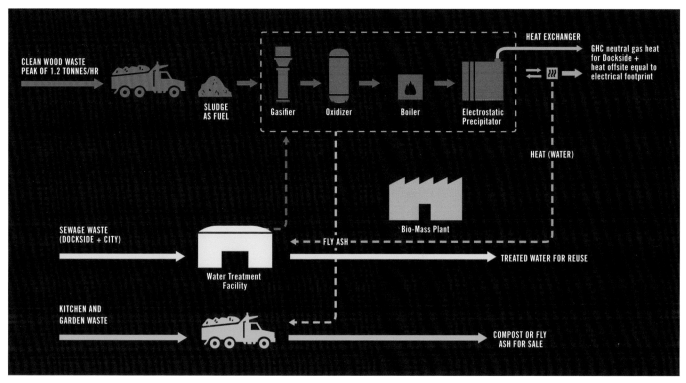

CLEAN WOOD WASTE
PEAK OF 1.2 TONNES/HR

SLUDGE
AS FUEL

Gasifier   Oxidizer   Boiler   Electrostatic
Precipitator

HEAT EXCHANGER

GHC neutral gas heat
for Dockside +
heat offsite equal to
electrical footprint

HEAT (WATER)

Bio-Mass Plant

SEWAGE WASTE
(DOCKSIDE + CITY)

Water Treatment
Facility

FLY ASH

TREATED WATER FOR REUSE

KITCHEN AND
GARDEN WASTE

COMPOST OR FLY
ASH FOR SALE

Dockside Green, Whole Systems Design, as-built

proposed (demand reduction should always be the first strategy considered). Significantly more efficient chiller plants that would include chilled water storage were also proposed. To reduce the GHG emissions related to operations, a gas fired cogeneration system was provided to reduce the use of grid electricity provided by coal and produce heat for building heating and absorption cooling. A waste-to-energy system was also proposed to produce additional power. Potentially based off-site, the waste-to-energy system would collect waste from the site and beyond for a larger, more economical system. The on-site sewage treatment system would produce cleaned sewage gas for use on-site and sludge that would be dried for fuel for the waste-to-energy system. As an entertainment venue, this property would have an abundant supply of both human and food waste. So we proposed a sophisticated, high-volume anaerobic digester that would run on organic waste as well as composted vegetative matter, producing biogas that will be used for vehicles and cooking on-site.

Key to the system (and a perfect example of operational interconnectedness) is an on-site sewage treatment plant that can process most forms of organic waste directly adjacent to the power plant, creating reclaimed water that can then be used to irrigate landscaping throughout the property. As the project developed, the owner negotiated for the sewage treatment services to be provided off-site, but the reclaimed water will be returned to the project. This is similar to the strategy of locating waste-to-energy plant off-site for larger scale economics then returning electrical power to the site. This was our first experience in extending our thinking about interconnectedness to capture synergies between partner agencies, not limited to ownership or project legal boundaries. Interconnectedness need not respect lot lines. Synergies are good wherever you can find them.

PROJECT SUSTAINABILITY: A TOTAL SYSTEMS SOLUTIONS
40% POTABLE WATER USE REDUCTION

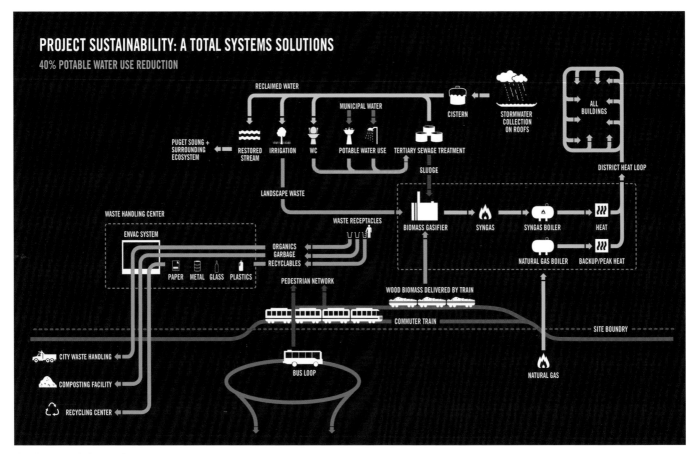

Point Wells, Whole Systems Design

Additional energy to meet the remaining needs of the project's overall energy demands will come from five purchased windmills at a regional wind farm. In addition, a pyrolysis plant will be constructed on the site to convert waste plastic into diesel fuel to operate certain vehicles that serve the project.

Water
Any water strategy designed to serve the multiple high-volume demands of a mixed-use property of this size and type would need to be complex. Complicating matters is the fact that the cleanliness of the region's water is compromised by various environmental conditions, as the rainwater, groundwater, and surface water in the area are all polluted to some degree.

To work around these obstacles, we decided to create a new surface water strategy to reflect the natural water culture of the region. A surface-level canal system wraps around the perimeter of the venue capturing rainwater and channeling overflow salt water that flows from nearby fields during flood conditions. Floating, natural, water treatment systems will clean the canal water system. All told, the sophisticated on-site system delivers five different levels of water cleanliness to serve the project's various demands:

1. A potable water treatment plant treats the city water so it is suitable for human consumption
2. Water at swimming pool cleanliness standards is used in areas of the property where guests and occupants will come in contact with but not consume the water

3. Tertiary treated, reclaimed water is used for landscaping
4. Bioswale treated water flows through the canals that wrap around the property
5. Non-potable reclaimed water is used to flush toilets

Food

As an entertainment venue, the project must be able to provide significant quantities of food to its guests. Knowing the owners were interested in true sustainability, we encouraged strategies that would create on-site and nearby farming opportunities to help meet the project's demands. After calculating the amount of food that would be consumed on the premises daily, we estimated the necessary acreage of farm land – approximately 70 hectares – necessary to cultivate the applicable crops. Rather than draw those ingredients from distant sources, we recommended that the farmers being displaced by the construction of the development be employed directly by the owner or a partner organization, hired to oversee in-house production of the agricultural products that would be in highest demand throughout the development. Clean water from the canals would feed the crops, further ensuring quality control within the food supply and connecting benefits from multiple systems to serve one another. At the time of this writing, it is not determined whether these food supply strategies will ultimately be implemented.

Overall Impact

All key systems in this planned development are interconnected. These synergies enhance the effectiveness of each individual performance area as well as the entirety of the operation. Waste creates energy, energy fuels the power plant, waste effluent provides the water, waste-to-fuel systems propel the vehicles, and so on.

In the case of this project, the client benefits greatly from a whole systems approach. Working together, the strategies mean secure sources of clean water, virtually limitless sources of renewable energy, less dependency on outside systems, less volatility in energy costs, and reduced operational costs. Just as importantly, this systems-oriented strategy actually generates jobs, since every on-site plant requires skilled labor in the construction, maintenance, and operational phases.

As of the writing of this book, the project is still in its construction phase. However, we have received word from the client that they are implementing over 90 percent of our proposed ideas. I consider that an enormous success and a testament to the power of whole systems thinking.

Sustainable Campus Planning

We were retained in 2007 to advise the University of British Columbia as to how they might reach their 2030 commitment, and ultimately get to carbon-neutral in operations. The report we produced, published in 2008, suggested a series of strategies based on our whole systems approach to communities.

The University of British Columbia's (UBC) Sustainability Office commissioned Perkins+Will to examine and recommend the most appropriate green building rating systems for new and existing institutional buildings on the UBC Vancouver Point Grey Campus with regards to the rating system's energy and greenhouse gas (GHG) emissions conservation standards and provide recommendations on how UBC can move towards carbon neutrality while minimizing the institution's need to purchase offsets.

Evaluation of Green Building Rating Systems for University of British Columbia: Greenhouse Gas Conservation Measure Recommendations; 2008

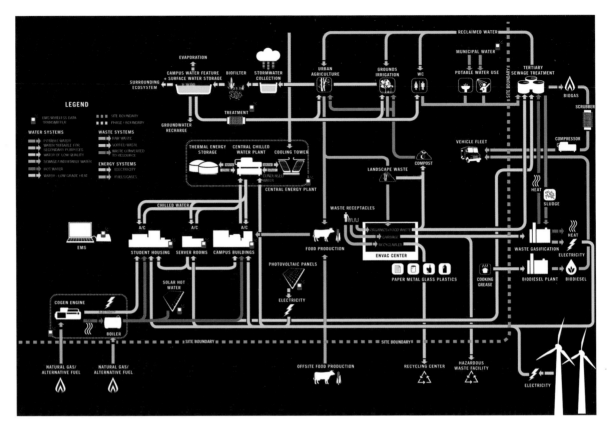

Sustainable Campus Diagram

The Provincial Government's commitment to ensure that all publicly funded projects become carbon-neutral by 2030 necessitated a closer examination of green building rating systems with regards to measuring and reducing carbon. As a publicly funded institution, UBC recognized that reducing the campus' carbon emissions profile was the first priority and that the purchase of carbon offsets was a secondary priority in achieving carbon neutrality. The University has already completed some of the most detailed CO_2 reporting of any campus and wanted to better refine the institution's ability to measure and reduce CO_2. As such, the report provided UBC with a potential strategy to move the Point Grey Campus to carbon neutrality without the purchase of carbon offsets by 2030. The strategy outlined a plan for reducing operating energy, building more energy-efficient buildings and switching the natural gas powered central plant.

To further the discussion about whole systems thinking and campus opportunities (read any kind of community, from healthcare campuses to office parks to town sites), we developed the following whole systems diagram in 2008 to illustrate the conceptual interconnectedness of the design possibilities. Note the advancement over the diagram (above) for Dockside Green. This diagram is also quite similar to the whole systems plan developed for the confidential project discussed above.

Blatchford Redevelopment: Community-Side Systems Thinking

In 2012, Perkins+Will entered an international competition to design a new carbon-neutral mixed-use community for 30,000 residents on the site of a decommissioned municipal airport in Edmonton, Alberta. After being shortlisted as one of five firms asked to submit a detailed plan (we were the only Canadian design team lead on the shortlist; other finalists hailed from the United States and

Europe), we won the Blatchford Redevelopment contract late that year, and spent all of 2013 securing community approvals and honing design and system plans. Early in 2014, the municipal airport was permanently closed and in late 2014 construction on the Blatchford Redevelopment project is due to begin.

Blatchford's ambitious scope has been challenging enough. Designing a carbon-neutral community in a region of the world known more for its oil sands than its lack of environmental commitments has proven to make the planning process even more complex. These project realities have only strengthened our resolve to show what is possible when it comes to large-scale whole systems design. We note that the political support of Edmonton's Mayor Don Iveson and Council has been instrumental in the development and approval of the project. More generally, we note that acceptance and development of advanced infrastructure proposals always requires strong political support, a lesson we first learned in Victoria for Dockside Green (Mayor Alan Lowe), and in Vancouver under Mayor Gregor Robinson and City Manager Sadhu Johnston. Politicians who get climate change and the need for innovation and action are crucial to the success of change going forward. May they proliferate!

Energy

We began the project's energy strategy by designing a district energy plant. An existing rail spur on the north end of the site provided the ideal location for the plant, which features biomass reactors. With plenty of agricultural waste (principally straw and corn stalks) generated by nearby farms, these renewable fuel sources will always be available and can easily be delivered to the site via rail.

For the second phase of the energy system design (when a critical mass of construction has been accomplished), we took advantage of a geological anomaly. Edmonton, it turns out, sits atop a lava dome, beneath which surges the extreme heat of the earth's lava mantle. The difference here, as in only a few other spots in North America (such as Yellowstone National Park, Mount St. Helens, and British Columbia's Mount Garibaldi) is that the dome formation brings the mantle's heat closer to the surface. At the Blatchford Redevelopment site, that natural heat sits a mere three kilometers beneath the ground.

Using drilling technology available through the local oil industry, we proposed a system of true geothermal wells to tap the earth's heat and circulate it through the site's district energy loop. Water will be pumped deep into the wells, where it heats to approximately 280 degrees C, then it is brought back to the surface to drive steam turbines. The waste heat from the turbines then powers the district heating system. Low-grade waste heat from that process could even, in turn, "heat the sidewalks." On its own, the geothermal system is powerful enough to provide more than the entire Blatchford Redevelopment community requires, so we proposed that surplus energy be delivered to Edmonton's downtown core to help offset municipal buildings' fossil fuel consumption. We estimate that over a 20-year period, the net carbon impact of the Blatchford Redevelopment district energy system will be approximately 3.2 million tons of averted carbon emissions. This is not just a "net zero" project; it marks a significant positive contribution to the climbing CO_2 emissions profile of the oil sands.

Water

Every drop of stormwater that falls on the Blatchford Redevelopment site is collected and delivered to a 20-hectare central pond system to be constructed at the heart of the community. In addition, supplemental stormwater is brought to the site via stormwater culverts converted to daylighted streams from adjacent neighborhoods. The system contains five different levels of ponds, each specifically

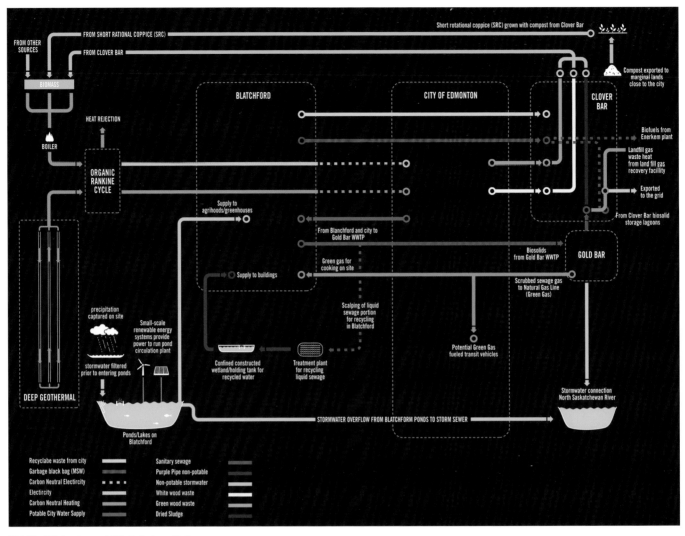

Blatchford Redevelopment, Whole Systems Design

engineered to serve a different treatment and/or cleaning function so that, in combination, they meet the large-scale needs of the entire community.

Since landscaping and farming are key to the community's self-sufficiency and operational performance, water strategies allow for significant amounts to be used for irrigation purposes.

Agriculture

The Blatchford Redevelopment plan includes strategies to allow individual neighborhoods to oversee their own mini-farms. These "agrihoods" will support the food needs of communities and help ensure plenty of green space throughout the development. Professional farmers will oversee larger-scale plots and will serve as information resources to all residents interested in learning more about how to plan and manage their own harvests. The project contemplates up to three farmers' markets operating in the summer and autumn months to deliver produce to the community.

Waste

To process the Blatchford Redevelopment community's refuse, we designed a centralized waste collection system that uses vacuum lines connected to all of the buildings on the site. (Although such systems are not in common use in North

America, there are many examples being used in Scandinavia that served as our inspiration.) The concept is simple: 450 mm diameter vacuum tubes are installed as infrastructure within all buildings, with groups of ports accessible from the interiors of each structure and leading to a centralized processing area adjacent to the district energy plant. Occupants place their garbage, recycling, and compostable material into one of five ports depending on the specific material being discarded. Recyclables are processed appropriately. Any biosolids that can be used for fuel are delivered to the bioreactors. Compostables are reserved for agricultural use. Metals, glass, and plastics are recycled. The centralized waste processing location saves floor space in individual projects that would otherwise have to be constructed, and minimizes the noise and emissions associated with vehicular refuse collection. At Blatchford, nothing is wasted.

The Blatchford Redevelopment project will benefit from a strong relationship with the City of Edmonton, which is already recognized for having one of the most progressive municipal waste treatment programs in North America. To support the development's green goals, the city will divert part of its organic waste stream to the site to provide additional fuel for the district energy plant. Also, Blatchford will be allowed to send some of its waste and recyclables to a municipal processing plant. This interconnectedness with local government will benefit both local and regional environmental efforts.

Overall Impact

Ten years after Dockside Green's systems were designed, we see the next generation of systems thinking coming to life at Blatchford Redevelopment. With a district energy system, renewable energy resources, waste streams supporting power and energy systems, a regional recycling industry, and a significant interconnectedness with metropolitan organic sewage and recycling streams, this 30,000-person community includes plans for the most sophisticated set of *whole systems* in our portfolio to date.

Local Politics Intervenes

Perkins+Will delivered the completed Master Plan and Guidelines to the City in spring 2013. Following a fall election that same year, the makeup of City Council changed. The City of Edmonton hired a consultant to implement civil engineering design shortly thereafter. The mandate of this consultancy was broadened to review the sustainability aspects of the plan. They reported back in mid-2014 that proposals were uneconomic (their report contained significant errors). Some members of the local development industry, more familiar with the low densities of single family housing associated with urban sprawl, lobbied council to reduce development densities to allow for their style of land use by giving up park space. The developers also lobbied for larger development parcels, to be achieved by removing roads. The same consultant was asked to amend the plan to accommodate these changes, drastically reducing open space and stripping out 13 kilometers of roads. Revised rezoning was approved by Council in July 2014, with many of our proposals and systems greatly compromised or removed altogether. Blatchford as it proceeds, will not be carbon neutral, not even close - an exceptional opportunity lost for Edmonton. In retrospect, we believe that ours was a game changing plan that can still lead the way for other community designs, if not for Edmonton. We will continue to publish and present our ideas for Blatchford in the public realm so that others may learn and hopefully emulate the progressive ideas that we developed for Edmonton.

Chaudière Island Master Plan, Ottawa, Ontario

The Site and Context

The Chaudière Master Plan is one of enduring beauty, great cultural and historic significance and thoughtful ecological stewardship. The plan for the former Domtar paper mill envisions a powerful link with the Ottawa River, a signature destination supporting urban growth and vitality for both Ottawa and Gatineau, which will connect people to the Ottawa riverfront in ways which have not been possible for generations.

The site includes property on both sides of the river. To the north, in Gatineau, the lands are within the downtown core and offer an opportunity to extend the urban fabric and grid of the city down to the riverbank. To the south, in Ottawa, the lands consist of Chaudière and Albert islands, physically disconnected from both cities by river channels and offering the opportunity to create a unique sense of place which connects both sides of the river.

The Master Plan

The Plan offers an unmatched choice of activities, magnificent views, and multi-season recreation for all residents and visitors. It will be a place where people from all over the region will come to play, relax, eat and stay. The site has numerous industrial buildings of various ages, several of which will be preserved and adapted for reuse in the development. Long-forgotten alignments of roads and plazas will be restored to public use as a reminder of the historic public realm. Portions of the existing urbanized river's edge will be returned to a more naturalized state to recall the original river ecology.

Development proposals include mixed-use, residential, commercial, retail, innovation incubator facilities and community amenities on both sides of the river.

Some of the best views in Canada are available from the site; Parliament Hill, The National Gallery, War Museum, Gatineau Park, both City skylines, the Falls and winter sunsets upriver. The siting and massing of buildings within the development has been particularly deferential to this unique asset by protecting and framing recognized view corridors across the site, by placing new buildings relative to each other to ensure the maximum exposure to views from within each building and by creating a new and varied skyline within the development to provide interesting views from the surrounding areas into the site.

The natural draw for all visitors will be the enhanced water's edge with a variety of gathering places, promenades, plazas and piers. A walk or a bike ride along new riverfront promenades will connect lively public spaces, quiet ecological zones and engaging waterfront destinations. Located in the heart of the Canadian capital, the Chaudière Master Plan deliberately builds on this remarkable asset by framing view corridors to the historic Parliament and other key government buildings on Capitol Hill.

One Planet Community

If everyone in the world consumed as many natural resources as the average person in North America, we would need five planets to support our lifestyles. One Planet Living is a model based on ten simple principles which provide a framework to make sustainable living easy and affordable for all. The Chaudière Master Plan will achieve the highest green building standards for materials, water, energy and indoor air quality to create a zero carbon sustainability showpiece. It includes creating habitat protection, outdoor recreation, community agriculture and connecting the site with adjacent open spaces. It also means having more local, organic, and fair trade products in restaurants and shops; providing cleaner transportation options; creating quality affordable housing and jobs; and making it easier to adopt healthy, green lifestyles.

The Perkins+Will team used the One Planet Community rating system to ensure that the Chaudière Master Plan is not just a model of great mixed-use, pedestrian oriented city design but is also a leading example of sustainable development with aggressive targets including:

- 100 percent of energy needs to be supplied from renewable sources by 2020
- All buildings to be net zero carbon by 2020
- 98 percent of all solid waste to be diverted from landfill
- Site related VMT to be reduced by 55 percent by 2020
- Carbon emissions from vehicles travelling to and from the site to be reduced by 75 percent by 2032
- Interior consumption of water to be reduced by 60 percent compared to local benchmarks
- 100 percent of exterior water to be from non-potable sources

Planning Principles

The Plan offers a chance to counter archaic, car-centric urban planning principles, high maintenance landscapes, and inefficient buildings that are highly consumptive of natural resources. The transformed place will be built on a strategy of ecological urbanism which can be defined as the re-thinking and re-structuring of the built environment in response to, and in collaboration with, the natural environment. Urban development and natural systems need not be mutually exclusive nor should people and their activities be separate from nature. The Plan is based on eight urban design principles:

1. Celebrate Heritage
2. Connect the Capital
3. Support Healthy Living
4. Build Ecological Systems
5. Invigorate Waterfronts
6. Complete Communities
7. Incubate Innovation
8. Create and Enhance Views

The Plan implements all of these principles to develop a community vision and to create a place where people will be able to live, work, and play and that will also become a destination for visitors to the National Capital Region.

Infrastructure Design

Perkins+Will led an interdisciplinary team in a collaborative process in the design and implementation of district-wide sustainability systems including energy, water and waste. The Infrastructure plan is designed for functionality and promotion of the One Planet approach through the use of Low Impact Development (LID) practices and sustainable design principles. The plan meets technical requirements outlined by the City of Ottawa and Ville de Gatineau and exceeds conventional grading, stormwater management and servicing strategies to set a precedent for water conservation and low impact development. Site grading is designed to limit disruption to the existing

Chaudière Island Master Plan, Ottawa, Ontario-Gatineau, QC; 2014

shoreline and surrounding infrastructure while ensuring a safe environment for pedestrians and cyclists. A variety of innovative stormwater management principles, including bioretention areas and bioswales, provide visual and environmental benefits including foliage and vegetation along right-of-ways and ensuring only clean water is entering the Ottawa River.

Energy

The neighboring Kruger plant uses thermal energy as a key part of its process in paper and cardboard production. The heat is used inside the plant for pre-heat of process water, freshwater for showers and heating coils on the air handling plant. Waste heat from these sources, plus heat from tissue machine exhausts and boiler plant flues, if fully captured, is estimated to be around 13.2MW, at a temperature of 55°C-60°C. This waste heat will be collected and piped to the Domtar Redevelopment Lands, meeting much of the heat loads of the development.

- Ontario: The recovered waste heat would be increased in temperature by a modular system of water-to-water heat pumps to supply a higher temperature (75°C/65°C) hydronic heating supply which would enable building services systems to be as conventional as possible, such as four-pipe fan coil units. It is proposed that the central heat pump system would be located on the Québec side for a number of reasons: to take advantage of low costs Hydro Québec electricity to run the heat pumps, and closer proximity to the Kruger plant.

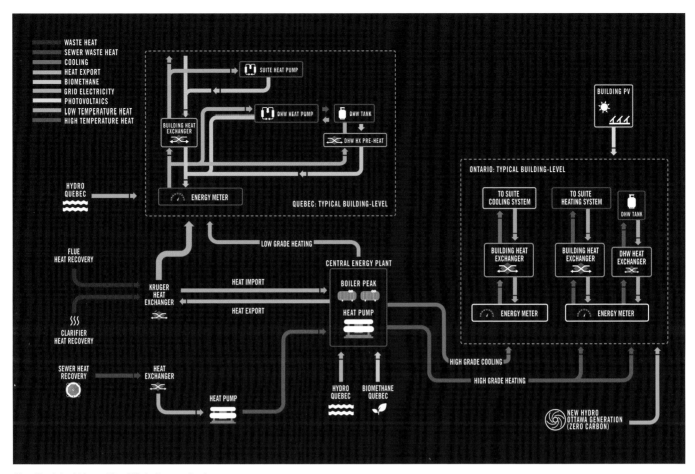

Chaudière Island Master Plan, Whole Systems Design

• Québec: Each building would have a direct connection (via heat exchanger) to the recovered waste heat from the Kruger plant. The lower temperature of 55°C/60°C supply from Kruger is suitable for direct use as pre-heat for domestic hot water services and also in-floor radiant heating systems. Where higher temperatures are required for the air handling plant and for domestic hot water heating, the temperature would be raised to the required servicing standards (75°C/65°C) by decentralized heat pumps located through each building.

Water Use

Systems have been designed to maximize water conservation within the development and meet or exceed all technical requirements set by the City of Ottawa and Ville de Gatineau. The development will employ an innovative solution to water conservation; namely, a purple pipe system which will be looped through the site supplying non-potable greywater for toilet flushing. More than 35 percent of all residential water consumption is from toilet flushing alone. The purple pipe system consists of pumping water directly from the Ottawa River and treating on-site for color and odor control. This purple pipe system, in combination with water-efficient appliances, will ensure that the development will be a leader in water conservation and reduce stress on the municipal water supply network.

Stormwater Runoff

Site hydrology and stormwater management for the site is unique; the majority of the development is on Islands within, or lands directly adjacent to, a major body of water, the Ottawa River. The site is also downstream of the Chaudière Falls which is used to generate electricity and control flows in the Ottawa River.

As rain falls it either turns into runoff, infiltrates the ground or evaporates. Runoff from the site will be managed to ensure that there is no increased risk of flooding. The existing site discharges all stormwater runoff to the Ottawa River with no control on the quality or quantity of water. The Plan will improve on existing conditions by implementing a highly efficient treatment train approach to ensure that all stormwater runoff from the site is treated with bioswales, bioretention areas and oil/grit separators, all used in series to minimize pollutants from vehicles and urban activity from entering the river. Bioswales are similar to grassed swales seen beside roadways in rural areas, but differ by containing a dense array of water friendly vegetation that filters runoff. Bioretention areas are similar to bioswales; however, instead of conveying water they collect and store it and use vegetation and soil layers to filter the water as it infiltrates to the ground. The oil/grit separator is the last treatment method removing sediment and oil before finally discharging the stormwater to the Ottawa River. This treatment approach will reduce the amount of Total Suspended Solids by more than 80 percent and greatly reduce the number of hydrocarbons and heavy metals entering the Ottawa River.

Whole Systems Benefit Whole Environments

Whole systems thinking is the future of architecture and engineering for buildings and communities. It is not a design solution that is yet owned by any specific discipline. Architects are uniquely positioned to design the systems planning, in collaboration with progressive mechanical and civil engineers, because we own the generalist's viewpoint. As a thought and design process, whole systems thinking should be used whenever any large project is designed, as it offers logical, holistic, sustainable performance solutions for even the most complex developments. Any project including 50,000 square meters or more of space can benefit from a district energy system or a modular on-site sewage treatment plant. As natural resources become scarcer and sustainable design becomes the norm, whole systems designs will provide the necessary efficiencies through their synergies. Whole systems design seeks to emulate nature, by considering input and output (waste) steams as potentials for interconnected solutions. Projects that incorporate whole systems thinking will be much more environmentally successful because they will be better equipped to mimic the beautiful simplicity of nature's own interconnected processes.

Sustainable Campus Design in a Climate of Change

Sustainable Campus in a Climate of Change was a self-directed research project which compared and contrasted programs and policies Canadian universities have implemented to mitigate climate change. The results from the survey informed a paper prepared and published in the April-May 2008 issue of Academic Matters.

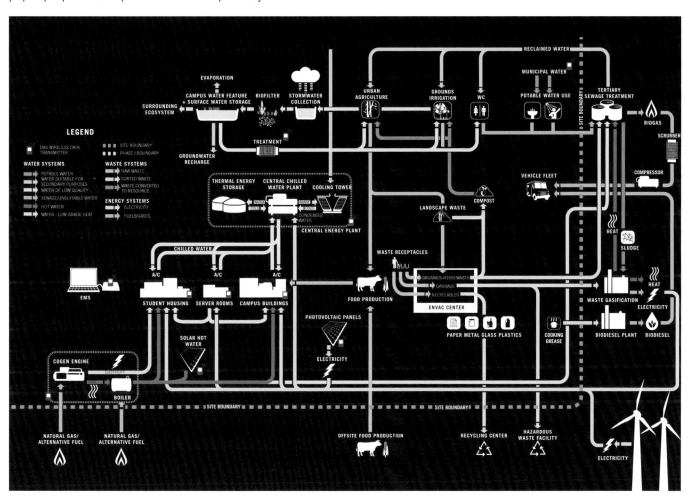

New Edge Innovations

The research and analysis required to complete the Sustainable Campus in a Climate of Change elevated our understanding of how whole systems thinking could be applied and scaled to any institution. The study highlighted that by changing the scale of our thinking, we can create solutions by connecting seemingly disparate systems and functions.

CLIENT Self-directed research, Perkins+Will
DATE 2008
DESIGN TEAM Perkins+Will: P. Busby, M. Driedger, K. Wardle, B. Wakelin
REFERENCE TO PUBLICATIONS
Brian Wakelin and Kathy Wardle, "Universities in a climate of change," *Academic Matters,* April/May 2008, p. 18-21.

Dockside Green

Victoria, BC

Dockside Green, the largest project ever developed in Victoria, British Columbia, involves the reclamation and redevelopment of 15 acres of formerly industrial waterfront property into 1.3 million square feet of commercial, residential, live/work, work/live, and light industrial uses.

Dockside Green, Synergy; Victoria, BC; 2009

In addition to the original master plan, Perkins+Will completed several phases of Dockside, including Phase 1: Synergy, the highest-scoring LEED Platinum project in the world at the time of certification; Phase 2: Balance, also LEED Platinum; and Phase CI1: Inspiration, which earned the highest LEED score for a Core and Shell building.

New Edge Innovations

The project was developed around the ideas of superlative sustainable design at the neighborhood level. Mixed uses featuring residential, retail, commercial, and industrial uses also included plans for senior living, childcare, and a hotel, resulting in a projected balance between homes and jobs. Social equity (15 percent affordable housing donated to not-for-profits) and employment opportunities for First Nations were created in the first phases of construction.

The site is oriented around a greenway and manmade water feature running parallel to the coast with a village plaza providing a focal point at the western edge of the development. Mixed-use residential towers to the west reach up to ten stories while the majority of development is three to seven stories tall.

The greenway is a functioning bioswale, polishing tertiary effluent from the on-site sewage treatment facility and stormwater detention ponds. Surplus naturally cleaned water is sold to an adjacent industry and returned to the ocean.

A district energy system fueled by biomass gasification of forestry waste pellets provides zero net carbon heating for the entire project, a first in North America. Surplus energy is shipped to an adjacent hotel, offsetting their carbon based energy, resulting in the net zero achievement of this project for both annual energy and carbon emissions.

From the project's inception, Perkins+Will recognized the unique opportunity the development represented, working in deep collaboration with the entire project team and stakeholder groups to create an exciting new community. The team's vision was a Dockside neighborhood that creates economic opportunities while promoting environmental responsibility and healthy, vigorous, dynamic urban living. As a result, the Dockside Green Development was selected as a model "Climate Positive Development" by the Clinton Climate Initiative, setting a compelling environmental and economic example for cities to follow.

With a LEED Platinum certification goal for each building on-site, this project is a global showcase for large-scale integrated sustainable development. In 2009 Dockside was certified LEED for Neighborhood Development at the Platinum level, making it one of only a handful of projects worldwide that have received this certification. By early 2015, 8 of the project's 26 projected buildings had been constructed. The water usage of the building was addressed by adding a greywater flushing system combined with low flow fixtures. The roof drainage system was modified to allow collection of this water for treatment and use for toilet flushing.

PROJECT Dockside Green
LOCATION Victoria, BC
CLIENT Windmill West, VanCity Enterprises
SIZE
SITE 15 acres / 6 hectares
TOTAL DEVELOPMENT 30,000 sm of built mixed-use space
SYNERGY (PHASE I) 178,680 sf / 16,600 sm
BALANCE (PHASE II) 155,215 sf / 14,420 sm
INSPIRATION (PHASE III) 20,160 sf / 1,874 sm
DESIGN AND CONSTRUCTION
SYNERGY (PHASE I) Design 2004-2005; Construction 2006-2008
BALANCE (PHASE II) Design 2005-2006; Construction 2007-2009
INSPIRATION (PHASE III) Design 2007-2008; Construction 2008-2009
DESIGN TEAM Perkins+Will: P. Busby, L. Chester, P. Cowcher, R. Drew, A. Fawkes, D. Kitazaki, R.

Dockside Green, Balance; Victoria, BC; 2009

Dockside Green, Balance; Victoria, BC; 2009

Maas, S. Patterson, J. Skinner, A. Slawinski, T. Williams, B. Wakelin, G. Underhill
STRUCTURAL ENGINEER Read Jones Christoffersen
MECHANICAL ENGINEER Stantec
ELECTRICAL ENGINEER Stantec
CIVIL ENGINEER Worley Parsons Komex
CIVIL ENGINEER RCL Consulting
ECOLOGY/STORMWATER Aqua-Tex Scientific Consulting
GREEN BUILDING BuildGreen Consulting
COST CONSULTANT Payne Group
LANDSCAPE ARCHITECT PWL Partnership
ENVIRONMENTAL SOILS Quantum Environmental Remediation
SURVEYOR Focus Group
GEOTECHNICAL CONSULTANT C.N. Ryzuk & Associates
TRAFFIC CONSULTANT Boulevard Transportation Group
CONTRACTOR Farmer Constructors, Inc.
INTERIOR DESIGNER False Creek Design
CODE CONSULTANT Gage-Babcock & Associates
ENVELOPE CONSULTANT Morrison Hershfield
PHOTOGRAPHER Vince Klassen
AWARDS RECEIVED
- Dockside Green was named one of the first carbon neutral projects by the Clinton Climate Development Initiative, 2009
- Architectural Institute of British Columbia Special Jury Award, 2009

- AIA Committee on the Environment (COTE), Top Ten Green Projects, 2009
- Royal Architectural Institute of Canada, Green Building Award of Excellence, 2009
- AIA Seattle Committee on the Environment (COTE), What Makes it Green?, Regional Top 10 Green Project, 2009
- GLOBE Awards for Environmental Excellence in Urban Sustainability, 2008
- BC Hydro Power Smart Excellence Award, Innovation in Sustainable Design, 2007
- Smart Growth of British Columbia Awards, Process/Proposal Award, 2006
- RAIC National Urban Design Awards, Merit Award, Approved or Adopted Urban Design Plan, 2006
- Canadian Architect, Award of Excellence, 2005
- Canadian Urban Institute, Brownie Award, Best Overall Project, 2005
- Canadian Urban Institute, Brownie Award, Green Design and Technology, 2005
- Planning Institute of BC Innovation in Site Planning and Design Award, 2005
SUSTAINABILITY RATINGS
- Synergy (Phase I): LEED Platinum. This phase reached LEED Platinum at 63 points, making it the highest-scoring LEED Platinum certified project in the world at the time.
- Inspiration (Phase II): LEED Platinum
- Balance (Phase III): LEED Platinum

REFERENCE TO PUBLICATIONS
- Kaid Benfield, "Is this the world's greenest neighborhood?" The Atlantic, August 24, 2011.
- Sara Hart, "Dockside Green: A Platinum Setting," GreenSource, January 2009.
- "Dockside Green," Metropolis, October 2008, p. 134.
- "Dockside Green," Urban Land, October 2008, p. 71.
- Dockside Green Achieves Highest LEED Score Ever," SABMag, September/October 2008, p. 7.
- Zach Mortice, "Busby Perkins+Will's Dockside Green Places Its Bets on Record-Shattering Sustainability," Architect, September 26, 2008.
- "Dockside Green's integrated design team celebrates groundbreaking achievement," Canadian Architect, July 23, 2008.
- "Dockside Green recognized for sustainable design," Globe Net, June 22, 2006.

Blatchford Redevelopment
Former Municipal Airport, Edmonton, AB

The winner of an international design competition, Perkins+Will's master plan for the redevelopment of Edmonton's Blatchford lands creates a global model for sustainable city-building and a truly vibrant live-work-play destination for Edmontonians, while providing homes, jobs, and recreational opportunities for 30,000 residents.

Blatchford Redevelopment, Site Plan; Edmonton, AB; 2013

Blatchford Redevelopment; Edmonton, AB; 2013

New Edge Innovations
Delivering on the City of Edmonton's Master Planning Principles, the plan repairs a 215-hectare rift in the city's urban fabric and incorporates four strands of sustainability-based principles of connectedness: cultural, ecological, social, and economic.

Cultural Sustainability -
Connecting to Site History:
Embedding the site's past in its future, the plan repurposes historical features of the site's former airport lands as new community amenities and reuses the runways as organizing elements.

Ecological Sustainability –
Connecting to Nature:
Preserving more than half of Blatchford as green space, the plan includes a destination park while neighborhood-scaled open spaces at the park perimeter extend into the city to knit together adjacent communities.

Social Sustainability –
Connecting Communities:
Extending surrounding street patterns through new neighborhoods, the plan connects future and current residents. A Light Rail Transit Line

(LRT) will connect the site to more distant neighborhoods while providing easy access to Edmonton's downtown.

Economic Sustainability –
Connecting to Growth Catalysts:
Fostering economic vitality, the plan creates both a mixed-use community and connects to the growth potential of four major catalysts: a planned LRT line, the Northern Alberta Institute of Technology (NAIT), a new rehabilitation hospital, and Kingsway Gardens Mall.

Perkins+Will's plan provided an innovative district energy strategy to reduce carbon emissions from the community by 3.2 million tons over 20 years while generating site-wide electricity through biomass and deep (true) geothermal sources. A "beyond carbon neutral" community is envisioned by selling surplus energy to public buildings in the area.

Water strategies are equally significant. Rainwater, snowmelt and daylit stormwater culverts from adjacent neighborhoods feed a vast central pond system. It detains and stores water for a community purple pipe system and irrigation. It has five stepped levels, each performing a natural cleaning process, which will allow overflow to enter the river system, fully cleaned. It also provides summer

and winter recreational opportunities for the community.

Urban agriculture is also embedded in all areas of the development, along with the creation of public markets for the sharing of produce.

In June 2014, City staff, without our involvement, presented a significantly amended plan to City Council which has substantially scaled back the fundamental sustainability strategies and innovations. Council has subsequently approved the reduced plan with an amendment to review and determine how and to what degree many aspects of the original sustainability strategies can be achieved over the life of the project.

PROJECT Blatchford Redevelopment
LOCATION Former Municipal Airport, Edmonton, AB
CLIENT City of Edmonton, City Centre Redevelopment
DESIGN 2010-2013
SIZE 531 acres / 215 hectares
DESIGN TEAM Perkins+Will: P. Busby, A. Charisius, J. Drohan, N. Friedman, C. Gomes, B. McCarry, M. Nielsen, P. Pinto, G. Silwal, Y. Sun, P. Vaucheret
COMMUNITY PLANNING Civitas Urban Design and Planning

Blatchford Redevelopment, Open space preserve; Edmonton, AB; 2013

LOCAL ARCHITECTURE AND URBAN DESIGN Group 2
Architecture Engineering Ltd.
TRANSPORTATION ENGINEER Nelson\Nygaard
Sustainable Building Design Archineers;
Integral Group
Geotechnical and Environmental Golder
Associates
Local Municipal Planning ISL Engineering and
Land Services
LAND ECONOMICS Pro Forma Advisors
PUBLIC CONSULTATION Soles and Co.
MECHANICAL ENGINEER Integral Group
ELECTRICAL ENGINEER Integral Group
HERITAGE CONSULTANT Alberta Western Heritage
LANDSCAPE ARCHITECTURE Phillips Farevaag
Smallenberg
RENDERINGS Foyd Architects
AWARDS RECEIVED
• Canadian Urban Institute Brownie Award, 2014
• Royal Architectural Institute of Canada, (RAIC)
  National Urban Design Awards, 2014
• Globe Awards - Excellence in Urban
  Sustainability, 2014
SUSTAINABILITY RATINGS Beyond carbon neutral
REFERENCE TO PUBLICATIONS
• Gorden Kent, "Trash vacuum, stormwater
  irrigation on the table in Blatchford project,"
  Edmonton Journal, March 21, 2014.
• Blair McCarry, "Blatchford Redevelopment,"

SABMag, December 24, 2013: http://
www.sabmagazine.com/blog/2013/12/24/
blatchford-redevelopment/
• Alix Kemp, "Downtown or Bust: Calgary and
  Edmonton attempt to revitalize their downtown
  cores," Alberta Venture, November 18, 2013.
URL City of Edmonton, Blatchford
Redevelopment website: http://www.edmonton.
ca/blatchford.aspx

Chaudière

Les Isles, Ottawa, ON / Gatineau, QC

The Chaudière Master Plan is one of enduring beauty, great cultural and historic significance, and thoughtful ecological stewardship. The plan for the former Domtar paper mill envisions a powerful link with the Ottawa River, a signature destination supporting urban growth and vitality for both Ottawa and Gatineau, which will connect people to the Ottawa riverfront in ways they have not been able to connect for generations.

Chaudiere; Les Isles, Ottawa, ON-Gatineau, QC; 2014

The Chaudière Master Plan offers an unmatched choice of activities, magnificent views, and multi-season recreation for all residents and visitors. It will be a place where the people from all over the region will come to play, to wander, to eat, and to stay.

Perkins+Will led an interdisciplinary team in a collaborative process in the design and implementation of district-wide sustainability systems including energy, water, and waste. The Chaudière Master Plan offers a chance to counter archaic, car-centric urban planning principles, high-maintenance landscapes, and inefficient buildings that are highly consumptive of natural resources. The transformed place will be built on a strategy of ecological urbanism which can be defined as the rethinking and restructuring of the built environment in response to and in collaboration with the natural environment. Urban development and natural systems need not be mutually exclusive nor should people and their activities be separate from nature. The Chaudière Master Plan is based on eight urban design principles:

1. Celebrate Heritage
2. Connect the Capital
3. Support Healthy Living
4. Build Ecological Systems
5. Invigorate Waterfronts
6. Complete Communities
7. Incubate Innovation
8. Create and Enhance Views

The Concept Master Plan implements all of these principles to develop the community vision and to create a place where people will be able to live, work, and play and that will become a destination for visitors to the National Capital Region.

New Edge Innovations
The Perkins+Will team used the One Planet Community rating system to ensure that the Chaudière Master Plan is not just a model of great mixed-use, pedestrian-oriented city design but is also a leading example of sustainable development with aggressive targets including:
- Supplying 100 percent of energy needs from renewable sources by 2020
- All buildings net zero carbon by 2020
- Divert 98 percent of all solid waste from landfill
- Reduce site related vehicle miles traveled (VMT) by 55 percent by 2020

- Reduce carbon emissions from vehicles travelling to and from the site by 75 percent by 2032
- Reduce interior consumption of water by 60 percent compared to standards use in surrounding communities.
- 100 percent of exterior water shall be from non-potable sources

If everyone in the world consumed as many natural resources as the average person in North America, we would need five planets to support our lifestyles. One Planet Living is a model based on 10 simple principles that provide a framework to make sustainable living easy and affordable for all. The Chaudière Master Plan will achieve the highest green building standards for materials, water, energy, and indoor air quality to create a zero carbon sustainability showpiece. It includes creating habitat protection, outdoor recreation, community agriculture, and connecting the site with adjacent open spaces. It also means having more local, organic, and fair trade products in restaurants and shops; providing cleaner transportation options; creating quality affordable housing and jobs; and making it easier to adopt healthy, green lifestyles.

Chaudière; Les Isles, Ottawa, ON-Gatineau, QC; 2014

The Infrastructure plan is designed for functionality and promotion of the "One Planet Action" through the use of Low Impact Development (LID) practices and sustainable design principles. A variety of innovative stormwater management principles including bioretention areas and bioswales provide visual and environmental benefits including foliage and vegetation along right-of-ways and ensuring only clean water enters the Ottawa River. A proposed greywater distribution system will supply non-potable water instead of clean municipal drinking water to flush toilets, reducing the stress on the municipal water supply network. The neighboring Kruger plant uses thermal energy as a key part of its processes in paper and cardboard production. The heat is used inside Kruger for pre-heat of process water, freshwater for showers, and heating coils on air handling plants. There are further potential opportunities for heat recovery from the existing Kruger plant. The waste heat will be collected and piped to the Domtar Redevelopment Lands, meeting much of the heat loads of the development.

Site hydrology and stormwater management is unique for the fact the majority of the development is on islands within, or lands directly adjacent to, a major body of water, the Ottawa River. The site is also downstream of the Chaudière Falls which is used to generate electricity and control flows in the Ottawa River. The proposed site development will improve on existing conditions by implementing a highly efficient train approach treatment to ensure that all stormwater runoff from the site is treated and exceeds City of Ottawa and Ville de Gatineau's water quality standards. The treatment approach consists of Low Impact Development (LID) practices such as bioswales and bioretention areas and conventional treatment methods such as oil/grit separator (OGS) units all used in series to minimize pollutants from vehicles and urban activity from entering the river. The treatment train approach described above will reduce the amount of Total Suspended Solids (TSS) by greater than 80 percent, and also greatly reduce the number of hydrocarbons and heavy metals entering the Ottawa River.

LOCATION Ottawa-Gatineau metropolitan area. The site is located on both sides of the river in Ottawa and falls partly within the City of Ottawa, Ontario and partly within the City of Gatineau, Quebec.
CLIENT Windmill Development Group

DESIGN June 2013 through April 2014
CONSTRUCTION 2015 through 2030
SIZE Site size: 38 acres / 15 hectares. PROPOSED DEVELOPMENT 3,000,000 sf / 279,000 sm mixed use
DESIGN TEAM Urban Design and Master Plan: Perkins+Will: P. Busby, D. Dornan, N. Friedman, L. Shifley, R. Song, J. Yong
LANDSCAPE PFS
PLANNING CONSULTANT Fotenn
CIVIL ENGINEER DSEL (Civil)
HERITAGE ASSETS Rubin Rotmann
TRAFFIC ENGINEER Delcan
SUSTAINABILITY ADVISOR Archineers
RENDERER Chris Foyd
SUSTAINABILITY RATINGS The project is designed to be the first One Planet Community in North America. In keeping with Windmill's sustainability commitments, all buildings will pursue the certification goal of LEED Platinum.
REFERENCE TO PUBLICATIONS
"Windmill unveils plans for 'world's most sustainable community' for former Domtar lands," *Ottawa Citizen*, April 22, 2014.

Regenerative Design

VanDusen Botanical Garden Visitor Centre; Vancouver, BC

Architecture Finds its Place in Nature

VanDusen Botanical Garden Visitor Centre, view of green roof with nodding onions, courtesy Sharp and Diamond Landscape Architecture; 2012

Sustainable design began as a practice of doing less damage to the planet through design and construction of the built environment. For over 20 years, those of us committed to sustainability focused primarily on wreaking less havoc on the natural world. When LEED was introduced, it broadened the scope of included issues and helped codify goals, calling for incrementally less degradation at each higher level of the standard. LEED Certified was better than nothing; LEED Silver and LEED Gold were less harmful than LEED Certified; LEED Platinum called for even less environmental injury.

More recently, new strategies have asked the question, "Rather than doing less harm with our work, shouldn't we strive to do no harm whatsoever?" Sustainability, in theory, implies the conceptual position of doing no harm to the environment, on the assumption that if humans do not violate it, nature remains intact, and our activity is sustainable. We have learned how to design and build "net zero" projects that aim to have no impact whatsoever on specific environmental targets. Drawing no off-site water, generating their own power, treating their own waste on-site and requiring no fossil fuels, these buildings – and sometimes entire communities – operate in harmony with nature with no adverse consequences on the environment.

But the continued deterioration of the biosphere reminds us that we are due for another paradigm shift. As carbon builds up in the atmosphere, garbage islands grow in the oceans, and the health of thousands of global species diminishes, it becomes increasingly apparent that we are losing time in the fight to save our planet. We now know that our planet needs more than a neutral partner. Nature needs humans to advocate for its health and sustainability.

While we are transitioning from doing less harm to doing no harm, it is also time to take the next step: to design buildings and communities that *give back* to the environment. Our work must have positive effects on natural cycles that we have previously conspired to break. The buildings and systems we create must be part of and one with nature, so that humans and their creations ultimately enter into a mutually nurturing relationship with the planet. In nature there is no waste, no garbage, and all living things depend on vast systems of support and balance. Biological organisms take care of the system that is going to support their offspring. The organisms of the natural world not only thrive, but they do so for millennia. Life in nature creates conditions conducive to life, building soil, cleaning air and water, all conditions for regeneration.

Humans were part of that natural balance for over 400,000 years. On that timeline, it is only recently and briefly, in particular since the industrial revolution, that we have grown to disregard nature and our place in it so callously. By bringing nature back into the equation, we can develop regenerative design. We have to find a way to meet our human needs while returning this world closer to Eden.

Defining Regenerative Design

Broadly speaking, the term "regenerative design" applies to any design process that ends up having a net benefit to the natural systems affected by the project. Several of our movement's visionaries have offered up their own interpretations of the concept, all of which focus on a common principle but come at it from slightly different perspectives. Here are some of the variations I find most useful, followed by my own definition:

Ray Cole: Regenerative Design relates to approaches that support the co-evolution of human and natural systems in a partnered relationship. It is not the building that is 'regenerated' in the same sense as the self-healing and self-organizing attributes of a living system, but by the ways that the act of building can be a catalyst for positive change within the unique 'place' in which it is situated. Within regenerative development, built projects, stakeholder processes and inhabitation are collectively focused on enhancing life in all of its manifestations – human, other species, ecological systems – through an enduring responsibility of stewardship. [1]

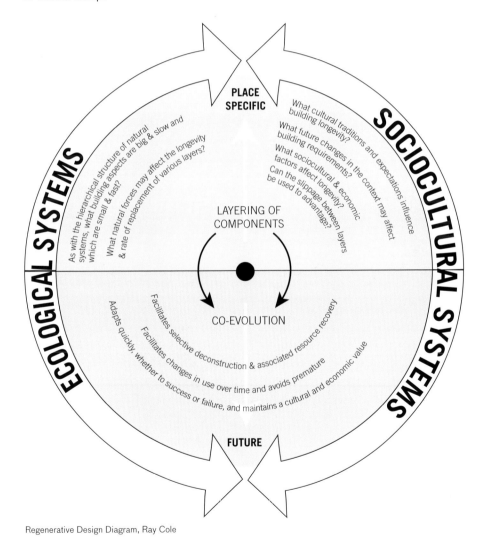

Regenerative Design Diagram, Ray Cole

1. Cole, Raymond J., "Regenerative Design & Development: Current Theory and Practice," *Building Research & Information*, 2012 40 (1), 1.

Bill Reed: Regenerative Development is a whole systems approach that partners people and their place, working to make both people *and* nature stronger, more vibrant, and more resilient. Becoming a Regenerative Practitioner is about seizing the potential, born of crisis, for transforming our role as designers, planners, builders and citizens. In particular, it is about learning how, in an increasingly unpredictable world, we can enable the places where we live and work to thrive, not just sustain a precarious balance. Practitioners of Regenerative Development believe it is not enough to aspire to mitigate the effects of human activity—people need to take their place again as a part of nature. From this perspective, Regenerative Development means harmonizing human activities with the continuing regeneration of life on our planet, even as we continue to develop our potential as humans. It seeks to reverse the degeneration of ecosystems caused by human activities, and to design a built environment and human systems that can co-evolve with natural systems. In this way it increases the overall expression and resilience of life. A core premise of Regenerative Development is that we cannot make the outer transformations required to create a truly sustainable world without making the inner transformations in how we think. Thus, Regenerative Practitioners weave together work on developing themselves (personal development), their work community (development of one's practice/team) and their effect in the world (making a meaningful and significant difference to the regeneration of our places).[2]

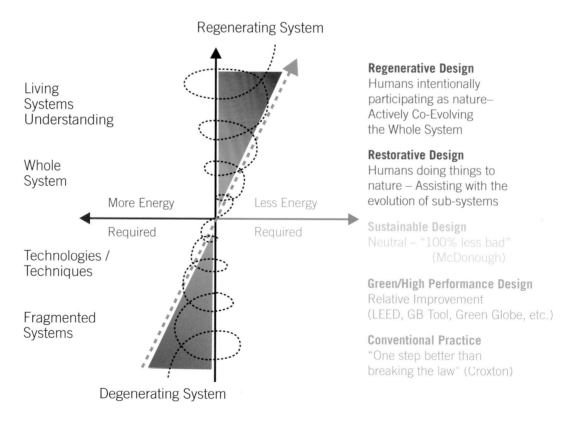

Regenerative Design Diagram Bill Reed

---

2. Pamela Mang, "Curriculum Materials, The Regenerative Practitioner, an educational series offered by Regenesis Group"

Sim Van der Ryn: Regenerative Design focuses on users and people as part of the design process from the beginning and learning to manage all components of the finished building and its natural systems. Regenerative literally means restoring natural systems to health and incorporating them into the design, in the same way users need to be incorporated in the design process. For Van der Ryn, the Living Building Challenge is the first step towards truly Regenerative Design.

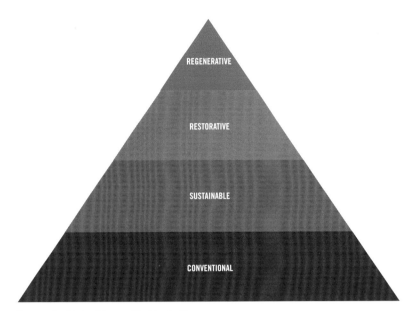

Regenerative Design Diagram, Sim Van der Ryn

Peter Busby: Regenerative design features human constructions that contribute positively to coexistence and restoration of natural cycles in our biosphere, to sustain all life.

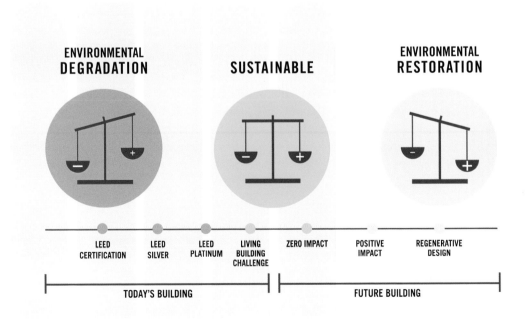

Regenerative Design Diagram, Peter Busby

Regenerative Design Tool, Place Diagram

Do We Need a Regenerative Design Standard?

Given the various sustainable design standards and green building measurement tools that already exist in our industry, some may question the necessity of adding yet another aspirational target to the crowded field. Indeed, there are scores of standards circulating around the globe designed to guide us toward cleaner, smarter solutions. (In addition to LEED, the Living Building Challenge, BOMA Go Green, and One Planet Living, more than two dozen separate standards are used everywhere from Europe to China to the United Arab Emirates.)

The problem with most of these tools, however, is that they tend to look at external issues rather than the natural systems affected by buildings and communities. In addition, they are structured using point systems, imperatives, and layers, which provides too limited a range of tackled issues and too rigid a construct for projects that strive to join nature's fluidity.

A regenerative design standard should be looser in its framework and methodology, allowing people to consider the impacts and benefits of every design-build-use-discard decision made. Instead of zeroing in on individual point-based targets, it must be designed to encompass entire interconnected ecological systems involving water, energy, materials, and land (earth). As such, it does not lend itself well to becoming a quantifiable, codified model. Still, because we feel strongly that the industry needs something definitive in this area, we have been working with Dr. Ray Cole to create a "tool that is not a tool," slated for release in 2015. (Ray has written extensively on the topic. See the Appendix 2 for his article, "A Regenerative Design Framework: Setting New Aspirations and Initiating New Discussions,"[3] coauthored with several of us at Perkins+Will.)

The first phase of the research and tool development ran from 2012 to 2013.

3. Raymond J. Cole, Peter Busby, Robin Guenther, Leah Briney, Aiste Blaviesciunaite, and Tatiana Alencar, "A Regenerative Design Framework: Setting New Aspirations and Inititating New Discussions," *Building Research and Information* (2012) 40(1), 95-111.

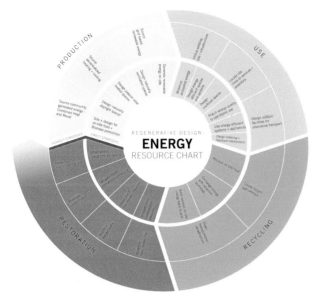

Regenerative Design Tool, Energy Resource Chart

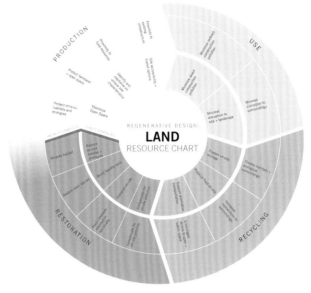

Regenerative Design Tool, Land Resource Chart

Regenerative Design Tool, Water Resource Chart

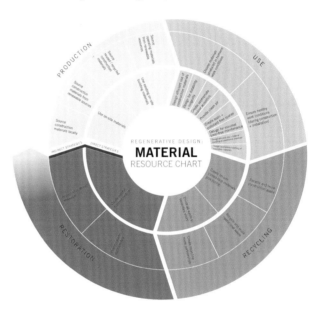

Regenerative Design Tool, Material Resource Chart

It concluded with a Regenerative Design Framework that established natural flows for Materials, Place Energy, Water, and Waste. Each flow, illustrated in the diagrams below, had a cycle of creation, use, return, and regeneration. "Rings" of information moved from the most specific (inner) to the most general and interconnected outer ring. Hundreds of strategies were documented, and the "non-tool" was tested on six prototype Perkins+Will projects in 2013, ranging from buildings to urban design projects. Mixed results followed, with the tool being found to be too broad or at times not detailed enough. Teams also wanted to enter (use) the cycles in parts, at multiple entry points, and seemed to avoid the implied commitment to visit the whole cycle (regenerate!). Ray and I also tested the ideas in public presentations in 2012 and 2013 to get feedback on the ideas from architects and engineers.

We have recently recommitted to each other that we will work further on a more applied version (less academic?) that will adapt to project goals, have links

Dr. John Gunn, indicating the depth of topsoil from 30 years ago

to other standards (LEED, the Living Building Challenge), and contain metrics. The true potential of this tool will be revealed over time.

A Commitment

No one has designed a regenerative building... yet. However, we and others now consider aspects of regenerative design in almost everything we do. We believe in it so strongly that it has become part of the fabric of our practice. Whether we are proposing, designing, or building, we start by determining the needs of the environment. All other decisions flow like water from that point.

Three key projects (the Vale Living With Lakes Centre for Applied Research in Environmental Restoration and Sustainability, Laurentian University; the Centre for Interactive Research on Sustainability, University of British Columbia; and the VanDusen Botanical Garden Visitor Centre) demonstrate our learning process and our commitment to regenerative design, each proving that the built environment can deliver beauty, performance, and health to its human occupants as well as contributing to the health of its natural surroundings.

The Vale Living With Lakes Centre for Applied Research in Environmental Restoration and Sustainability

This research laboratory for ecologists in Sudbury, Ontario gave us our first opportunity to consider upfront regenerative design in the planning and design process. We requested and received full access to a team of ecologists (led by our client, Dr. John Gunn) who have been in place in the region for decades studying how to mitigate the impacts of Sudbury's nickel mines' famously disastrous environmental legacy.

The town's smelting operation, which powered its economy and once boasted the tallest smokestack in the world, decimated local flora and fauna over the span of the 20th century. At its worst, pollution from the mill was so extensive that it virtually extinguished most non-human life forms downwind of the plume for nearly 100 miles. The area was so desolate of natural growth in the 1960s that NASA used it as a testing ground for lunar vehicles. Fervent regreening efforts (led by our clients and others) began in Sudbury during the 1970s and life forms gradually began to return to the Sudbury basin in the years that followed after Inco (the mine owners) incorporated pollution abatement and dispersion measures. Today, the average height of vegetation is 20-30 feet high, where once there stood an extensive boreal forest. Although the regeneration of this region is gradual, it is measurable.

When we arrived in Sudbury, Dr. Gunn and his colleagues shared with us their key findings so that we could design a structure that did more than just avoid further harm to the area, but actually began to repair past damage. They were particularly concerned about two issues: abundant heavy metals from the polluted air that had acidified rainfall over the years, moving heavy metals directly into local lakes with every storm event; and the continued imbalance of the lakes' acidity. The delicate life forms in the lakes were extremely compromised as a result of both problems.

So we set out to create a laboratory that would not only house the ecologists' world renowned ecological research efforts but actively heal the lakes themselves – both Ramsey Lake, which sits adjacent to the building, and the 330 lakes that are spread throughout the city of Sudbury.[4] The learning experience for us

4. http://www.greatersudbury.ca/living/lakes-facts/

Living With Lakes; Sudbury, ON; 2011

was profound. While the Vale Living With Lakes Centre for Applied Research in Environmental Restoration and Sustainability, Laurentian University (Living With Lakes) was our first experience collaborating with ecologists, now we routinely add ecological expertise to our planning and design teams.

We spent significant time mapping the ecological systems that occurred in the area surrounding the site: the movement of rainwater and snowmelt as it traveled from the sky to the lake; the various types of plants and vegetation that occupied the nearby hills and depressions; the subtle ecological differences between the reforested high ground and the wetlands at the lakes' edges. Every part of the ecosystems was considered; nothing was deemed inconsequential.
By the time the design was complete, three key strategies drove the project's regenerative mission:

Rainwater adjustment: Instead of channeling rooftop rainwater down a pipe and into the ground or lake, we sent it over a base course of the building made of limestone. Interacting with the alkaline limestone alters the pH of the acidic rainwater, which measures 5.60 when it falls from the sky and 7.96 by the time it has run across the stone. After traveling through the project's bioswale, the newly cleaned water flows into the lake, gradually altering the pH balance. So every drop of rainwater that falls on this building is affected by the building

Living With Lakes, Bioswale; Sudbury, ON; 2011

Living With Lakes, green roof; Sudbury, ON; 2011

and landscape, then helps to correct the acidity of the lake that sits by the structure's side. Nature benefits from human construction.

Heavy metal separation: In a second rainwater cleaning process targeting what falls beyond the roofline of the building, water runs into a landscape filter constructed of natural rocks and plants that work together to separate heavy metals. To correct the effect of pollution attaching to rainfall in the air or on the ground, we created a three-tiered trench system that simplifies the process of separating and removing the harmful metals isolated by the filters. Heavy metals trapped here can be periodically removed mechanically. The rainwater then exits the bioswale and enters an enlarged wetland (richer and more biologically diverse than we found it) and then into the lake.

Green roof: We deliberately planted the roof surfaces with native blueberry species – a specific vegetation that benefits from the acidic, moist conditions present at the site. Now thriving, the bushes lure fauna from the nearby hillsides to the structure's roof, which is connected directly to the landscape as the building is nestled into a hillside. Deer and other animals stroll up the land bridge and feed on the berries, receiving a direct nourishing benefit from the building.

These three strategies may seem like small steps, but they constitute our start at deliberate design to heal the environment.

Living With Lakes, diagram showing pH Balance

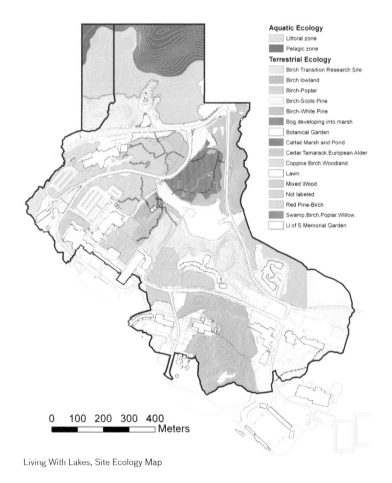

Aquatic Ecology
- Littoral zone
- Pelagic zone

Terrestrial Ecology
- Birch Transition Research Site
- Birch lowland
- Birch-Poplar
- Birch-Scots Pine
- Birch-White Pine
- Bog developing into marsh
- Botanical Garden
- Cattail Marsh and Pond
- Cedar,Tamarack,European Alder
- Coppice Birch Woodland
- Lawn
- Mixed Wood
- Not labeled
- Red Pine-Birch
- Swamp,Birch,Poplar,Willow..
- U of S Memorial Garden

0 100 200 300 400 Meters

Living With Lakes, Site Ecology Map

Centre for Interactive Research on Sustainability, University of British Columbia, Vancouver, BC; 2011

Centre for Interactive Research on Sustainability, University of British Columbia, Entry; Vancouver, BC; 2011

Centre for Interactive Research on Sustainability, University of British Columbia, Stormwater collection; Vancouver, BC; 2011

The UBC Centre for Interactive Research on Sustainability

It is not an exaggeration to say that the Living With Lakes project awakened in us a desire to apply regenerative design principles whenever and wherever possible. We also learned the inherent value of working closely with ecologists, biologists, arborists, and other experts, all of whom can add their specialized science and environmental skills to enhance the regenerative nature of any built project. These new collaborative opportunities pushed our practice to an exciting new edge.

When we were asked by Dr. John Robinson at the University of British Columbia to design the Centre for Interactive Research on Sustainability (CIRS), we were committed to establish regenerative design as a specific goal for the project. The CIRS building would end up being much more urban than Living With Lakes, due to its 100 percent site coverage mandate, but we remained true to regenerative principles for the campus structure designed to house research and outreach efforts on urban and building sustainability. The building would help demonstrate and further the mission of its occupants: researchers and academics committed to the future of sustainable design.

Given the fact that the CIRS project would be a zero lot line building on a site that was devoid of flora and fauna, we needed to find ways to create and maintain connections among systems, ultimately achieving net zero energy and zero carbon in this very urban setting. We believed then and now that every project has the potential to be regenerative. Our goal was to create measurable support for ecosystems and species on a site where none had recently existed. Four key regenerative design strategies from the CIRS project include:

Stormwater collection: All rainwater on the project flows from the roof through visible open channels to a bioswale planted with native vegetation and teeming with insects and other species at the entrance of the building. Locating the bioswale in such an obvious location was an intentional decision, as it reminds every student, teacher, and visitor entering the building of the importance and role of water and nature throughout the building. Overflows from the bioswale are directed to a nearby well and pumped down to the water table. In our pre-construction research, we learned that the site's water table has been shrinking dramatically in recent decades. The water strategies at CIRS actually help replenish the aquifer, as rainfall is channeled back underground rather than being syphoned away from the site into the ocean. In a new program, the entire UBC campus now connects all of its buildings to a series of wells that support the effort of recharging the aquifer.

Planting wall: The green wall on the western face of the CIRS building serves multiple purposes. The wall is constructed of a grid that supports a series of molded containers housing rich soil and a healthy vertical foliage of chocolate vines (*Akebia quinata*). In the wintertime, these deciduous vines defoliate and allow for passive solar gain throughout the building. In the summertime, the lush and colorful blooms do more than just shade the interior space, as the vines' fruit is a favorite food source among a number of local bird species. So a renewable living system supports the building's heating and cooling functions while simultaneously supporting ecological systems. Nature and building provide service to one another. The chocolaty aroma and visual beauty of the CIRS planting wall create additional aesthetic and inspirational benefits.

Green roof: The green roof over the CIRS lecture hall is planted with a number of native species, sedum being the most prominent. These various flora would

Winter

Spring

Summer

Autumn

Centre for Interactive Research on Sustainability, University of British Columbia, Planting Wall

otherwise not have the opportunity to exist on this urban site. But on the CIRS roof, they bloom, grow and thrive in a newly vigorous rooftop ecology. A portion of the roof has even been planted with lettuce varieties that are cultivated specifically for use in the ground-level café.

Blackwater treatment system: At the heart of the CIRS on-site water strategy is a solar aquatic sewage treatment tank located at the southwest corner of the building, clearly visible at the main entrance. Surrounded by glass to allow the sun's rays to support the life forms inside, the tank houses all processes required to treat and clean the human waste generated in the building. Algae, snails, and other species interact with the waste to clean the water and produce sludge, which is periodically exported to the green houses used by the university's horticultural programs in buildings across the street. Greywater from the tanks travels back into the CIRS structure to service toilets before returning through the same cycle once again. The overall process benefits the small species that dwell inside the tanks, the human species studying the biological systems, and the operational performance of the building itself. In the summer (when building occupancy drops), the tanks are "fed" by sewage drawn from the general campus network.

CIRS has many other sustainable design strategies that make it one of the greenest buildings in North America. Constructed on a site largely devoid of biosystems, CIRS is an urban building that also pointedly demonstrates that nature can be regenerated through design and operation of a dense development.

Centre for Interactive Research on Sustainability, University of British Columbia, Green Roof; Vancouver, BC; 2011

Centre for Interactive Research on Sustainability, University of British Columbia; Vancouver, BC; 2011

VanDusen Botanical Garden Visitor Centre, Water Systems; Vancouver, BC; 2012

VanDusen Botanical Garden Visitor Centre

Arguably our most dramatic and important building contribution to the regenerative design discussion to date, the VanDusen project was an opportunity to weave together natural and architectural themes into a single elegant project. Working on the grounds of a botanical garden allowed us to play with multiple natural themes that served the aesthetic and operational goals of the building. Most profoundly, we were able to support a high degree of biodiversity that had not previously existed on the site.

Regenerative ideas are implanted virtually everywhere on the site in, on, under, and around the VanDusen building. Everything about the design and performance of the structure focuses on human needs in the context of natural systems.

Energy systems: The building is powered by photovoltaic panels and solar hot water heating tubes that create energy and warmth throughout the interior. Solar hot water is also delivered to an adjacent building, where it offsets that structure's use of fossil fuels (a gas-powered heating system). So, by supporting its neighbor, the Visitor Centre enjoys a net-positive impact on the emissions and a total reduction of carbon emissions.

Solar Chimney: Biophilic by nature, the solar chimney serves as the lungs of the building while also contributing to the building's memorable character. Located in the center of the atrium, and exactly at the center of the building's radiating geometry, the solar chimney highlights the role of sustainability by form and function. Natural ventilation is assisted by a solar chimney, composed of a 13.5 meter-high glazed oculus and a perforated aluminum heat sink, which converts the sun's rays to convection energy. The heatsink suspended in the oculus is painted with a pattern, based on the sun path, which maximizes heat gain to encourage air movement due to temperature differentials in the building. As the heat sink heats up, the air flow in the building increases in response. The heat sink is sculpturally derived to precisely mimic the tracking angles of the sun.

Rooftop: The design of the expansive and curvaceous roof of the VanDusen building is based on the elegant structure of a native orchid. The roof is comprised of five different ecosystems spread out across the different roof "petals." On one, we worked with Cornelia Hahn Oberlander to choose plants that would support a species of endangered indigenous butterflies. Other sections of the roof contain more luxurious and varied foliage supporting other types of flora and fauna. One part of the roof surface slopes gently toward the ground via a "land bridge" to encourage animal species to explore what the roof has to offer them. We know this is successful, as coyotes have been spotted on the roof, evidence of a full ecosystem at work. We have seen through the project's first few years of operation that the bioregion's natural cycles are fully and robustly echoed on the VanDusen roof surfaces. Springtime brings vigorous growth and flowering species. Guests witness these naturally occurring phenomena as part of the overall visitor experience at the gardens, gaining important understanding that these seasonal cycles are healthier than a grassy surface that stays artificially green throughout the year. Intentionally unkempt with many native ecosystems, the VanDusen roof reflects the type of grassland meadow that was native to southwestern British Columbia a century ago.

Landscaping: The vegetation surrounding the VanDusen building includes a rich mix of plant varieties, including several endangered species. Madrona (locally

VanDusen Botanical Garden Visitor Centre, Water Systems; Vancouver, BC; 2012

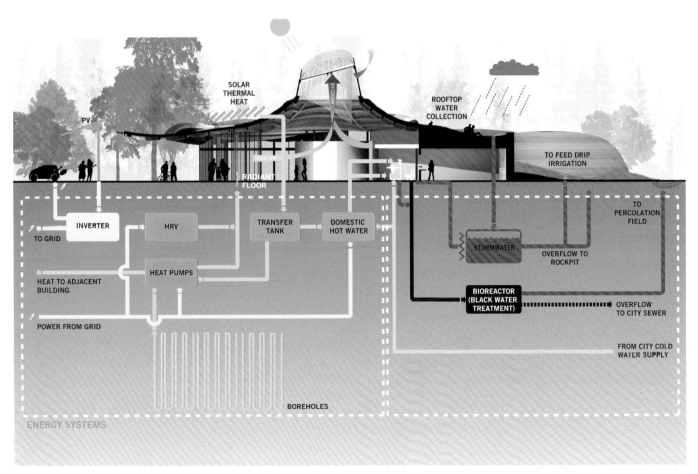

VanDusen Botanical Garden Visitor Centre, Energy; 2012

VanDusen Botanical Garden Visitor Centre, Rain Garden, Sharp & Diamond   VanDusen Botanical Garden Visitor Centre, Solar Chimney; Vancouver, BC; 2012

referred to as Arbutus) trees, once ubiquitous in this region, have become increasingly susceptible to pollution and human interventions in the land. The project's landscape designers carefully reestablished them in the context of the larger botanical garden, reminding visitors about the extent and beauty of the bioregion's native vegetation. Traditionally, botanical gardens have symbolized a human place in the natural world. Botanical gardens were typically organized into plant classifications based on research and education, medicinal and food plants of horticultural significance, as well as aesthetic beauty. The principal role of a botanical garden was to maintain and document collections of living plants for the purposes of scientific research, conservation, display, and education.

The VanDusen Visitor Centre has a larger goal of connecting visitors with the environmental issues of the 21st century while relating to the significance and beauty of Vancouver's native ecology. By highlighting local flora, the garden emphasizes the importance of low maintenance and low water-consuming plants.

Unlike a conventional botanical garden, the Visitor Centre landscape is designed to function as it would in nature, displaying seasonal changes. The varying spaces around the Visitor Centre form the Cascadia Garden - a series of distinct ecological zones ranging from wetland to woodland to Garry Oak meadow. Each zone has been carefully designed and planted using only native plants that were identified and documented by naturalist Archibald Menzies on the 1792 expedition up the coast with Captain George Vancouver.

The gently sloping site was carefully re-graded to preserve the many significant trees in the garden's collection and to facilitate a system of wetlands, rain gardens, and streams that allow rainwater to infiltrate naturally. A series of plazas frame views of the building and the larger landscape. Every bench, structure, stone, and plant has been locally sourced and reused (from materials found on site where possible). The team was unanimous that the building and roof must appear seamless and appear to grow out of the site. Seventy-five percent of the significant trees, many of them towering Douglas firs, were retained to enhance this experience. Large chestnut and walnut trees within the sloping fescue meadow create a shady wildlife corridor and habitat for butterflies, critters, and bird life ultimately linking the site to the building.

VanDusen Botanical Garden Visitor Centre, Green Roof; Vancouver, BC; 2012

Rammed earth: Incorporating rammed earth (a low-cement form of concrete pounded in layers around an insulating cavity) helps reduce the overall carbon impact of the project. (Cement production requires ultra-high heat and fuels burned to create that heat constitute over eight percent of global greenhouse gas emissions.) Our initial design intention was to mix native clay soils found on the site with cement and blend it with clay that we would dredge from the adjacent pond. Dredging the pond, we calculated, would deepen it and thereby increase its resistance to extreme temperatures during summer and winter. While some dredging did take place and did aid in the pond's resiliency, the removed clay proved to be unsuitable for the structure's rammed earth walls. We opted, instead, for alternative local materials. Still, we made measurable improvements to the ecological health of the pond, enhanced by constructed wetlands at the water's edge that act as a natural filter for the water and promote biodiversity.

Water systems: Water is collected from the building's roof and the surrounding areas before being put to a variety of good uses. A significant portion of the rainwater is channeled to the south of the project, where a beautiful artificial wetland has been created within the sightlines of all pedestrian traffic entering the property. After being cleaned by the wetland's plant and animal species (all native to the region), the water feeds into the adjacent lake, which is part of the botanical garden's larger ecological system.

A treatment plant inside the building processes blackwater from interior toilets and provides greywater for irrigation and toilet flushing. The system draws additional effluent from a sewage line on 37th Avenue nearby, reducing flows to the city's central sewage treatment facility, and providing more consistent irrigation water flows. Nutrients from this waste treatment process are mixed with compost and used in gardens throughout the property, while treated tertiary water helps to irrigate the plants and landscapes. Looking at the overall give-and-take of the on-site water systems, we can see that the human use and occupation of the building produces nutrients and water that serve the flora and fauna that exist on the property. Instead of shipping human waste to a remote sewage treatment plant, we return what we can to the on-site species that can benefit and flourish. The VanDusen building gives more to nature than it takes.

VanDusen Botanical Garden Visitor Centre, Rammed Earth; Vancouver, BC; 2012

VanDusen Botanical Garden Visitor Centre, Rammed Earth; Vancouver, BC; 2012

VanDusen Botanical Garden Visitor Centre; Vancouver, BC; 2012

VanDusen Botanical Garden Visitor Centre, Landscape; Vancouver, BC; 2012

REGENERATIVE DESIGN

Nicola Valley Institute of Technology, Merritt, BC; 2001

Telus Office Building; Building-Integrated Photovoltaics; Vancouver, BC; 2001

Regenerative Design Examples are Everywhere

As we focus more of our firmwide work on regenerative design, we can look back at earlier projects that were regenerative in some degree. We consider any building that eliminates waste, repurposes stormwater, or even reintroduces plant species to a bioregion to be a regenerative success. Wherever there is evidence of beneficial systems, we have made a small improvement. In a thinly veiled attempt to give you regenerative ideas for your projects, here are a few examples of projects we have covered in more detail elsewhere in the book, but that offer aspects of regenerative design:

Nicola Valley Institute of Technology, Merritt, BC
This building's site was in an area of historic First Nations pit houses. In an effort to replicate the relationship between nature and human occupancy, we embedded the library into the side of the hill and extended natural vegetation from the hillside across the library's roof. This design provided insulation as well as an expanded home for the ecology of the Okanagan hillside.

Telus Office Building, Vancouver, BC
This structure's ventilated façade is powered by building-integrated photovoltaics. When the sun shines, it creates electricity that powers a series of fans operating at the top of the atrium space, assisting natural cooling systems. On cloudier days or at nighttime, when the temperatures are lower and the cooling effect is not needed, the electricity does not flow and the ventilation does not occur. Tapping the solar energy allows us to create a mechanical system that requires less carbon. Although this feature is less about regenerative effects, the technology points to the many ways building components (in this case the ventilation fans) can respond to naturally occurring environmental phenomena in ways that are beneficial to both. Imagine buildings in the future that respond more fully to sunpath, opening and closing like many flowers, or turning to follow the sun like sunflowers.

White Rock Operations Centre, White Rock, BC
This building is located near the beach, where conditions are dry and sandy. During its first year of operation, we noticed three pairs of nesting sandpipers on the green roof, which had been generously planted with sedum. As we observed and studied their nesting patterns, we discovered that human (and dog) use of the nearby beach was disturbing the nesting patterns of the sandpipers, interfering with their ability to raise their offspring. They turned to the White Rock roof for more favorable conditions. Since then, the operators have deliberately kept the rooftop dry during the nesting months to provide a safe haven for this local species.

Center for Urban Waters, Tacoma, WA
This project was located along a seaway that once served as a nesting ground for osprey. In designing the building, we also had jurisdiction over the seawall edge. So we created a rock wall specifically designed to support the sea life that dwells below the high tide level. Through a network of cavities and underground structures, fish and other species were given a safe habitat where they could also clean the water through organic processes. In addition, we recovered four tall snags from the nearby forest and placed them alongside the water's edge, enticing the osprey back to their former home. A nest was visible within the first year of operation. Native bees that bore individual cavities in standing dead wood also found and soon populated the standing snags.

Center for Urban Waters, Tacoma, WA; 2010

White Rock Operations Centre, White Rock, BC; 2010

Vancouver Convention Centre, Vancouver, BC

Blair McCarry, Ray Cole, and I were members of a sustainability advisory team for the Vancouver Convention Centre. We contributed many ideas to a great building principally designed by LMN Architects and PWL Landscape Design. It ended up certified at LEED Platinum. The roof of the project is a well-researched and designed native grassland that, at over 10 acres, supports vibrant ecological systems. In particular, the sustainability team looked at potential problems associated with the seawater areas located beneath the building that would be devoid of sunlight and unable to support life. Together with our colleagues, the team designed a series of intertidal "steps" to be installed as a skirt around the entire site. The steps descend into the water at various levels and support life to approximately four meters below low tide. The strategy has been very successful; today, this site boasts the greatest amount of underwater diversity in the entire Vancouver harbor. A relatively small act of design created significant benefits to many of the life-forms that exist in and around this man-made structure. The precursor to this idea was a series of gravel intertidal "shelves" designed into the north false creek seawall between Burrard and Granville streets for BC Place in 1982-84 while I served as the Crown Corporation's chief architect. These shelves still support a rich variety of intertidal life that interests seawall pedestrians today.

Oltremare; Riccione, Italy; 2004

Oltremare; Riccione, Italy; 2004

Dockside Green, Stream; Victoria, BC; 2009

OltreMare, Riccione, Italy

Researching the local flora and fauna for the bioregion surrounding this entertainment venue and dolphinarium in Riccione, a city in the province of Rimini, Italy we established an outdoor living exhibit that displays the pre-Roman natural habitat of the Po Valley. We discovered that the original native habitat had been destroyed centuries ago by the Romans when they built canals and drained the land for agricultural use. We were able to reintroduce many of the species to the site as part of our restoration work. This repatriation reinforced the park's mission to educate the public about how to support local natural systems, whether they be plants, dolphins, or other species.

Samuel Brighouse Elementary School, Richmond, BC

As part of our design for this Richmond, BC school, we created an artificial wetland with an observation deck designed to facilitate ecology and nature studies. Today, students have direct on-site access to bulrushes, red-winged blackbirds and various other species of flora and fauna that are native to the area and have returned to the site specifically because of this project. Studying these species on their own campus instills in the students a sense of protectiveness and a personal interest in ecological conservation.

We have also applied our growing body of regenerative design ideas on a larger scale, expanding some of the same concepts to housing developments, campuses, and entire planned communities. Along the way, we continue to ask

Dockside Green, Balance waterway; Victoria, BC; 2009

Blatchford Redevelopment; Edmonton, AB; 2013

ourselves: What else can we do using only renewable local resources to modify building operations on a daily, monthly, or annual basis that offer our creations and the surrounding natural context a mutually beneficial relationship?

Dockside Green, Victoria, BC

The artificial stream at the heart of this project, which receives stormwater and treated tertiary water from the on-site sewage treatment plant, is an engineered series of landscaped basins containing different ecological systems providing the required level of natural cleaning processes for the water. All surplus water from the site descends through these basins before flowing into the ocean. The landscape design team chose plants and animal species for the basins based on how they would perform for a specified cleaning process. The evidence demonstrates that the system works. The outfall is clean and the natural species that populate the basins are thriving. (Following a surprising but very Darwinian development, in which sea otters arrived from the harbor and regarded the basins' fish residents as theirs for the taking, we substituted fish with snails that perform the same cleaning function.) We even planted eelgrass below the intertidal zone to finish the "polishing" of the greywater as it returned to the ocean.

Blatchford Redevelopment, Former Municipal Airport, Edmonton, AB

There are multiple ways that this net zero energy, zero carbon project will have a beneficial effect on the region's flora and fauna. For 80 years, the airfield that has sat on the site has been devoid of most organic life, as airfields tend to be. (Flora attracts fauna and birds that do not mix with aircraft, so the absence of one leads to an absence of the other.) Our redevelopment plan will channel stormwater from the site as well as from adjacent neighborhoods in daylit streams into a lake system that will restore ecological health to the land. The lake system is a much larger version of the Dockside design, also by PWL Landscape design. The site lies in a major flyway for migrating birds that do not use coastal routes. The native species that will be planted at the park in the center of the property will allow migrating bird species to rest on the lakes and recuperate while on their way north or south. Every resident will be within a five-minute walk from a park, and urban agricultural plots will be abundant. Nature, at Blatchford, will become an explicit part of urban life, experienced inside and outside of every built structure on the property.

Life-giving Design

Compiling these examples of regenerative design has been encouraging. As architects, engineers, landscape designers, and ecologists, we are just beginning to think about the countless areas where we can have a *positive* impact on nature. Making conscious choices in the way we design and build and operate our buildings and communities can make profound differences. We have seen it in our own work and it is exciting.

From the sandpipers spontaneously nesting on the roof of the White Rock Operations Center to the deliberate development of a 76-acre wetland and resting place for migratory species at Blatchford, we are experiencing the joy of seeing nature flourish as a direct result of our efforts. Architecture's new edges are brimming with life, and architecture is finding its place in nature.

Blatchford Redevelopment, Site Plan showing lake system; Edmonton, AB; 2013

The Vale Living With Lakes Centre
Sudbury, ON

The Vale Living With Lakes Centre (LLC) represents the next step in the evolution of Laurentian University's Cooperative Freshwater Ecology Unit (CFEU). An internationally recognized research center, CFEU focuses on the restoration of ecology, environmental protection, and aquatic resource management and is a collaborative effort between Laurentian University, Environment Canada, and Natural Resources Canada.

Living With Lakes; Sudbury, ON; 2011

Located on the shores of Ramsey Lake, a body of water historically damaged by neighboring mining smelters, the LLC reflects the energy of scientific discovery and the character of the campus as a whole. Perkins+Will worked closely with CFEU's scientists to create a working environment conducive to creative and collaborative research, to minimize the building's ecological footprint, and to assist in the restoration of Sudbury's ecosystems, including Ramsey Lake. The building includes basic and applied research labs, collaborative meeting spaces, and a multimedia theater for teleconferencing, extending the center's outreach to the million lakes of Canada's Boreal Shield ecozone.

In keeping with the nature of the CFEU and its programs, the new facility is designed as a restorative building, moving forward from a facility that simply does less harm to the notion that a building can have a positive effect on its surrounding environment. Particular attention has been paid to shoreline management along Ramsey Lake and water quality protection within the site context.

New Edge Innovations
With climate change a focus of the LLC's research, the building is also designed to adapt to a 2050 climate. Some of the design features that address energy and water conservation include: green roofs to reduce stormwater runoff;

a high-performance thermal envelope; a ground source heat pump; hydronic radiant floor heating; passive heating and cooling; solar domestic water heating; stormwater and greywater treatment; permeable paving for driveways and parking lots; natural daylighting; energy-efficient lighting and appliances; smart building systems; and the use of non-toxic materials.

The building fabric responds to ecological and regenerative design ideas. Green roofs are accessed by fauna for feeding, acidic rainwater is directed over limestone walls to reduce pH levels before returning to the lake through expanded and constructed wetlands.

The LEED Platinum project also has the smart building sensor technology necessary to

Living With Lakes; Sudbury, ON; 2011

monitor the effectiveness of these environmental strategies. Results are conveyed through web-based media and interpretive exhibits at Science North, Sudbury's internationally renowned science center.

PROJECT The Vale Living With Lakes Centre for Applied Research in Environmental Restoration and Sustainability
LOCATION Sudbury, ON
CLIENT Laurentian University
DESIGN 2006-2009
CONSTRUCTION 2009-2011
SIZE Site Area: 440,610 sf / 40,934 sm
PROJECT AREA 28,441 sf / 2,643 sm
DESIGN TEAM Perkins+Will:

P. Busby, S. Bergen, R. Holt, G. Lim, N. Shuttleworth, S. Schou, B. Wakelin
Joint Venture Architect: J.L. Richards & Associates Limited
STRUCTURAL ENGINEER Fast + Epp / J.L. Richards
MECHANICAL ENGINEER Stantec Engineering / J.L. Richards
ELECTRICAL ENGINEER K.L. Engineering
CIVIL ARCHITECT J.L. Richards
PHOTOGRAPHER Tom Arban
AWARDS RECEIVED
- Wood WORKS! Ontario Green Building Wood Design Award, 2012
- Canadian Consulting Engineers (CCE) Award of Excellence Building Category, 2012
- Holcim Award for Sustainable Construction,

Bronze Award, 2008
SUSTAINABILITY RATINGS LEED Platinum. The Vale Living With Lakes Centre is designed to be adaptable to a 2050 climate.
URLS http://www3.laurentian.ca/livingwithlakes/community/video/

Centre for Interactive Research on Sustainability (CIRS)
Vancouver, BC

Located on a dense site at the University of British Columbia, CIRS houses 200 researchers from University, private, public, and non-government sectors working together under a common mission: to accelerate sustainability.

Centre for Interactive Research on Sustainability, University of British Columbia; Vancouver, BC; 2011

Including laboratory space, academic offices, meeting rooms, and social spaces, CIRS is organized around two four-story wings linked by an atrium that serves as a building lobby and the entry to a daylit 450-seat auditorium and "social condenser" space.

New Edge Innovations
An integrated design process involving the client and entire project team produced a number of innovative and synergistic design strategies aimed at achieving key net positive goals related to construction, water and energy use, operations, health, and productivity. With occupant behavior intricately linked to these goals, CIRS also seeks to transform users from passive occupants into active inhabitants.

Utilizing wood as a primary building material, CIRS achieves its low-embodied energy and low-carbon impact goals while becoming the first large, multi-story wood building on campus. As the only building material made by the sun, wood allows CIRS to store over 900 tons of carbon, reducing its carbon footprint by more than 90 percent of the average UBC building. A wood-based moment frame provides a column-free interior ensuring greater flexibility of uses and durability to seismic events.

The building is net zero for energy on an annual basis, based on waste heat capture from adjacent buildings, geoexchange heating/cooling and the return of 600-megawatt hours of annual surplus energy to the campus. BIPVs are embedded in the skylight glazing and solar shading devices. The roof houses conventional PV arrays and solar hot water tubes. The building is 100 percent daylit through form and sunlight harvesting. Rainwater is harvested for irrigation, toilet flushing, and to recharge an underlying aquifer. Potable water is created through the purification of rainwater and blackwater in an on-site solar aquatics biofiltration system.

By putting sustainable systems on display, CIRS serves as a living laboratory for testing the performance of sustainable technologies while promoting shifts in occupant behavior in response to the test findings. More than a building, CIRS is a research tool that demonstrates the possibilities in sustainable design, serving as a catalyst for change.

LOCATION Vancouver, BC
CLIENT University of British Columbia
SIZE 61,085 sf / 5,675 sm
DESIGN 2008-2009
CONSTRUCTION 2009-2011
DESIGN TEAM Perkins+Will:
P. Busby, M. Cocivera, W. Dahl, R. Drew, B. Gasmena, J. Gravenstein, R. Holt, H. Lai, B. McCarry, T. Miller, M. Nielsen, J. Peacock, A. Pilon, R. Rheaume, M. Richter, S. Schou, Z. Smith, K. Wardle
PROJECT MANAGER Alberto Cayuela, P. Eng., PMP, University of British Columbia
CONSTRUCTION MANAGEMENT Heatherbrae Construction
STRUCTURAL ENGINEER Fast + Epp
MECHANICAL ENGINEER Stantec
ELECTRICAL ENGINEER Stantec
LANDSCAPE ARCHITECT PWL Partnership
CIVIL ENGINEER Core Group Consultants
GEOTECHNICAL CONSULTANT Trow Associates, Inc.
INTERIOR DESIGN Perkins+Will Canada
BUILDING ENVELOPE Morrison Hershfield Limited
CODE CONSULTANT LMDG Building Code Consultants
ACOUSTIC CONSULTANT BKL Consultants
QUANTITY SURVEYOR Spiegel Skillen
AUDIO VISUAL CONSULTANT MC Squared System Group
FURNITURE, FIXTURES AND EQUIPMENT Haworth
OWNER REPRESENTATIVE UBC Properties Trust
WASTEWATER CONSULTANT Eco-Tek Ecological Technologies
RAINWATER CONSULTANT NovaTec Consultants
PHOTOGRAPHER Martin Tessler
AWARDS RECEIVED
• SAB Magazine, 2014 Canadian Green Building Award, 2014
• Wood WORKS! BC Wood Design Awards, Green Building Award, 2013

Centre for Interactive Research on Sustainability, University of British Columbia, Entry; Vancouver, BC; 2011

- Delta Management Group, Clean50, Top 5 Project, 2013
- World Architecture News WAN Sustainable Building of the Year, Longlist, 2013
- North American Wood Design Award, Canadian Wood Council Award, 2012
- IStructE (Institute of Structural Engineering) Commendation - Award for Education or Healthcare Structures, 2012
- National Council of Structural Engineering Associations Awards, $30-100 Million Category, 2012
- AIBC Innovation Award, 2012
- GLOBE Awards for Environmental Excellence, Excellence in Urban Sustainability Finalist, 2012
- Treehugger Best of Green: Best Office or Commercial Design & Reader's Choice Winner, 2012
- Treehugger Best of Green: Design and Architecture, 2010

SUSTAINABILITY RATINGS LEED Platinum with a strong score of 56 points. Pursuing Petal Recognition through the Living Building Challenge v1.3. The building has completed the Preliminary Audit process, and expects to finalize LBC certification when one year of operations monitoring is complete.

REFERENCE TO PUBLICATIONS

- Zachary Edelson, "Architecture That Drives Ecological Innovation" *Architizer,* August 13, 2013.
- "Centre for Interactive Research on Sustainability," *Arch Daily,* March 13, 2013. http://www.archdaily.com/343442/centre-for-interactive-research-on-sustainability-perkins-will/
- Paige Magarrey, "Higher Learning," *Azure,* November/December 2012, p. 72-73.
- "Centre for Interactive Research on Sustainability," *Wood Design & Building,* September 6, 2012, p. 15-17.
- Suzanna Morphet, "Making a Positive Impression," *Innovation Magazine,* July/August 2012, p. 16-19.
- Paula Melton, "Whole-Building Life-Cycle Assessment: Taking the Measure of a Green Building" *BuildingGreen.com,* May 6, 2012.
- Frances Bula, "The Building that's Beyond Green," *Globe and Mail,* April 20, 2012, E6-E7.
- Sean Ruthen, "Regenerative Design," *Canadian Architect,* March 1, 2012, p. 26-33.
- Edward Keegan, "Centre for Interactive Research on Sustainability," *Architect,* March 2012. http://www.architectmagazine.com/sustainability/the-centre-for-interactive-research-on-sustainabi.aspx?dfpzone=projects.sustainability
- "UBC - Educating today to ensure tomorrow," *Canadian Journal of Green Building and Design,* January/February 2012.
- "The Centre for Interactive Research on Sustainability opens at the University of British Columbia," *Canadian Architect,* November 8, 2011.
- Heather Amos, "UBC opens North America's most sustainable building," *UBC Report,* November 1, 2011.
- Michael Cockram, "The Living Lab," *GreenSource,* September/October 2011, p. 100-106.

URLS

- CIRS Handbook – A Technical Manual and website (www.cirs.ubc.ca) further disseminate information with lessons learned, on-going updates, and actual performance data from the project.
- The process of creating CIRS has reshaped UBC's vision for its campus and its role as an institution; the results from CIRS are helping move the world toward a more sustainable future.
- http://cirs.ubc.ca/building/building-history
- https://www.youtube.com/watch?v=uz_au8JvCO8

VanDusen Botanical Garden Visitor Centre
Vancouver, BC

Inspired by organic forms and natural systems, the VanDusen Botanical Garden Visitor Centre seeks to create a harmonious balance between architecture and landscape, from both a visual and an ecological perspective.

VanDusen Botanical Garden Visitor Centre; Vancouver, BC; 2012

The dynamic single-story structure includes an innovative prefabricated roof form that appears to float above the building's curved rammed earth and concrete walls. Metaphorically representing undulating petals, the building form flows seamlessly into a central oculus and the surrounding landscape.

Located on the Garden's prominent southeast corner, the 19,000 square foot Visitor Centre transforms the site's entrance to heighten public awareness of the Garden, its conservation mandate, and the importance of nature. The building houses a café, library, volunteer facilities, garden shop, offices, and flexible classroom/rental spaces.

New Edge Innovations
The Visitor Centre is the first building in Canada to apply for the Living Building Challenge. The building uses on-site, renewable sources to achieve near net zero energy on an annual basis. Wood is the primary building material,

storing carbon dioxide for the life of the building. Rainwater is filtered and used for the building's greywater requirements;

LEED certified to the Platinum level, the Visitor Centre is pursuing the Living Building Challenge—the most stringent measurement of sustainability in the built environment. The Visitor Centre uses on-site, renewable sources—geoexchange boreholes, solar photovoltaics, solar hot water tubes—to achieve net zero energy on an annual basis. Wood is the primary building material, sequestering enough carbon to achieve carbon neutrality. Rainwater is filtered and used for the building's greywater requirements; 100 percent of blackwater is treated by an on-site bioreactor—the first of its kind in Vancouver—and released into a new percolation field located in the garden. The building is 100 percent naturally ventilated; to enhance ventilation further, located in the center of the atrium, and exactly at the center of all the building's various radiating geometry, a solar

chimney highlights the role of sustainability by form and function. It is a heat sink that responds to solar altitude and azimuth hourly, using passive solar energy to drive ventilation rates.

LOCATION Vancouver, BC
CLIENT Vancouver Board of Parks and Recreation
SIZE
PROJECT AREA 183,000 sf / 17,000 sm
BUILDING AREA 19,483 sf / 1,810 sm
DESIGN 2007-2008
CONSTRUCTION 2009-2012
DESIGN TEAM Perkins+Will: S. Bergen, P. Busby, P. Cowcher, R. Drew, R. Glover, H. Grusko, J. Ho, R. Holt, J. Huffman, P. Martyn, J. Peacock, M. Richter, S. Schou
GENERAL CONTRACTOR Ledcor Construction
STRUCTURAL ENGINEER Fast + Epp
MECHANICAL ENGINEER Integral Group
ELECTRICAL ENGINEER Integral Group
CIVIL ENGINEER R.F. Binnie & Associate
CODE CONSULTANT B.R. Thorson, Ltd.

VanDusen Botanical Garden Visitor Centre, Interior with solar chimney; Vancouver, BC; 2012

COST CONSULTANT BTY Group
ENVELOPE CONSULTANT Morrison Hershfield
LANDSCAPE ARCHITECT Sharp & Diamond
Landscape Architecture, Inc. with Cornelia
Hahn Oberlander
LIGHTING DESIGN Total Lighting Solutions
ECOLOGY CONSULTANT Raincoast Applied
Ecology
ACOUSTICAL CONSULTANT BKL Consultants
COMMISSIONING AGENT KD Engineering Co.
COMMISSIONING AUTHORITY KD Engineering Co.
PHOTOGRAPHER Nic Lehoux
AWARDS RECEIVED
- World Architecture News (WAN), Sustainable
  Building of the Year, 2014
- SAB Magazine, 2014 Canadian Green
  Building Award, 2014
- International Green Roof Association, Green
  Roof Leadership Award, 2013
- Metal Architecture Design Award, Metal
  Roofing Category, 2013
- Wood WORKS! BC Wood Design Awards,

Wood Innovation Award, 2013,
- Globe Award for Excellence in Urban
  Sustainability, Finalist, 2013
- World Architecture News (WAN) Engineering
  Awards, Winner, 2012
- Lieutenant-Governor of British Columbia Merit
  Recipient, 2012
- Lieutenant Governor's Award for Engineering
  Excellence, ACEC-BC, 2012
- Sustainability Ratings: LEED Platinum. Pursuing
  certification through the Living Building
  Challenge v.1.3.

REFERENCE TO PUBLICATIONS
- Peter Busby and Harley Grusko, "How Does
  Your Building Grow? The VanDusen Botanical
  Garden Visitor Centre, *Trim Tab,* v 2.1, April
  2014.
- "VanDusen Botanical Garden Visitor Centre,
  Arch Daily, March 20, 2012. http://www.
  archdaily.com/215855/vandusen-botanical-
  garden-visitor-centre-perkinswill/

- Edward Keegan, "VanDusen Botanical Garden
  Visitor Centre," *Architect,* March 2012.
URLS https://vancouver.ca/parks-recreation-
culture/vandusen-botanical-garden.aspx

The Future of Cities

Sustaining Life

Prior to World War II, thriving North American cities typically grew from well-defined ports or rail lines. Transit-related infrastructure, principally streetcars and, for larger cities, extensive subway systems, provided enough support for growth to develop around an established urban core. (Think Chicago, Winnipeg, New York and Toronto – each a busy maritime port and/or railway hub.) Cities were naturally busiest at their centers, where mixed-use buildings met both commercial and residential needs. Waterways and railroads helped people and cargo travel beyond city limits. Essential services for all residents were either within walking distance or accessible via streetcars.

Amazingly, the 1928 Bartholomew Plan for Vancouver (the city's first master plan, developed by Harland Bartholomew and Associates) foresaw a city of smaller communities defined by their walking distances from schools. Almost all of these schools were actually built and remain in use today, helping the underlying pedestrian fabric of the city that, to a certain extent, remains in place.

In the period immediately following World War II, the structure of North American cities underwent a dramatic change with the emerging dominance of the automobile. Automotive designs and technologies became more sophisticated just as the economic boom made car ownership more feasible for a greater number of households. The rise in automobile production was followed by the construction of a sprawling interstate highway system. (President Eisenhower's Federal-Aid Highway Act of 1956 created a 41,000-mile network of expressways that was said to allow "speedy, safe transcontinental travel" and was deemed "essential to the national interest."[1]) This reorientation to growth and expansion of suburbs defined by automobile movement was matched by the tragic and duplicitous destruction of the tram and streetcar systems in most North American cities, often at the hands of entities funded by the automobile industry.

Modern cities were quickly redefined according to post-war sensibilities. As the highways spread people farther afield, new zoning regulations began to change downtown sectors. City centers were now expected to serve as central business districts only, with separate zones designated for commerce and industry. Residential zones would be at the cities' perimeters, reachable only by car in many instances. Retail developments grew in clusters, which progressed in the 1970s and 1980s to full-scale shopping malls that threatened and often destroyed "Main Street" businesses and pedestrian-based neighborhood shops.

Thanks in large part to the highway systems, our cities were no longer defined by their cores; they were defined by their roadways.

In 2008, we proposed EcoDensity, a radical plan to reduce the carbon footprint of Vancouverites based on zoning changes that moved away from the "CBD/suburban" model of the 1950s. We were able to show city officials that if most residents lived within 400 meters of a transit hub, the overall annual carbon footprint of Vancouver could go from an average of five and a half tons

---

1. http://www.history.com/topics/interstate-highway-system

Vancouver Town Planning Commission; Harland Bartholomew and Associates, *A Plan for the City of Vancouver, British Columbia, including a General Plan of the Region* (1928) "Existing and Proposed Playgrounds," page 192, plate 44. City of Vancouver Archives. Available online: https://archive.org/details/vancplanincgen00vanc

Aerial view of Vancouver, courtesy Google earth. Note that the schoolyards and the local commercial highstreets are largely still visible in this satellite view.

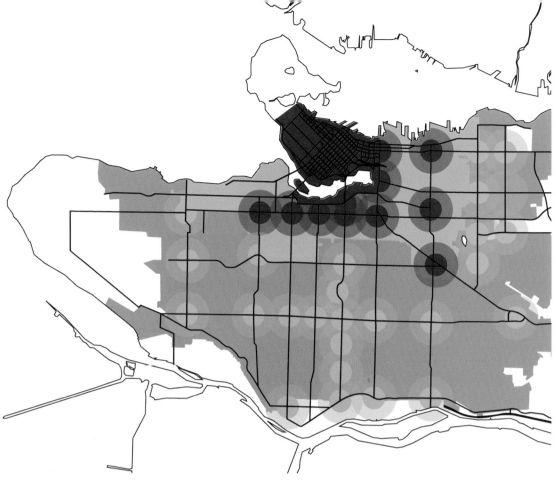

EcoDensity: A Plan to reduce Vancouver's emissions to 3 tons/person/per year. Vancouver, BC; 2008

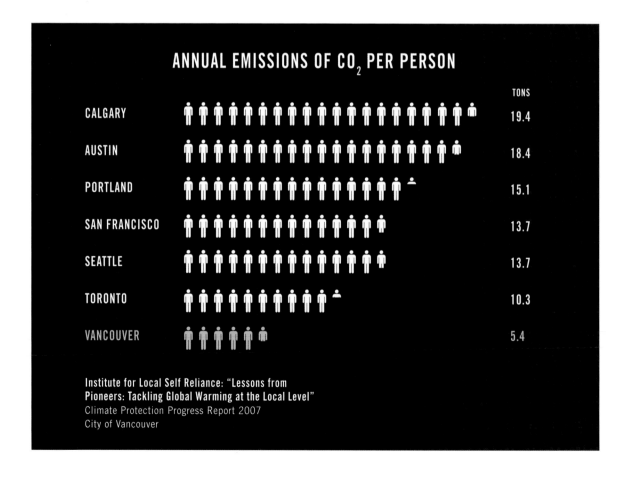

ANNUAL EMISSIONS OF CO_2 PER PERSON

		TONS
CALGARY		19.4
AUSTIN		18.4
PORTLAND		15.1
SAN FRANCISCO		13.7
SEATTLE		13.7
TORONTO		10.3
VANCOUVER		5.4

Institute for Local Self Reliance: "Lessons from
Pioneers: Tackling Global Warming at the Local Level"
Climate Protection Progress Report 2007
City of Vancouver

per person to less than three tons per person, in line with the city's commitment to Ed Mazria's 2030 plan. This is not an unrealistic scenario. A number of European cities, with vibrant, pedestrian-friendly and mixed-use cores, have carbon footprints of four to five tons per capita per year.

By re-planning around a transit infrastructure rather than an automobile infrastructure, we could make a significant difference in the short and long-term health of the city and its residents – all with a negligible impact on commuting times. Prioritizing transit within the culture of the city bumps the car down the hierarchy, diminishing the need for freeways, bringing all individual modes of transportation to the same street/bike/pedestrian level.

Embracing a New Urbanism

Today, we feel there must be a new armature for cities; a framework built primarily around transit systems rather than the automobile. Rather than building new business districts defined largely by commercial and industrial facilities and an absence of housing, we need to zone our cities around their transit infrastructures. An urban core should decentralize and become distributed around transit nodes, featuring a built environment that returns to the high-density, mixed-use model of the pre-war era while accommodating 21st-century realities. In addition, those unsustainable late 20th-century malls that ring our cities should be connected to transit and refashioned into viable Transit Oriented Development (TOD) communities.

Perkins+Will has had the opportunity to participate in several projects that explore these ideals in Vancouver, the two most dramatic examples of which are Marine Gateway and the EcoDensity project. Both exemplify the notion that cities can and should be planned differently; that communities can and should exist independent of the automobile. We can return our cities to their former (sustainable) glory and recommit to transit infrastructure as a way of re-purposing suburban and exurban properties that were designed to suit a disappearing and antiquated auto-centric society.

The EcoDensity Project was a pro bono study demonstrating how density could be increased in the City of Vancouver. In light of significant projections in population in the region, Perkins+Will's study was a response to an open call for architects to envision how these new citizens would be housed. EcoDensity proposed significant up-zoning of neighborhoods around the city's transit infrastructure, using the new Canada Line as a case study. Based on 400 meter walkability criteria, we demonstrated that over 30 percent of the 2035 projected residential population and nearly 25 percent of the increased job base was possible within walking radii of the six stations in the Vancouver portion of the line. EcoDensity was presented to City Council in 2008 and helped precipitate a formal two-year policy plan by the Planning Department. Sanity prevailed over NIMBY forces, and rezonings have subsequently been approved for millions of square meters of density at these stations, many under construction. All the ensuing developments feature mixed-use formats and unprecedented low levels of parking. These residents just will not need cars.

In a similar effort that applied the same approach to the San Francisco Bay Area, our urban design group, led by Noah Friedman, prepared a public response to Plan Bay Area, a regional planning document projecting growth for the region over the next three decades. While the City of San Francisco resembles a traditional, urban downtown core, the Bay Area has morphed over the past 30-plus years into a sprawling, auto-oriented, mega-region. As a result of recent development patterns, nearly 80 percent of the region's population still drives

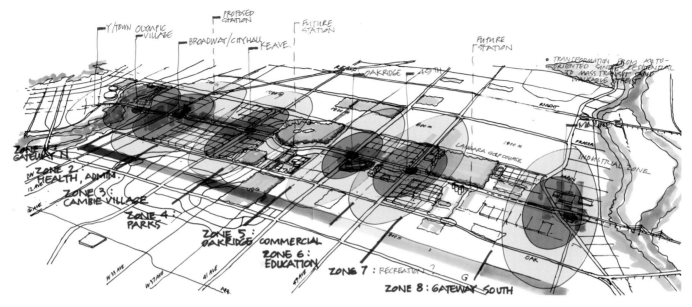

EcoDensity study, showing nodal development zones, Vancouver, BC, 2008

alone to work and private automobile use accounts for the largest portion of a typical Bay Area resident's carbon footprint.

California's landmark 2008 climate law (SB 375, Steinberg) requires communities throughout the state to decrease greenhouse gas emissions from cars and light trucks, and to accommodate all needed housing growth. Most of the scenarios presented in Plan Bay Area predict reduced per-capita CO_2 emissions from cars and light-duty trucks by 15 percent by 2040 and an adequate housing supply to house 100 percent of the region's projected population growth. However, we felt that these targets did not go far enough. As a region, we are already experiencing the irreversible effects of climate change and achieving housing affordability in the Bay Area has long been considered a myth.

At Perkins+Will, we have been fortunate to work on some of the most transformative projects in Northern California. According to Plan Bay Area, our Treasure Island project will be the single largest housing producing project in the region over the next 30 years. Similarly our Warm Springs / South Fremont Innovation District will be the single largest jobs-producing project. This project is located on the extension of the Fremont Bay Area Rapid Transit (BART) line, which will connect San Francisco to Silicon Valley. Our strategy was to locate the highest intensity residential and jobs-producing uses within a five-minute walk of transit and locate the entire project (which targets 20,000 jobs and 4,000 dwelling units) within a comfortable ten-minute walk. The remainder of the new district will be dedicated to light industrial and manufacturing uses allowing for the continued production of innovative new products similar to the electric cars that are being made at the current Tesla Motors factory at the south end of the district.

The result could be dramatic reductions in carbon footprint. Co-locating housing and jobs-related uses reduces this impact even further to achieve a carbon footprint of almost five and a half tons per person per year. This is far below the current impact of over 13 tons per year. Unfortunately, these aggressive project targets are not financially feasible today. To address this predicament we devised a mechanism of phased master plans, where land owners and developers can began their projects today at lower intensities than desired while reserving land for future growth and development at higher intensities. Ultimately, the goal is to achieve project targets of 8 tons for residential uses, 3.3 tons for jobs-related uses and a combined 5.6 tons per person per year. Going beyond the numbers, this level of intensity will result in a vibrant, walkable community where people, not cars, are at the center of life.

Transportation Equity

Over time, different modes of transportation have shifted within the North American cultural hierarchy. First, humans relied only on our own two feet for travel. Then we called on horses and other animals to move us around, which bumped pedestrian power one rung lower on the ladder. We invented the wheel, the horse-drawn carriage, time progressed and bicycles provided a wonderful transportation alternative, especially for city dwellers, until streetcars came along and took over the top spot. Then came the automobile, which eclipsed virtually every other mode of short- and medium-distance transportation.

In a sustainable city, there needs to be transportation equity. By that, I mean that we all should be given an equal right to get where we need to go via clean, safe, reliable methods. Whether going by bicycle, rail line, electric vehicle, or on foot, everyone deserves easy, safe access to the places in the city where they live, work, shop, socialize, relax, and recreate.

We are beginning to see personal transportation choices transition away from private automobiles to alternatives that are both greener and more affordable. As car ownership becomes increasingly expensive relative to average incomes, people are looking with renewed interest at bikes, motorized two and three-wheeled vehicles, and transit systems. As our transportation priorities realign, it is up to city planners and designers to ensure that suitable and fairly distributed infrastructure is available to accommodate all of these modes. Land and access that was once reserved for cars (more than 33 percent of all land in most North American cities) must now be reallocated. Street-side parking places will give way to bicycle racks; parking lots will feature electric car charging stations; multi-lane roadways will be reconfigured to allow a mix of pedestrians and clean-powered vehicles. In short, safety and convenience will be granted to all citizens, however they choose to move around the city.

Most profoundly, the sustainable future city will be devoid of freeways. Perkins+Will has had the privilege of contributing to the efforts to remove freeways in multiple major cities, with each endeavor helping prove the point that there is no longer any need for them. Cases in point:

San Francisco Embarcadero Freeway Removal Project
The 1989 Loma Prieta earthquake expedited this freeway removal project, (the granddaddy of all freeway removal projects) damaging the double-decker elevated span and hastening its demolition (which the community and local government had been discussing and debating for years prior). Eliminating the elevated roadway opened up a beautiful section of the city's waterfront adjacent to its historic Ferry Building and dozens of neglected waterfront piers. Streetcars, pedestrians, bikes and vehicles are now all accommodated along the boulevard that stands in the freeway's place. Most importantly, San Francisco's vehicle traffic simply shifted away, once the Embarcadero Freeway was no longer there, proving that there was no need to replace it with expensive alternate infrastructure. The city has adapted and is immeasurably better for it. The myriad of public waterfront open space now known simply as The Embarcadero is the armature of

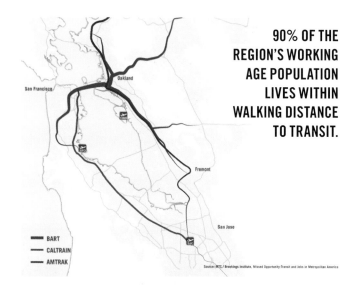

90% OF THE REGION'S WORKING AGE POPULATION LIVES WITHIN WALKING DISTANCE TO TRANSIT.

BART
CALTRAIN
AMTRAK

Source: MTC / Brookings Institute, Missed Opportunity: Transit and Jobs in Metropolitan America

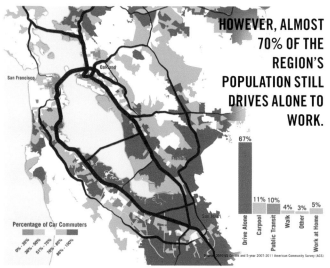

HOWEVER, ALMOST 70% OF THE REGION'S POPULATION STILL DRIVES ALONE TO WORK.

Percentage of Car Commuters

0% - 39%   39% - 50%   51% - 79%   78% - 80%   80% - 100%

67%

11% 10%   4%   3%   5%

Drive Alone | Carpool | Public Transit | Walk | Other | Work at Home

Source: 2010 US Census and 5-year 2007-2011 American Community Survey (ACS)

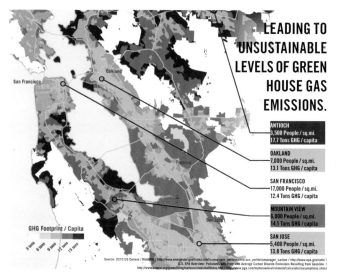

LEADING TO UNSUSTAINABLE LEVELS OF GREEN HOUSE GAS EMISSIONS.

GHG Footprint / Capita

3 tons   6 tons   9 tons   12 tons   15 tons

ANTIOCH
3,500 People / sq.mi.
17.7 Tons GHG / capita

OAKLAND
7,000 People / sq.mi.
13.1 Tons GHG / capita

SAN FRANCISCO
17,000 People / sq.mi.
12.4 Tons GHG / capita

MOUNTAIN VIEW
6,000 People / sq.mi.
14.1 Tons GHG / capita

SAN JOSE
5,400 People / sq.mi.
13.8 Tons GHG / capita

Source: 2010 US Census / BAAQMD / http://www.energystar.gov/index.cfm?c=evaluate_performance.bus_portfoliomanager_carbon / http://www.epa.gov/rvfei /
U.S. EPA Overview: Pollutants and Programs Average Carbon Dioxide Emissions Resulting from Gasoline /
http://www.nature.org/greenliving/carboncalculator/index.htm / http://www.pge.com/myhome/environment/calculator/assumptions.shtml

Perkins+Will Plan Bay Area Response; San Francisco, CA; 2014

HOW WILL THE NEXT 2 MILLION INHABITANTS OF THE BAY AREA LIVE?

S.F.
120 Square Miles
17,000 People / sq.mi.
+23M Tons GHG / year

OAKLAND
280 Square Miles
7,000 People / sq.mi.
+26M Tons GHG / year

ANTIOCH
580 Square Miles
3,500 People / sq.mi.
+33M Tons GHG / year

Source: 2010 US Census / BAAQMD

every visit to the City. San Francisco leaders are now exploring ways to remove all of the remaining freeways over time. Perkins+Will has just been selected as part of a team to study the future removal of the remaining I-280 elevated freeway in the city, along with the redevelopment of the Caltrain yards once high-speed rail makes it to the Transbay Transit Center, now under construction.

The San Francisco Embarcadero Freeway removal proves that traffic is like water: it will always find another route, some portion dissipates when alternatives are provided, and automobile capacity reduction as part of urban renewal is a viable strategy.

Boston's "Big Dig" Project
Boston's decision to replace its elevated interstate highway through the downtown with an underground route succumbed to the private vehicle lobbies and proved to be the most expensive highway project in United States history. At the same time – following a Corridor Master Plan by Perkins+Will, – the resulting urban fabric is healed, the City is reconnected to its waterfront, the noisy barrier of the highway is gone, and adjacent neighborhoods are bringing their distinctive personalities to the form and use of this new public realm.

Seattle Alaskan Way Viaduct Removal Project
Very similar to the former Embarcadero Freeway in San Francisco, the Alaskan Way Viaduct is a double-decker elevated roadway that runs along Seattle's waterfront district. In 2004, I was honored to lead one of the original charrettes for Seattle's Central Waterfront Plan that explored plans to remove this seismically risky, aesthetically dreadful, ecologically harmful stretch of road. We proposed a system similar to the Embarcadero in San Francisco: a broad boulevard with surface rail enhancement. Unfortunately, Seattle's voters and politicians have opted to replace the viaduct with a tunnel rather than allow traffic to find other ways into the city's center. Replacing traffic capacity is not the answer; we have seen cities remove automobile-only roadways and adapt to the change. Vehicles begin by finding other routes, then eventually decrease in absolute numbers when freeways are removed. Still, Seattle will benefit when pedestrians, bicycles and streetcars are prioritized along its waterfront.

Vancouver Dunsmuir Viaduct Removal Project
We have been involved in the process of removing the Dunsmuir Viaduct, the only stretch of freeway constructed within the Vancouver city limits. (An ambitious freeway engineering project was planned in the 1960s and stopped by citizens in a pivotal standoff in 1968, just as the "viaduct" reached Chinatown.) Our study identified abundant new opportunities for public parks and open space, as well as the recovery of city land for housing and community facilities that removal of the viaduct would provide. The proposal is inching forward through a planning and political process that is taking far too long.

Toronto Gardiner Expressway Removal Project
Perkins+Will is part of a large consultant team working with Waterfront Toronto and the City of Toronto to study the future of the eastern section of the elevated Gardiner Expressway. "The Gardiner" was built between 1955 and 1964 to link the Queen Elizabeth Way and the Don Valley Parkway in downtown Toronto. With six major exits leading into the city's core, the downtown and the surrounding neighborhoods are heavily congested during commute times. We are proposing to remove the Gardiner and replace it with an eight-lane,

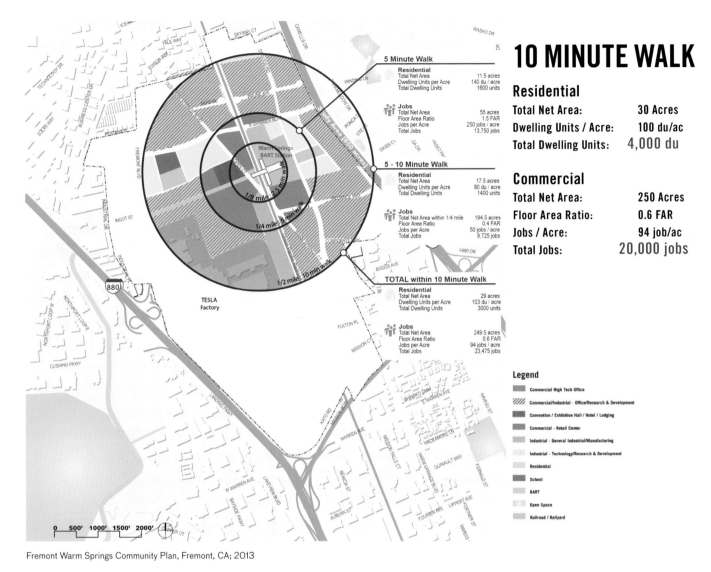

10 MINUTE WALK

5 Minute Walk

Residential	
Total Net Area	11.5 acres
Dwelling Units per Acre	140 du / acre
Total Dwelling Units	1600 units

Jobs	
Total Net Area	55 acres
Floor Area Ratio	1.5 FAR
Jobs per Acre	250 jobs / acre
Total Jobs	13,750 jobs

5 - 10 Minute Walk

Residential	
Total Net Area	17.5 acres
Dwelling Units per Acre	80 du / acre
Total Dwelling Units	1400 units

Jobs	
Total Net Area within 1/4 mile	194.5 acres
Floor Area Ratio	0.4 FAR
Jobs per Acre	50 jobs / acre
Total Jobs	9,725 jobs

TOTAL within 10 Minute Walk

Residential	
Total Net Area	29 acres
Dwelling Units per Acre	103 du / acre
Total Dwelling Units	3000 units

Jobs	
Total Net Area	249.5 acres
Floor Area Ratio	0.6 FAR
Jobs per Acre	94 jobs / acre
Total Jobs	23,475 jobs

Residential

Total Net Area:	**30 Acres**
Dwelling Units / Acre:	**100 du/ac**
Total Dwelling Units:	**4,000 du**

Commercial

Total Net Area:	**250 Acres**
Floor Area Ratio:	**0.6 FAR**
Jobs / Acre:	**94 job/ac**
Total Jobs:	**20,000 jobs**

Legend

- Commercial High Tech Office
- Commercial/Industrial - Office/Research & Development
- Convention / Exhibition Hall / Hotel / Lodging
- Commercial - Retail Center
- Industrial - General Industrial/Manufacturing
- Industrial - Technology/Research & Development
- Residential
- School
- BART
- Open Space
- Railroad / Railyard

0   500'   1000'   1500'   2000'

Fremont Warm Springs Community Plan, Fremont, CA; 2013

10-20 YEARS : 7.1 TONS / PERSON
PROJECT BASELINE : 13.8 TONS / PERSON

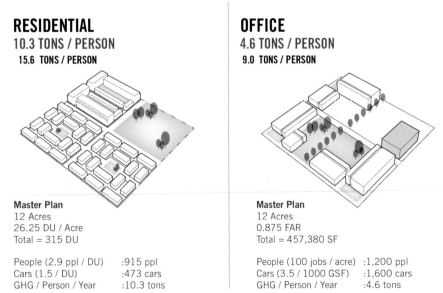

RESIDENTIAL
10.3 TONS / PERSON
15.6 TONS / PERSON

Master Plan
12 Acres
26.25 DU / Acre
Total = 315 DU

People (2.9 ppl / DU)	:915 ppl
Cars (1.5 / DU)	:473 cars
GHG / Person / Year	:10.3 tons

OFFICE
4.6 TONS / PERSON
9.0 TONS / PERSON

Master Plan
12 Acres
0.875 FAR
Total = 457,380 SF

People (100 jobs / acre)	:1,200 ppl
Cars (3.5 / 1000 GSF)	:1,600 cars
GHG / Person / Year	:4.6 tons

194

Fremont Warm Springs Community Plan, Fremont, CA; 2013

signature, tree-lined boulevard with transit and bike lanes that will dramatically transform Toronto's waterfront district. The goal is to provide an attractive urban multi-modal boulevard that is a pleasant experience for all, with abundance of light and air in the Lake Shore Boulevard corridor, reduced noise levels, improved air quality, and an enhanced and engaging public realm. In addition to removing the blight of an elevated roadway, the project will help distribute vehicle traffic evenly through the city streets and return Toronto's core to a gridded plan that is well connected to its vibrant waterfront. Transportation modelling studies indicate that this change will add approximately ten minutes' time for 15 percent of the city's workers commuting during peak periods, but will have an overall smoother flow for all traveling in and out of downtown Toronto. In reality, these computer predictions are flawed, habits will change and, like San Francisco, commuter vehicular traffic will melt away. City politics in Toronto are currently governed by suburban interests, which has made the decision-making process for the Gardiner removal option slow to realize.

View of San Francisco with Embarcadero Freeway, Wikipedia; 1982

View of San Francisco after removal of Embarcadero Freeway, Perkins+Will; 2014

North End Parks, Boston, MA, Wikipedia/Rose Fitzgerald Kennedy Greenway Conservancy; 2008

Rose Fitzgerald Kennedy Greenway, Boston, MA, Wikimedia Commons; 2008

Key Components of Healthy Cities

As we envision the sustainable and healthy future city, we consider its foundational elements: significantly reduced energy consumption, efficiently engineered district energy systems, radically reduced waste disposal, careful water management, abundant urban agriculture and available ubiquitous information infrastructure. Together, these strategies and technologies have the power to sustain populations and urban cultures alike.

The Energy-Efficient City

The future of green urban buildings will involve mandated energy performance. We are beginning to see such requirements in places like California, where Title 24 mandates energy efficiency standards in a state-wide building code, at periodically revised ever more demanding rates of performance. Title 24 is far and away the most stringent energy performance code for buildings in North America, and it has negligible impact on the economic activity around development and housing (the reasons usually cited in opposition to strong energy codes). Municipalities such as Seattle, Vancouver, Portland, New York, and Philadelphia are calling for higher levels of energy performance in renovation and new construction projects within their city limits. And across Europe, a growing number of cities are folding energy performance requirements into the permitting process, as EU-mandated building performance standards come into effect. (In Holland and Belgium, for example, residential building permits require proof that the project will consume no more than 72 kW hours per square meter per annum. If actual performance outcomes do not reach targets, developers lose their performance bonds.) The EU has mandated that actual energy performance figures be attached to title of all properties in all member countries, in an effort to link this data with building value, long a dream of environmentalists.

"Smart" energy meters help measure performance within buildings, and we will see more of them being used in new and renovated urban buildings. Such tools monitor actual usage in real time, engaging occupants in the act of energy conservation. Smart meters are proliferating, as energy supply utilities move to time-of-use pricing (a conservation and capacity restriction strategy). The meters also facilitate feed-in systems and pricing, anticipating a future where every roof is a generator and every hybrid/electric car plugged in a garage is a peak load energy storage device.

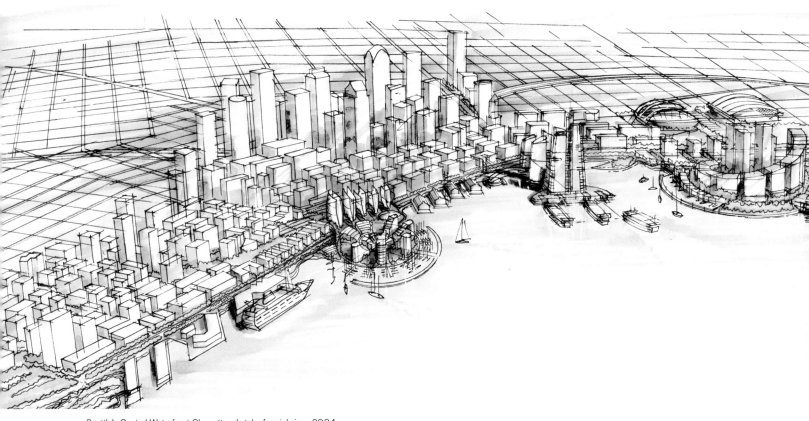

Seattle's Central Waterfront Charrette; sketch of aerial view; 2004

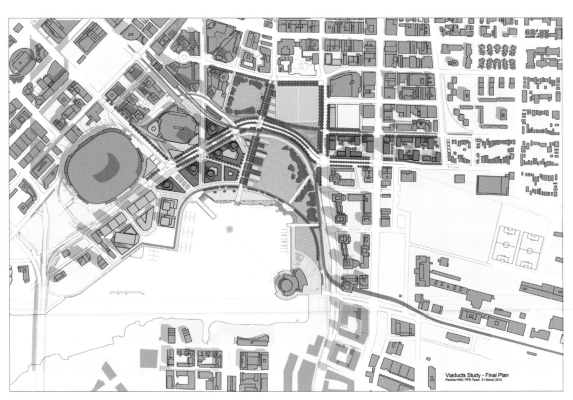

Vancouver Dunsmuir Viaduct Study; 2012

Rendering of Proposed Gardiner Expressway
Replacement Boulevard; Toronto, ON; 2015

Future of Gardiner Expressway Study;
Toronto, ON; 2015

It is also important to note that we can track energy usage and improve energy performance in every building, whether it is new or historic. Given most cities' inventory of decades- and (sometimes) centuries-old structures, we can gradually incorporate energy-saving mechanisms as we upgrade the building stock. At predictable intervals, we force change and improve existing buildings with proven, efficient, sustainable technologies. To be specific, we have the opportunity to swap in green solutions the next time maintenance projects are performed:

- We repaint every five years. At the next interval, use non-VOC options.
- We re-carpet every ten years. At the next interval, use the latest technology and non-toxic supplies.
- We replace windows every 25 years. At the next interval, improve daylight infiltration and thermal energy performance and add shading devices.
- We change out the mechanical systems every 30 years. At the next interval, replace them with the latest technology and efficiency models.
- We upgrade building envelopes every 50 years. At the next interval, re-skin with sustainable high-performance alternatives.

Currently, buildings consume more than 40 percent of all energy in North America. We have the knowledge and technology to reduce that number in most climates to zero. So we can and should set demanding standards for all new buildings. But 95 percent of the building stock is not new. We could collectively determine that by the end of a 50-year cycle, we could transform a 19th- and 20th-century historic fabric into a 21st-century model of energy efficiency without changing the important role a building plays within its city's larger cultural story. We can build energy efficiency into new structures and rehabilitate existing structures so they meet comparable performance goals. All buildings can then be part of the low carbon future and overall healthiness of the cities in which they stand. Imagine a concerted effort to systematically upgrade the entire building stock over the next 50 years. Think of the many positive impacts such a strategy would have, ranging from employment growth to a 40 percent carbon emissions reduction!

District Energy Systems and Distributed Generation

Naturally, energy efficiency relies on state-of-the-art energy systems. We addressed the topic of the design and interconnected possibilities of district energy systems in more detail in Chapter 4, but the subject is worth a mention in the context of this discussion as well. The future of energy and power in cities must include localized district energy loops that will include power production from renewable resources and waste energy generated by urban buildings. The idea is to link energy generators with energy users in a mutually beneficial loop, much like a heat pump system in a single building. At any given moment, all across the fabric of a city, different types of building use, size, orientation, and occupancy rates affect whether structures need heat or cooling at the same time. District energy loops can move that energy around efficiently, resulting in a significant overall reduction in new energy consumption, thought to be in the order of 30 percent. We use this strategy now in large mixed-use projects (like Marine Gateway and Crossroads) where we deploy energy loops serving the entire project, moving energy around among retail, commercial, and residential uses.

District energy systems are not a new concept; they were used in many North Americans cities prior to World War II when underground loops ran from central coal-burning boilers to deliver steam energy to downtown buildings. Most systems have been decommissioned (in part because of their polluting effects), but the infrastructure still exists in many of our urban areas. Modernizing these systems with more localized, lower-temperature, adaptable energy inputs and outputs will allow us to deliver clean power to our cities' structures while also aiding in civic resiliency by decentralizing the delivery mechanism.

Distributed energy generation (fueled by feed-in tariffs) will become part of the landscape. Sources will vary but photovoltaic building skins will proliferate. The price per watt of installed solar energy has dropped by over 80 percent in the last five years, and we can anticipate now a point in time, say in three to four years, when solar energy production will be as cheap as any source, and the skins and roofs of all buildings will be fitted to produce energy and revenue.

City Waste Be Gone

Across most of the world, municipalities "pick up the trash." Even the expression is outdated! Let's try "harvest internal resources." Green cities of the future will handle their garbage, as zero waste to landfill strategies are implemented, and as they lease their former landfill sites to mining companies.

Managing waste responsibly is first about minimizing it, then creating infrastructure to recycle, compost, or reuse as much of it as possible. The City of Edmonton, Alberta offers a very sophisticated model. As much as 90 percent of that city's collected garbage is recycled in one form or another, facilitated in large part by many partnerships between the city and local businesses. Recycling operations that are co-located near the trash sorting facilities "farm" useable product flows from the waste stream, minimizing the volume of garbage that ends up in landfills. There is nothing stopping every city from emulating Edmonton's economic and business model for success.

In Stockholm, Sweden, beautiful one-story recycling stations are set up in many neighborhoods, where the act of sorting and depositing one's "trash" becomes an opportunity for social interaction as members of the community incidentally meet in a spotlessly clean and comfortable location.

The idea in cities – or anywhere – is that whatever can be recycled, composted, or reused should be. As our resources diminish, so-called garbage

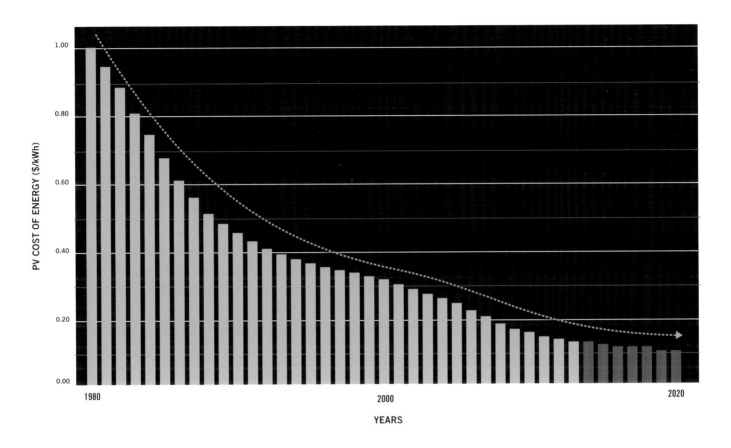

becomes increasingly valuable for the promise it offers. Eventually, we will see a day when dump sites will be mined for the buried treasure they contain. There is potential value in nearly everything we consider tossing away today.

Part of the full future picture must include municipal or regional construction of waste-to-energy plants to produce electricity and heat, large-scale composting to produce soil and nutrients, and the construction of anaerobic digestion plants that can produce biogas. Again, Swedish, Danish and German examples abound where these facilities operate economically, and reduce waste to landfill to nearly zero. The knock on waste-to-energy plants in North America usually features political debate about flue gas emissions, but the Swedes have demonstrated that emissions can be scrubbed to exceptionally high levels (scrubbing technology constitutes 70 percent of the capital costs of their waste-to-energy plants). Taking one contaminant as an example, all the flue gas emissions from all the waste-to-energy plants in all of Sweden operating for a full year produce less dioxins than one domestic wood fireplace operating for two hours.

Water: Eventually Liquid Gold

Water, arguably our most precious resource, is expensive and getting more so; it is often polluted and getting more so; and clean supplies of it are scarce and getting more so in many parts of the world. So we must begin using our available water resources in a more decentralized and conservation-oriented manner. In most American cities, municipalities collect or extract water from central sources using costly processes, then supply that water to residents through aging infrastructure. The results are significant system-wide losses as well as biological infiltration that threatens human health. These negative consequences arise in spite of abundant rainfall in most cities, with plenty of opportunities to capture and treat greywater.

Our future cities should feature decentralized systems of rainwater and greywater capture. We are already seeing some communities experimenting with these technologies. San Francisco, for example, has connected whole neighborhoods to "Purple Pipe" systems, which add an extra color-coded pipe to the municipal water system for the collection, treatment, and reuse of greywater on a localized basis. (Purple is recognized as the color associated with reclaimed water.) California's drought concerns make it an ideal laboratory for such approaches, as nature has necessitated a change from the wasteful water systems of old. In Australia, Dubai, and other areas of the Middle East, treated sewage effluent (TSE) is returned for use in Purple Pipe systems. In Australia, TSE treated to potable water standards is referred to as "sweet water." We believe that Purple Pipe initiatives and other innovations will be incorporated into a growing number of municipal water systems as supplies and sources diminish and populations become increasingly aware of the urgency of water conservation.

Climate change has different effects in different regions, but generally it will mean more overall precipitation on most areas (and much less in a few). Based on annual rainfall amounts, most North American cities (except those located in desert climates) could exist off the rainfall that currently falls on them, if we assume sufficient storage capacity. Storage capacity can be sized for anticipated drought duration periods. Current municipal design standards vary widely, but often are between 500 and 700 l/person/day. The Swiss use 165 l/person/day. We estimate per capita water use could be reduced from the current average levels of 350 l/person/day to 150 l/person/day through education, revised appliance standards, reclamation and rainwater harvesting. Potable water is also embodied energy (for treatment and transportation) so efficiencies count twice for climate change impacts. Sadly, many cities and institutions still do not even meter consumption.

Multifunctional Landscapes

When it comes to landscaping, future strategies will take advantage of the operational potential of the greenery that surrounds us. Plants will be used to enhance stormwater system performance, increase biodiversity, and regulate air quality. Landscapes will be used to absorb water and take the brunt of storms and floods as the impacts of climate change force our cities to become more resilient. At present the number one crop use of irrigation water in North America is lawns, and they only have aesthetic value. There will be no appropriate place for thirsty, drug-dependent lawns or inedible gardens. Instead, we will surround ourselves with indigenous plants, drought-resistant vegetation and waste-treating functional wetlands. Landscapes will bring us back to nature, nourishing ecological systems and supporting biodiversity.

The Blatchford Redevelopment project features a multifunctional landscape that helps reintegrate what was once an airport back into the area's rich ecological network. We are working to restore the 500-acre site's natural regional bird habitat by creating a significant patch of open space with a diverse array of landscape types and also to reinvigorate the site's ecological function by creating wetlands and natural open spaces within the urban fabric. The site features various ecological zones including Aspen Parkland, Wild Prairie, Skater's Pond, Stormwater Ponds and Wetlands, The Rills, and Furrows and Hedgerows. The diverse landscape zones will function as active landscape elements that benefit residents – some will provide rainwater retention, while others will offer recreational activities such as pedestrian and cycling paths, and lakes for boating in the summer and ice skating in the winter, or offer opportunities for local agriculture and open space – while actively increasing the site's ecological value for birds and animals that had been driven off the site in its previous manifestation. Blatchford highlights the benefits of creating beautiful and diverse working landscapes that can benefit both the human and natural ecological systems.

Urban Agriculture

Making healthy future cities means thinking about urban agriculture and the many important related topics. Nutrition, the cost of food transportation, the carbon emissions associated with moving food miles to the city, how to repurpose underutilized land for farm use, and localized produce markets all factor into the discussion.

For example, as part of this discussion, it may be argued conceptually that there should be a small farmed plot on the roof of every city building, that every patch of manicured grass should be replaced with a vegetable garden, and that every piece of underutilized urban land should be converted into community plots. It is important to implement city-wide agriculture strategies that promote biophilia and enhance community health. Our future cities depend on them.

In the Blatchford Redevelopment, described in more detail in Chapter 4, we carefully incorporated the concept of farm-driven neighborhoods, which we called "agrihoods." Each has a resident farmer who helps tenants plant, tend and gather their own vegetables, as well as tending larger community plots. We liken these consultants to local librarians; they are community resources available to offer information, experience and assistance. Urbanites have generally forgotten how to farm, knowledge that has sustained mankind for millennia.

We added valuable data to our growing urban agriculture knowledge base when we explored converting an existing building design into a fully "self-feeding", self-sufficient community. Katrina Sutcliffe, a student at the University of Calgary, used a dense Calgary downtown project of ours as her research thesis focus, exploring what design changes were required to make it self-sufficient from a food standpoint. She started with our design for a development, a proposed 181-unit, 20-story development capable of housing 435 people. As thesis mentor, I was excited to help Katrina explore the ideas and appreciate the results. According to her calculations and design, the refashioned building would need to shrink to an 11-story structure with a double basement. The basements would be dedicated to hydroponic farming and food storage, and solar aquatic waste management. Solaria would be attached to every unit and all available ground space surrounding the building would be farmed. Chicken runs would line a portion of the site, and the animals' waste could be used for fertilizer. Biowaste treatment on-site would yield cooking gas and heat. Our initial design featured 181 units; that dropped to 90 units in Ms. Sutcliffe's "self-sufficient for food" design, and occupancy numbers went from 435 to 162, but not one of those tenants would be hungry.

Dwelling of Permanent Culture demonstrates that it is possible to grow food and meet significant needs within an urban multi-residential dwelling in the predominantly winter city of Calgary, Alberta.

Accommodating an agenda of urban living and food production on the same site requires simultaneous consideration of the context, building systems, needs of the occupants, and requirements of the agricultural components from the very beginning of concept and design development.

The design follows concepts and theory generated from alternative agricultural practices, while balancing the programmatic and technical needs of a residential development to create a graceful continuity of balanced spaces and materials.

The landscape is designed to contribute to the food supply and vastly increase the biodiversity of the site. The architecture extends the landscape opportunities vertically providing generous built-in growing spaces on each level. The building vegetation provides shade and absorbs the sun's heat, contributing to the cooling of environments, both interior and exterior.

The southeast entry is flanked by formal gardens, decorative but edible plants, from which the central patio introduces an airy structure for the main entry. Organic mulch garden paths protect the ground from extreme temperatures, encourages water infiltration, and contributes to cooling in the summer. The chicken coop sits low in front of the main structure with its green roof sloping into the earth and adding to the grazing area of the chicken run.

Through the shared expertise and collaborative efforts of live-in professionals, the Demonstration Project stands poised as a testament to the great potential of its successful operation. The project exemplifies and explores foundational values of education and community as pivotal aspects and connections to its greater context. The site and design depict unprecedented testing grounds advocating the development of such dwellings of permanent culture, ultimately revolutionizing the urban condition for future generations.

Dwelling of Permanent Culture, Katrina Sutcliffe

We found Ms. Sutcliffe's report to be fascinating and inspirational, because it demonstrated the potential to aggressively ramp up all concepts of urban agriculture. If food is treated like renewable energy (where there are cycles of production, and the community gives to and takes from the "grid"), we will be in a stronger position to feed our cities' residents in the future.

Smart Cities

In the coming decades, more cities will build digital information infrastructure into their urban landscapes. The "smart cities" revolution is underway, with Cisco, IBM and Siemens among the notable leaders developing and deploying technology. Wireless transmitters attached to streetlamps and the sides of buildings throughout our cities will deliver more than free universal Internet ultra-high-speed broadband connectivity. They will usher in profound societal changes born of social equity. How could knowledge, accessible to everyone, do anything other than contribute to the collective intelligence and resilience of our communities? Add steadily more affordable hardware (the $100 tablet is near!), clever smartphones, Siri, Google Glass and other future ubiquitous technology tools, and the "connected city" gets real.

Technology is changing transportation too. Google and others are pioneering driverless cars. The computational power, video and sensory capabilities are there, holding the promise for a future that has a fraction of the current traffic and pedestrian fatalities, and even less frequent DUIs. At the Chaudière Island Master Plan project in Ottawa (detailed in Chapter 5), we are looking to create the first community in North America designed to facilitate driverless vehicles.

Remapping Cities for Demographic and Social Change

Our cities need to keep up with our societal patterns and demographic changes. As we map the cities of the future, it is important that we take into consideration our modern-day regimens and the patterns of contemporary households. Fewer family routines still revolve around nuclear families with conventional patterns of work and childcare. Urban populations in many western cities feature growing numbers of single parent families, singles living alone and various gender pairings. Two-career households number above 80 percent of family homes, and seniors live typically 30 years past retirement. Sweeping physical, social and infrastructure changes are occurring to address these changes. Our cities need to adapt with community care, decentralized healthcare, daycare infrastructure, denser and more varied accommodation offerings, better transit and more mixed-use developments so that generations can live in proximity to each other. The NIMBY forces in our political theatres, of course, oppose these changes, but they will get old too (sooner than they think!) and they may want their children and doctors to be nearby.

One-dimensional civic zoning (where all the housing types are the same) must be changed in favor of wide ranges of housing type and affordability. City blocks must be dotted with parks where people can play and relax, daycare centers where children can be nurtured and safe, senior housing where older citizens can age affordably, mixed-use buildings where sustainable urban density can be accommodated, and transit stops where anyone can get where they need to go. In other words, amenities throughout the healthy future city need to evolve along with the society it serves. One particularly enjoyable observation of mine is that when daycare and seniors facilities are co-located seniors lives and happiness are demonstrably improved. Let's put that idea into every urban and community plan we create!

RDoC: A Resilient Health Clinic

Extreme weather events such as Superstorm Sandy are stark reminders that for all our building standards and advanced technology, our communities are not as resilient as we would like to think.

Places such as hospitals or fire stations are designed to be more resilient than the average office building and are "hardened" to survive such events relatively intact, but New York City's experience during Sandy exposed the threat to "non-hardened" community health organizations and the populations they serve. For example, as dialysis facilities went off-line with the rest of the power grid, patients with chronic kidney diseases were compelled to go to emergency rooms for treatment, increasing the strain on the acute-care emergency response system.

Interruptions during an emergency constitute a significant public health challenge, in addition to breaking important links in the chain of community resiliency by separating communities from caregivers.

To address this problem, Perkins+Will, in conjunction with Degenkolb Engineers, Mazzetti Engineers, Public Architecture, and Alliance Health of San Francisco, developed a concept for a rapidly deployable health clinic – "RDoC" – and pharmacy that can be used as a replacement venue for critical ambulatory health services in the aftermath of a seismic or severe weather event. Deployed after an event, this temporary clinic would be available to community organizations whose staff would relocate there until their home facilities can reopen.

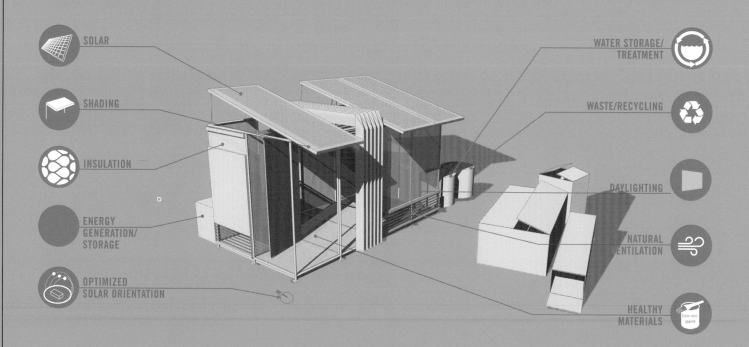

SOLAR

SHADING

INSULATION

ENERGY GENERATION/ STORAGE

OPTIMIZED SOLAR ORIENTATION

WATER STORAGE/ TREATMENT

WASTE/RECYCLING

DAYLIGHTING

NATURAL VENTILATION

HEALTHY MATERIALS

low-voc paint

Blatchford Redevelopment, Urban Agriculture, Perkins+Will

Now and Future Healthy Cities

Every city has experienced the phenomenal growth of its annual "marathon" over the last 20-plus years. Now, myriad charitable and competitive runs, walks, swims, bike races and other public expressions of physical activity dot the calendar in every city. Boomers want to live forever so they are working out, exercising and eating better, while younger generations just want to be healthier than their parents. They are all demanding healthier cities in which to live, and they see no limits to being fit and healthy in an urban lifestyle.

Parks, running, biking and boarding trails and facilities are being reshaped and constructed to fit this wave of public interest. Public open space is a right, not a luxury. Streams are being daylit, forests replanted, and street tree planting schemes abate civic heat islands. Matched with the repurposing of civic automobile space for the pedestrian realm discussed above, it's all about getting outside, and getting healthy.

Inevitably, this interest, combined with increasing urbanization in all countries, is forcing politicians to enact air, water, and litter pollution strategies to clean up civic and urban environments. Litter-free campaigns are succeeding in educating a more careful and caring generation. In North America and Europe, air quality standards are steadily improving. Industry and automobile manufacturers are being compelled to improve their emissions. Brownfields have all been identified and a generation-long cleanup effort is well underway. New brownfields will not be created as the general consensus is for tighter pollution and dumping laws and responsibilities. Electrification of trains, trams, buses, and private vehicles will result in lower levels of CO_2 and other pollutants in the urban environment. Plug-in recharging stations for electric vehicles will become as common as parking meters. Over a thousand cities and communities in North America have committed to the 2030 Challenge, a commitment that obligates them to a gradually reduced carbon footprint ending in a zero carbon future by 2030.

Resilient Urbanism: Opportunities for the [Under] Ground.

Design: Garen Gary Srapyen, at Harvard Graduate School of Design (now Perkins+Will San Francisco)

Known as one of the most heavily used transportation systems in the United States, the New York City MTA caters to over 5,000,000 people per day. Due to poor design and planning, more than 300 stations –as well as its tunnels–were deemed unsafe in the aftermath of Hurricane Sandy. That is, in that moment of panic, the MTA–and millions of New Yorkers–had no confidence in the country's most powerful transit system. The MTA later spent over five billion dollars in repair costs due to major flooding in almost all 468 stations across Manhattan. Resilient Urbanism: Opportunities for the [Under] Ground sought to find ways of addressing safety and resilience through the relationship between technicality and the poetics of design. In investigating several subway stops in Manhattan, the project attempted to uncover the symbiotic relationship between resilience and design poetics. Can this enhanced solution inform ways to use subway stations, not just as a utility but also as a better public space? While technical solutions have been defined by experts post-Sandy, the endless possibilities of design have yet to be investigated. Resilient Urbanism is not interested in a system that fights a natural disaster, but instead identifies a hybrid model that attempts to accept and adapt to New York's future climate. This investigation defines existing subway entrances' typologies and hydraulic infrastructure, generates small-scale recommendations for the most common subway entrances, and finally renders large-scale visionary solutions for re-thinking the future for New York City subway typologies.

A subway entrance near a small urban park provides maximum flexibility and opportunity to take advantage of the green space for flood mitigation and resilience. The undulating landscape includes a permeable amphitheater that acts as a vital public space for outdoor activities, while also being able to retain large amounts of water during major storms and hurricanes.

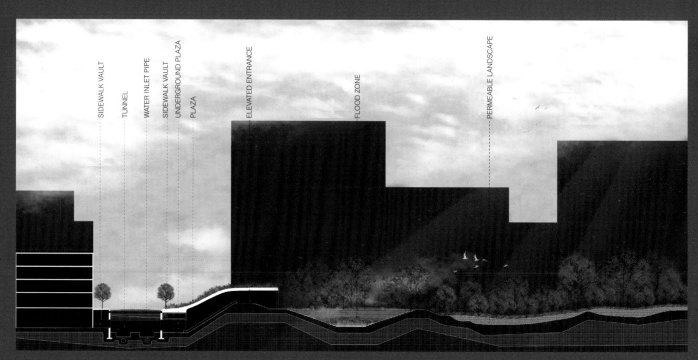

Resilient Urbanism: Opportunities for the [Under] Ground, Garen Gary Srapyen; 2013

The world is generally horrified at the levels of urban pollution being experienced in growing urban centers in the developing world, particularly China (with way too many coal-fired power plants) and India, which is likely to cause a dramatic reaction by the authorities in these countries, evidence of which can be seen in China at the moment.

Healthiness extends to the design of communities. New York City pioneered this type of effort with the study and publication in 2011 of the "Active Design Guidelines," a seminal document that is having a continent-wide impact. Stairs are the new "cool" and elevators are hidden from sight and buildings, communities, and public parks are littered with fitness equipment and opportunities. Most cities have banned smoking in buildings, and are moving to bar smoking in outdoor shared public spaces. Life expectancy has risen in cleaner Western economies from the mid-60s in 1960 to the mid-80s today, an astonishing fact unparalleled in human history.

Western democracies are increasingly bureaucratic and distant to most voters. Federal, state, and provincial governments take years to enact environmental legislation but not so at the community level. Cities collect the garbage, run the buses, clean the streets, provide the water and sewer services, maintain the parks, and oversee the public spaces. City politicians and planners are reachable by and accountable to the civic voter; they are close at hand and can be held to account. It is no wonder that at the civic level we see the most progressive implementation of sustainable design strategies and requirements. A dozen North American cities are vying to become the "greenest city" on the continent. Portland seems to be in the lead at the moment!

All of this civic initiative is very encouraging, as it corresponds with the increasing health of all natural systems in the urban environment. When we can swim on our beaches and enjoy birds and butterflies in our parks, nature, ecological systems, biodiversity, and the systems that sustain human life all prosper.

Resiliency and Cities

Cities and urban life are part of nature, much as we might pretend otherwise. Climate change and global warming has the seas rising, and storms and precipitation are increasing in amount and ferocity. Events such as Hurricanes Katrina and Sandy and the Calgary floods in 2013 all point to the need for change in the relationship between urban life and nature. We must restore forests in watersheds, rebuild natural foreshores to buffer from storms, reduce asphalt, deploy natural stormwater systems, and build urban resiliency by employing nature. District systems and interdependencies discussed in Chapter 4 on Whole Systems Thinking are a part of urban resiliency, as are photovoltaics on every roof, cisterns in every building, and urban agriculture on every horizontal opportunity. Understanding these natural forces in the context of social change heralds a bright future for cities. Two resiliency idea projects follow, both of which explore the social, physical, and natural aspects of civic resiliency.

The future of cities is in flux. Climate change, demographics, and social changes are forcing change for the better. The design of cities has been largely static for 40 years, but now there are exciting new trends developing. And designers are leading the way, with new approaches to zoning, transportation, landscapes, urban design, energy and waste systems, health, and resiliency. Civic design and urban living has new edges.

Plan Abu Dhabi 2030
United Arab Emirates

Abu Dhabi, the capital city of the United Arab Emirates, controls more than 10 percent of the world's proven oil reserves, and the income they provide has had a profound effect on the city.

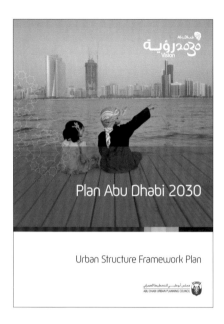

Fifty years ago, the majority of citizens lacked access to healthcare, education, electricity, and running water; today, the city is a bustling modern capital, with planned development for the next decade exceeding $100 billion USD in value. As a result of this rapid transformation, the city was in urgent need of a plan to direct development.

Perkins+Will, together with Larry Beasley (former Head of Planning for the City of Vancouver), and CIVITAS Urban Design and Planning Inc., developed an urban structure framework plan to address Abu Dhabi future development.

The planning process began in December 2006 with a series of preparatory studies: an economic analysis; an infrastructure review; an environmental audit; a transportation summary; an assessment of existing built form, develop-ment patterns, and open space distribution; and a broader examination of the challenges and opportunities facing the city. In February 2007, the team conducted a five-day charrette with planners and rulers from Abu Dhabi and a group of international experts, developing three large-scale plans based on the preparatory studies' projections. Following the charrette, these concepts were combined and distilled for an additional charrette in March, which included planning exercises at the regional, district and individual block levels. This process resulted in a policy framework for how the city will handle growth over the next 25 years.

Since Plan Abu Dhabi 2030's adoption as official government policy in 2007, the consortium of Beasley and Associates, CIVITAS Urban Design and Planning, Inc. and Perkins+Will have produced 2030 plans for the nearby City of Al Ain, the western region of Al Gharbia, and the country's eastern region, resulting in a comprehensive set of planning documents for the entire Emirate.

New Edge Innovations

We designed a city- and state-wide plan for a transit-oriented, mixed-use urban fabric for three million people. We eliminated freeway plans (nearing construction), proposed three levels of transit infrastructure, and developed pedestrian realm and building design guidelines. Our work resulted in a national set of marine and desert ecological preserves, and environmental laws of all types. Urban design excellence requirements resulted in the establishment of a Design Review Panel, and a strong planning authority. We even made proposals to the authorities illustrating how they could return the Emirate to a low carbon footprint.

LOCATION Abu Dhabi, United Arab Emirates
CLIENT Abu Dhabi Executive Affairs Authority Development Co., Ltd
DATES (DESIGN) 2006-2010
DESIGN TEAM Perkins+Will: P. Busby, M. Cocievera, J. Loewen, M. Nielsen, A. Slawinski
DESIGN PARTNERS
- L. Beasley, Beasley and Associates, Vancouver, Canada
- Civitas Urban Design and Planning, Vancouver, Canada

- John Buck, John Buck Company, Chicago, USA
- David Camp, London, UK
- Herbert Dreiseitl, Atelier Dreisleitl, Ueberlingen, Germany
- David Fields, Nelson/Nygaard Associates, New York, USA
- Michael Flanigan, City of Vancouver, Vancouver, Canada
- Jacquie Forbes-Roberts, City of Vancouver, Vancouver, Canada
- Robert France, Harvard Graduate School of Design, Cambridge, USA
- Alan Jacobs, Cityworks, San Francisco, USA
- Huub Juurlink, Juurlink & Geluk, Rotterdam, The Netherlands
- Lon LaClaire, City of Vancouver, Vancouver, Canada
- Elizabeth MacDonald, Cityworks / University of California at Berkeley, Berkeley, USA
- Paul Murphy, ARUP, Manchester, England
- Jaakko van't Spijker, Sputnik, Rotterdam, The Netherlands
- Jeffrey Tumlin, Nelson/Nygaard Consulting Associates, San Francisco, USA

AWARDS RECEIVED
- Planning Institute of British Columbia Award, 2008
- Canadian Institute of Planners Award, 2008
- GLOBE Award, Excellence in Urban Sustainability Finalist, 2008

REFERENCE TO PUBLICATIONS
Kathryn Engle, "The Canadians," *Slick World,* September/October 2010, p. 20-25.

Ten Big Ideas to Make Vancouver the Greenest City in the World

Perkins+Will worked closely with the City of Vancouver to develop significant, useable strategies to begin its conversion into one of the world's greenest metropolises.

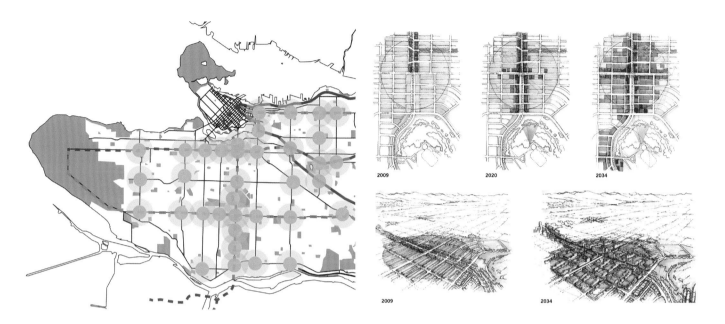

2009 · 2020 · 2034 · 2009 · 2034

Moving beyond the era when cities competed according to how numerous their parking places, how extensive their freeways, and how busy their ports, this document helps chart Vancouver's course as a leader in sustainable city development, and their "Greenest City" objective.

LOCATION Vancouver, BC
CLIENT Self-directed research, Perkins+Will
DESIGN 2010
DESIGN TEAM Perkins+Will: R. Bragg, P. Busby, D. Dove, M. Driedger, M. Sachs, K. Wardle

New Edge Innovations

The ideas presented included creating a walkable city, transportation equity, zero waste, a focus on district and renewable energy, innovative greywater and blackwater strategies, encouraging and requiring sustainable design, reintroducing native species and encouraging urban agriculture, enhancing the connection between the city and nature, and broadening planning and transportation perspectives to the regional level, all with a focus on data and implementation.

The innovative strategies and research provided by Perkins+Will were presented to City Council in late 2010, helping the City of Vancouver position itself as a global competitor for healthy and sustainable city making. The Ten Big Ideas research project was completed to help establish civil infrastructure and policies that support citizens and the community at large, sustainable design progress, pedestrian and bicycle priorities, urban agriculture, sustainable water practices, and the protection of precious natural resources and spaces.

The City of Vancouver adopted their own version of these ideas soon after and continues to roll out their "Greenest City" Plans today.

10 BIG IDEAS +↗
To Make Vancouver the
Greenest City in the World

BUSBY
PERKINS
+WILL

Ottawa Confederation Line
Ottawa, ON

The Confederation Line is a new 8-mile electric light rail transit line from Ottawa's Tunney's Pasture Station in the west to Blair Station in the east via a 1.5 mile downtown transit tunnel.

Ottawa Confederation Line, Ottawa, ON; 2017 (projected)

Commissioned by the City of Ottawa, Perkins+Will, in collaboration with Capital Transit Partners consortium, provided preliminary station design and carried forward design development to 30 percent on seven of the stations.

The stations are designed to be efficient, universally accessible, and provide residents and visitors with convenient links to a variety of community and city-wide destinations. The stations are also designed to provide future flexibility, accommodating potential changes to the program, needs, and ridership.

The designs emphasize comfort, experience, quality, accessibility, convenience, and sustainability in their built form, materials, and details. Stations exhibit a unified design approach across the system while expressing an individual distinctiveness in response to each station's individual context. Each station will contribute to and act as a catalyst for the integration and improvement of the surrounding urban fabric.

New Edge Innovations
Each station embodies the principles of holistic sustainable design—including the environmental, cultural, social, and economic aspects of sustainability. The design team pursued innovative, integrated, locally relevant, and appropriate sustainable solutions that promote energy efficiency, greenhouse gas reductions, environment quality, and sensitive material selection.

Station design was built around a computationally driven analysis of environmental and physical constraints. A modular "kit of parts" hybrid wood and steel structural and envelope system was developed for all stations. Details included stormwater collection, lighting, windscreens, platform furnishings, signage, and wayfinding. Every station design included TOD neighborhood development opportunity assessments, to anticipate future urban design needs.

We received project approval from all authorities, and the project was bid to P3 concessionaires in 2012. We reviewed and evaluated bids on behalf of the client organization.

LOCATION Ottawa, ON
CLIENT Capital Transit Partners

DESIGN 2010-2012
CONSTRUCTION 2014-2017
AREA 13 stations (10 above / 3 below grade), 394 f / 120 m platforms each
DESIGN TEAM Perkins+Will:
J. Belisle, J. Bielun, L. Briney, S. Briney, S. Bryce, P. Busby, M. Cunningham, J. Doble, B. Engle-Folchert, L. Espino, M. Haberli, A. Knorr, S. Kohut, M. Lampard, E. Ma, Y. Madkour, T. Martin, M. Nielsen, C. Osbourne, R. Piccolo, M. I. Thicke, E. Wolpin, J. Yum, F. Zahr
STRUCTURAL ENGINEER URS
MECHANICAL ENGINEER URS
ELECTRICAL ENGINEER URS
RENDERINGS Atchain
AWARDS RECEIVED Gold Award for Transportation Innovation, Canadian Council for Public-Private Partnerships, 2013
REFERENCE TO PUBLICATIONS "Realism And Excellence / Awards of Excellence 2013," Canadian Architect, December 2013: p. 11-18: http://www.canadianarchitect.com/news/awards-of-excellence-2013-realism-and-excellence/1002793990/?&er=NA
URLS http://ww.confederationline.ca

Eau Claire Market Redevelopment
Calgary, AB

Adjacent to high-density residential, mixed-use developments, millions of square feet of commercial space, and many of Calgary's major natural amenities, the Eau Claire Redevelopment is ideally positioned to become a major iconic destination and economic generator for the city.

Eau Claire Market Redevelopment; Calgary, AB; 2017 (projected)

The winning design in a competition for Harvard Developments, Perkins+Will's redevelopment concept envisions a thriving 2.5 million square foot mixed-use development, rich in office, hotel, and residential uses and more than a million square feet of retail that seamlessly integrates into the surrounding urban fabric. Included in the concept is the repurposing of the existing Eau Claire Market, an entertainment retail center that has struggled since opening in the 1990s largely due to its lack of connectivity to the community. Perkins+Will's revitalized Eau Claire rethinks these earlier shortcomings by creating a destination and community hub that fosters deep synergies with adjacent office, hotel, and residential users for mutual benefit and prosperity.

The project will be multi-phased to accommodate several tenants across the five main buildings, allowing for the facilitation of development while maintaining operation of as much of the existing market as possible.

New Edge Innovations
The project will incorporate its own district energy loop. The thriving mixed-use development will establish a new benchmark for social, pedestrian, and entertainment uses in the city. The iconic architectural design has won accolades in the city public venues and press and throughout the approval process.

LOCATION Calgary, AB
CLIENT Harvard Developments, Inc.
DESIGN 2013-2017
CONSTRUCTION 2015-2025 (three phases)
SIZE 2,500,000 sf / 232,000 sm overall
(950,000 sf / 88,300 sm for Phase I)
DESIGN TEAM Perkins+Will: J. Bamberger, R. Beal, S. Bryce, P. Busby, A. Chan, J. Chang, K. Donaldson, R. Drew, J. Drohan, D. Hawthorne, G. Tierney, J. Till, S. Yu
Architectural Consultant: MBAC, Gibbs Gage Architects
STRUCTURAL ENGINEER JC Kenyon Engineering, Read Jones Christoffersen, Fast+Epp
MECHANICAL ENGINEER WSP Group
ELECTRICAL ENGINEER SMP Engineering
RENDERINGS Atchain
SUSTAINABILITY RATINGS Registered with the certification goal of LEED Gold.
REFERENCE TO PUBLICATIONS

Rhiannon M. Kirkland, "New proposed plan for Eau Claire Market," *Avenue Calgary,* online, November 15, 2013.
URLS https://www.youtube.com/watch?v=VWZM1wdWV5c

Marine Gateway

Vancouver, BC

Marine Gateway is a transit-oriented, mixed-use development located at a significant new transit node in south Vancouver. It includes a neighborhood plaza, a 12-story office tower, a 3-story retail podium, an 11-screen theater complex, non-market rental units, and 31-story and 27-story market residential towers.

Marine Gateway; Vancouver, BC; 2015 (projected)

Central to the design is the accommodation of transit-related functions, including a bus loop and the new above-grade Canada Line transit station. Two neighborhood plazas and pedestrian mews provide a unique sense of place, concentrate pedestrian activity around the retail stores, and provide a legible connection to SW Marine Drive and the residential neighborhood to the north.

Residential towers include a variety of units that allow for a diversity of residents, including extended families and students.

New Edge Innovations
The significance of this project is related to the dense development of mixed-use at a transit node; Transit Oriented Development (TOD) is the pattern for future urban growth. We have to focus residential, commercial, entertainment, and retail opportunities in configurations that support transit-based utilization. Marine Gateway is a demonstration of the future of TOD.

An aggressive sustainable design strategy also includes geoexchange heating and cooling system with an ambient heat recovery energy loop, thermal mass, and sun shading devices. Marine Gateway provides district energy heating and cooling for the immediate neighborhood.

LOCATION Vancouver, BC
CLIENT PCI Developments
DESIGN 2005-2009
CONSTRUCTION 2012-2015
SIZE 860,000 sf / 81,300 sm
DESIGN TEAM Perkins+Will:
A. Baldwin, A. Boivin, R. Bragg, L. Briney, P. Busby, A. Charisius, D. Dove, M. Haberli, J. Ho, H. Lai, D. Newby, R. Piccolo, M. Richter, K. Rowe, J. Rudd, S. Schou, A. Shum, N. Shuttleworth, J. Tomas Nunez, Y. Watanabe, E. Wolpin
STRUCTURAL ENGINEER Glotman Simpson
MECHANICAL ENGINEER MCW Engineering
ELECTRICAL ENGINEER Nemetz S/A & Associates, Ltd.
LANDSCAPE ARCHITECT PWL Partnership
CONTRACTOR Ledcor Group
ACOUSTIC CONSULTANT Brown Strachan
GEOTECHNICAL CONSULTANT MMM Group
TRAFFIC CONSULTANT MMM Group
WIND/ODOR CONSULTANT RWDI

AWARDS RECEIVED
- Precast Concrete Architectural Recognition Firm Award, Canadian Precast/Pre-stressed Concrete Institute, 2012
- Sustainability Ratings: Registered with the certification goal of LEED Gold
- URLs: http://marinegateway.com

Marine Gateway; Vancouver, BC; 2015 (projected)

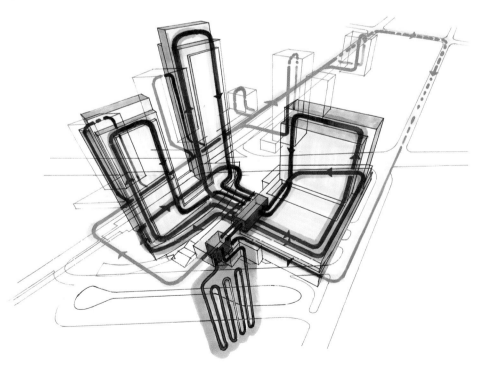

Marine Gateway, geoexchange heating and cooling diagram; Vancouver, BC; 2015 (projected)

THE FUTURE OF CITIES

7

The Future Face of
High-Performance Design

The Future Face of High-Performance Design

I began my career at the nadir of modern architecture, when the original invention, creativity, and social purpose of the movement had been lost. Modern architecture was focused on buildings as objects. There was virtually no relationship between buildings and context – natural, climatic, or otherwise – and some of the world's most famous and classically beautiful projects epitomize that. The famous buildings by Mies Van Der Rohe in the 1950s and 1960s were astonishing acts of vilification of our natural world. His admiration of nature's beauty shown in the selection of travertine and oak paneling belied a Renaissance world view; nature was to be subjugated, disciplined, and brought within square edges. And those were the good ones. Michael Graves and Charles Jencks turned architecture into six-inch-thick fashion shows, with the lipstick and hats of post modernism. They made architecture so trivial they almost killed it. Versions of the same exist today as in the Burj Khalifa and Burk Al Arab in Dubai: architectural objects that get built, but will ultimately be discarded.

Since I embarked on my professional journey, I have seen a lot of changes, many of which have been driven by accelerating technologies and design process changes. But all of it has contributed to the changing nature of the field and the redrawing of its boundaries.

On the technology of design, I started out as a young architect using ink on Mylar, scratching away mistakes in a most laborious hand drawing process, then transitioned in 1984 to AutoCAD 1.4 loaded onto on my 64 Kb ram IBM AT (which cost me $25,000). From there, we have witnessed the evolution of software that supports our design processes at an accelerating rate of change, stepped up to advanced 3D visualization, performance modeling, Revit, BIM, building analytics, CFD modeling, Rhino, and now Grasshopper, computational and parametric design. Our best designers are computer wizards; perhaps unfortunately, there is shrinking interest in traditional design tools and visualization methods.

Currently, Perkins+Will is focused on the evolving world of Design Technology. We are developing design analytics tools that assist our clients like Stanford and Genentech understand their needs and opportunities with real data collection and analysis. These process simulation exercises reinforce the importance of welcoming into our design practice lateral thinkers who can "problem solve" using unconventional digital tools. Simio allows us to model passenger flows for our transit designs. dRrofus is a comprehensive database tool for defining and managing project information. 3D printers and laser cutters have replaced cardboard and x-Acto blades in our model shops.

Approval processes, too, have changed. Unilateral permitting and zoning decisions that were once made by small groups of people slowly began (through the 1970s and 1980s) to require the approval of committees and neighborhoods. Now, entire communities, both real and virtual, get involved in the design and building decisions that affect them directly. When I started working, the approval documents for the entire City of Vancouver were found in two very small binders and approvals were easy to obtain. Five years ago, these same documents occupied approximately 15 feet of shelf space and included thousands of bylaws and requirements from municipal, provincial, federal, and environmental agencies, most of which were out of date. Today, current documentation is only available on the internet, and if we printed out all those reports, bylaws, drawings, et cetera, we could fill buildings. We have shifted our focus from an individual to a collective approach to architecture and planning. Today, everyone has a voice and the ability to be heard. Data supports debate, knowledge, and intervention. Architecture is part of an evolving knowledge ecology.

The most sweeping change has come to the industry as a result of the push for sustainable design. The rise of climate change discussions and the concern of design leaders about the role of buildings in the carbon problem has driven research, invention, standards, creativity, politics, and opportunity. There is no serious design competition or award program in the world today that does not weigh environmental attributes of submissions with gravity. LEED, established in 1998 and more broadly implemented beginning in 2000, has had a profound and beneficial impact on the global building industry, along with dozens of parallel environmental standards for building design around the world. Buildings have suddenly started looking different, sporting exterior shading, photovoltaic hats, grassy roofs, green walls, respecting orientation, wind, sun, rainfall, acting in concert with the passage of the day and seasons. Current design concerns focus on health and the welfare of building inhabitants, not just rent or return on investment. It is a very encouraging change, returning value to architects' creativity, innovation skills, and concerns about social responsibility. Just like the modern movement in the 1930s, architecture has striking new edges.

Some of us are committed to the idea today that buildings and human constructions need to be thought of as explicit parts of nature. We recognize nature as the most powerful imperative, accept the fragility of the biosphere, admit how good we are at damaging it, and acknowledge how profoundly we depend on it. Within this context, we can start to think of communities and buildings as organisms and ecosystems with lifecycles of their own, entities that we can create and reshape over time, and that can nurture all life in turn.

Buildings and communities need to function in many of the same ways living organisms do.

- They must **sustain** themselves to breathe, eat, prosper and survive.
- They must **adapt**, changing over time in order to be resilient.
- Finally, they must **prosper** to support future generations.

VanDusen Botanical Garden Visitor Centre, Vancouver, BC; 2012

Sustain

VanDusen Botanical Garden Visitor Centre, Solar Chimney; Vancouver, BC; 2012

In terms of sustaining buildings and relating to how they might change over time, we now have access to a variety of sustainable design standards. It began with LEED, which has gone through many iterations since its launch in the 1990s. We now also have the Passive House Standards, the 2030 Challenge, Net Zero Certification, the Climate Positive Development Program, and the Living Building Challenge – all of which have a dramatic impact on architecture. Today, we are diving deeper into the tenets of regenerative design in an attempt to make what was once a strictly academic concept into something that is usable and practical, linking human (construction) activity with the natural world on which our survival depends.

LEED projects have become a huge part of the marketplace in North America. An estimated 60 percent of buildings now have some kind of LEED rating in North America, and LEED-driven standards and features are appearing in an increasing number of buildings around the world.

In the early days of LEED, the buildings did not look very different. That began to shift as LEED became more widely adopted. As proof, one need only look at a LEED Platinum building to see the difference in architectural style. Take the Phillip Merrill Environmental Center at Chesapeake Bay, the very first building to receive LEED Platinum certification. Loaded with interesting features that

VanDusen Botanical Garden Visitor Centre, Entry; Vancouver, BC; 2012

VanDusen Botanical Garden Visitor Centre, Green Roof; Vancouver, BC; 2012

VanDusen Botanical Garden Visitor Centre, Vancouver, BC; 2012

Earth Sciences Building, University of British Columbia; Vancouver, BC; 2011

you never see on traditional buildings, this project shows how sustainability has driven architectural change. The VanDusen Botanical Garden Visitor Centre, our first project aimed at Living Building Challenge certification, is another example. To achieve the rigorous imperatives of the Challenge, the building simply could not assume a traditional form and rely on traditional systems.

The cumulative effect of all of these different standards on architecture will continue to be profound. It was only a few years ago when one of the largest "green" projects in the world was a building in Holland with three megawatts of photovoltaics. Today, we see an enormous investment in renewables; large corporations and communities at all levels that have made organizational commitments to low-carbon futures. Sustainable technologies are improving and costs are declining, which is helping to drive these trends. Our clients are coming to expect higher levels of performance in the buildings we design, which is gradually changing the physical nature of architecture. As sustainable practices become more commonplace, we are inching closer to a world of carbon neutrality in the built environment.

Adapt

The second big idea related to the new edge of architecture is adaptability. Similar to the way plants, humans, and other species evolve, the built environment also needs to adapt to a changing climate.

There are many ways that we can help buildings be adaptive and change over time, with hourly, daily, and seasonally variable design features that support both ecological and building-specific systems. In other words, we have the technology and expertise to create buildings that work with nature over time and adapt to nature's impact on them.

Resiliency is the current buzzword for adaptability in building and community design. As the impacts of climate change increase in severity and duration, resiliency will be seen to be the relationship between man's creations and the biosphere we depend on. This relationship between buildings and nature has many layers. Green walls and green roofs were the start; biophilic design and biomimicry are the sophisticated evolution of these ideas. The incorporation of urban agriculture and local food supply systems into the design of communities allows a mutually beneficial balance between humans and nature. Nature survives with our help, and we survive with its help. This interconnectedness becomes part of everything we do as designers and planners.

Prosper

A prosperous built environment, like all organic species, hinges on the health, survival, and propagation of the species itself. In our world, we relate this to material health. At Perkins+Will, we have become increasingly focused on material transparency, particularly through the development of our Precautionary List. Given what we now know about the built environment's effects on human health, we feel this is one of the most critical aspects of our changing industry. The material cycle in design and construction needs to be researched, revealed, studied, exposed, and cleaned up. Resource utilization is about regeneration; about choosing and configuring materials that support regenerative design.

Buildings can be designed to promote health: stairs should be attractive and easy; elevators should be hidden away; the landscape should offer opportunities for physical health and recreation. All of these ideas are about helping buildings and their occupants prosper.

Energy, Environment, Experiential Learning, University of Calgary, Calgary, AB;

Every building should be designed and nurtured like a living organism. It should enter into a mutually dependent relationship with the humans who occupy it, support it and thrive within it. It should provide function and beauty at the same time, and stand as a physical and metaphorical symbol of the healthy, prosperous, sustainable community it serves.

In the midst of a changing industry, architects are in a new and exhilarating position to act. We must continue to change the relationship between society and our practices, helping to make our chosen field more important, more viable, and more connected. We must use technology to support what we do, creating healthy, sustainable places to live and work. We must continue to push the new edges of our craft further outward, forever cultivating a healthy balance between the built and natural worlds. Because this is the only way we can heal our planet and live in harmony with nature.

The simplest organisms on earth while living and thriving create soil, clean the air and water, and exchange atmospheric gasses for the benefit of all others. And they do so for millennia. Given that we, as humans, have more control and skills and intelligence than any species ever, can we create the same relationships in the conduct of our own lives going forward, and ensure the health of our species for millennia? Let us hope so.

To return the discussion finally to what we do, this is a statement of optimism about the future. It takes courage to believe in the future, and our ability to look ahead. As architects we have a responsibility to be optimists because our whole lives are devoted to creating for a future that will extend beyond our lifetimes.

Blatchford Redevelopment; Edmonton, AB; 2013

Chaudiere; Les Isles, Ottawa, ON-Gatineau, QC; 2014

Blatchford Redevelopment, Edmonton, AB; 2013

2001
ONE WALL CENTRE
Wall Financial
Corporation
Vancouver, BC

TELUS HOUSE
TELUS
Vancouver, BC

**COMPUTER
SCIENCES BUILDING**
York University
Toronto, ON

**GILMORE SKYTRAIN
STATION**
Rapid Transit Proje[
Office
Burnaby, BC

**NICOLA VALLEY INSTITU[
OF TECHNOLOGY**
Nicola Valley
Institute of
Technology
Merritt, BC

PROFILE X F1 PODIUM
Profile Projex
International, Inc.

**BRENTWOOD SKYTRAI[
STATION**
Rapid Transit Proj[
Office
Burnaby, BC

1989
**MACMILLAN BLOEDEL
RESEARCH CENTRE**
MacMillan Bloedel, Ltd.
Burnaby, BC

1987
EBCO AEROSPACE CENTRE
Ebco Industries, Ltd.
Delta, BC

URBAN EXPRESSO KIOSK
Urban Expresso, Inc.
Vancouver, BC

**STANLEY PARK TROPICAL
COMPLEX**
Vancouver Parks
Board
Vancouver, BC

PEMBERTON AIR TERMINAL
Municipality of
Pemberton
Pemberton, BC

VANCOUVER VIEW STUDY
City of Vancouver
Vancouver, BC

VIDEO RECORDING KIOSK
Videogram International
Vancouver, BC

1992
CAPE ROGER CURTIS
The Burke and Frith
Families
Bowen Island, BC

EYEMASTERS STORES
Eyemasters Canada
Various Locations

WEST 1ST AVENUE
1650 Holdings, Ltd.
Vancouver, BC

1985
**2001 COMMUNICATIONS
SALES MODULE**
2001
Communications, Ltd.
Vancouver, BC

1996
**METRO MCNAIR CLINICAL
LABORATORY AND OFFICE**
MDS Metro
Burnaby, BC

1999
MATERIALS TESTING LABORATORY
City of Vancouver
Vancouver, BC

**GREAT NORTHERN WAY
TECHNOLOGY PARK**
Finning International, Inc.
Vancouver, BC

1984
**1216 GRANVILLE
STREET OFFICE**
Peter Busby
Architect
Vancouver, BC

1986
ROYAL ACADEMY KIOSK
London, UK

1988
EBCO TABLE
Ebco Industries, Ltd.
Delta, BC

1991
L-01 'GILL' WALL SCONCE
Designlines Canada, Ltd.
Vancouver, BC

1995
1650 WEST 2ND AVENUE
Busby Bridger
Architects
Vancouver, BC

APEGBC HEADQUARTERS
APEGBC
Burnaby, BC

MUNICIPAL CITY HALL
District of North
Vancouver
North Vancouver, BC

**RAIL YARD OFFICES AND
CONTROL TOWER**
British Columbia Rail
Corporation
North Vancouver, BC

1998
GIRAF TABLE
Componance, Inc.
Vancouver, BC

AIBC HEADQUARTERS
440 Cambie Street
Development Group
Vancouver, BC

REVENUE CANADA OFFICE
Public Works and
Government Services
Surrey, BC

1050 HOMER STREET
Busby+Associates
Architects
Vancouver, BC

2000
1220 HOMER STREET
Busby+Associates
Architects
Vancouver, BC

**CONCORD PACIFIC
PAVILIONS**
Concord Pacific
Developments
Vancouver, BC

Index

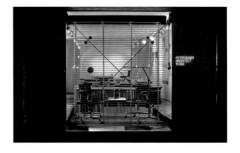

2 Bryant Street, Perkins+Will San Francisco, San Francisco, CA (2013-2014)

PROJECT 2 Bryant Street, San Francisco office of Perkins+Will
LOCATION San Francisco, CA
CLIENT Perkins+Will
DESIGN 2013-2014
CONSTRUCTION 2013-2014
SIZE 21,170 sf / 1,966 sm
DESIGN TEAM
Perkins+Will:
- S. Andersen, P. Busby, T. Campbell, R. Clocker, D. Hawthorne, A. Hoffert, C. Leighton, Y. Matsushita, R. Muir, K. Raines, S. Schou, A. Wolfram
CONTRACTOR NOVO Construction
STRUCTURAL Holmes Culley
MEP Integral Group
PHOTOGRAPHER Mariko Reed
SUSTAINABILITY RATINGS Registered with the certification goal of LEED® Platinum. Pursuing the Living Building Challenge (LBC) Petal Certification for Site, Energy, Health, Materials, Equity, and Beauty. We intend to achieve the Water Petal in the future. The project meets the 2030 Challenge at the 2030 level.

1050 Homer Street, Vancouver, BC (1998)

PROJECT 1050 Homer Street
LOCATION Vancouver, BC
CLIENT Busby + Associates Architects
DESIGN AND CONSTRUCTION 1998
DESIGN TEAM
Perkins+Will (formerly Busby + Associates Architects):
- P. Busby, J. Huffman, M. McColl, S. Schou, D. Thiruchitampalam
CONTRACTOR David Mitchell
MECHANICAL ENGINEER Keen Engineering
PHOTOGRAPHER Busby + Associates Architects

1216 Granville Street, Vancouver, BC, (1984-1987)

PROJECT 1216 Granville Street
LOCATION Vancouver, BC
CLIENT Peter Busby Architect
DESIGN 1984
CONSTRUCTION
- Phase I: June 1984 to November 1984
- Phase II: June 1987 to September 1987
SIZE 1,356 sf / 126 sm
DESIGN TEAM
Peter Busby Architect
- P. Busby
CONTRACTOR P. Busby
STRUCTURAL ENGINEER John Rockingham Engineering
PHOTOGRAPHER P. Busby
AWARDS RECEIVED
- Interior Designers Institute of British Columbia, Award of Merit (1986)

1220 Homer Street, Perkins+Will Vancouver, Vancouver, BC (2000)

PROJECT 1220 Homer Street, Vancouver office of Perkins+Will
LOCATION Vancouver, BC
CLIENT Busby + Associates Architects
DESIGN 2000
CONSTRUCTION 2000
SIZE 23,400 sf / 2,174 sm
DESIGN TEAM
Perkins+Will (formerly Busby + Associates Architects):
  • P. Busby, D. Dove, S. Gushe, S. Ockwell, A. Minard, S. Schou, R. Wu
STRUCTURAL ENGINEER Glotman Simpson
SKYLIGHT CONSULTANT Fast + Epp
ELECTRICAL ENGINEER Flagel Lewandowski
MECHANICAL ENGINEER Keen Engineering
PHOTOGRAPHER Michael Elkan
AWARDS RECEIVED
  • IIDA LIGHTING DESIGN Awards, BC Section Award and Pacific Regional Section Award of Merit, 2002
SUSTAINABILITY RATINGS LEED Platinum
REFERENCE TO PUBLICATIONS
  • "1220 Homer Street," *New Life for Old Buildings,* December 2009, p. 18-20

1315 Peachtree Street, Perkins+Will Atlanta, Atlanta, GA (2009-2010)

PROJECT 1315 Peachtree Street, Atlanta office of Perkins+Will
LOCATION Atlanta, GA
CLIENT Perkins+Will
DESIGN 2009
CONSTRUCTION 2009-2010
SIZE 78,000 sf / 7,246 sm
DESIGN TEAM
Perkins+Will:
  • Architecture: K. Chamness, K. Duckworth, M. Finn, S. McCauley, B. McEvoy, D. Reynolds
  • Branded Environments: B. Erlinder, E. Maddox, B. Weatherford
  • Interiors: V. Logsdon, R. Miles, T. Moore, D. Sheehan
  • Planning and Strategies: J. Barnes, K. Farley
  • Urban Design and Landscape Architecture: J. Cooper, Z. Stewart
  • Sustainability Charrettes: P. Busby, B. McCarry, P. McEvoy
STRUCTURAL ENGINEER Uzun & Case
MEP Integral Group
CONTRACTOR Brasfield & Gorrie
PHOTOGRAPHER Eduard Hueber
AWARDS RECEIVED
  • Top Ten Green Projects, American Institute of Architects Committee on the
  • Environment (COTE), 2012
  • Development of Excellence Award, ULI-Atlanta, 2011
  • Design Award, AIA-Georgia, 2011
  • Development of Excellence Award, Atlanta Regional Commission and the
  • Livable Communities Coalition, 2011
  • Award of Excellence for Sustainability, Atlanta Urban Design Commission, 2011
  • Golden Shoe Award, PEDS (Pedestrians Educating Drivers on Safety) For Pedestrian-friendly Site Redesign, 2011
SUSTAINABILITY RATINGS LEED Platinum
REFERENCES TO PUBLICATIONS
  • Sheila Kim, "Perkins+Will Atlanta," *Contract,* September 18, 2012. http://www.contractdesign.com/contract/design/features/PerkinsWill-Atlanta-7742.shtml#

  • "1315 Peachtree Street: 2012 AIA COTE Top Ten," *Architect,* August 23, 2012. http://www.architectmagazine.com/award-winners/2012-cote-1315-peachtree-street.aspx
  • Emily Badger, "How to Green Southern Cities Built in the Age of Cars and Air Conditioning" *CityLab,* April 18, 2012. http://www.citylab.com/design/2012/04/how-green-southern-cities-built-age-cars-and-ac/1619/
  • Paula Vaughn and Grzegorz Kozmal, "Designing for Design Perkins+Will Offers Up Opportunities and Insights from designing its own LEED Platinum-Certified Spaces" *ECOBuilding Pulse,* June 3, 2011: http://www.ecobuildingpulse.com/commercial-projects/designing-for-design.aspx

  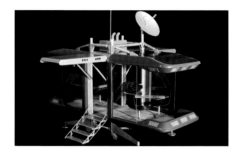

1650 West First Avenue, Vancouver, BC (1989-1992)

PROJECT 1650 West First Avenue
LOCATION Vancouver, BC
CLIENT 1650 Holdings, Ltd.
DESIGN 1989-1991
CONSTRUCTION 1991-1992
SIZE 26,500 sf / 2,462 sm
DESIGN TEAM
Perkins+Will (formerly Busby Bridger Architects):
  • P. Bridger, P. Busby, J. Huffman, J. Keen, R. Maas, U. Mueller, D. Wolfe
CONTRACTOR Norwood Construction
STRUCTURAL ENGINEER Fast + Epp
MECHANICAL ENGINEER Yoneda & Associates
ELECTRICAL ENGINEER Falcon Engineering
GEOTECHNICAL CONSULTANT Macleod

1650 West Second Avenue, Vancouver, BC (1989-1995)

PROJECT 1650 West 2nd Avenue
LOCATION Vancouver, BC
CLIENT Busby Bridger Architects
DESIGN 1989
CONSTRUCTION 1993-1995
SIZE 9,700 sf / 900 sm
DESIGN TEAM
Perkins+Will (formerly Busby Bridger Architects):
  • P. Bridger, A. Brown, P. Busby, B. Hryhorczuk, J. Huffman, C. Knichel, J. Konkin, R. Maas, C. Ramsay, S. Schou, G. Tovey
STRUCTURAL ENGINEER Fast + Epp
MECHANICAL ENGINEER Vel Engineering
CIVIL AND ELECTRICAL ENGINEER Reid Crowther and Partners
LANDSCAPE ARCHITECT Wendt Land Planning

2001 Communications Sales Module, Vancouver, BC (1984-1985)

PROJECT 2001 Communications Sales Module
LOCATION Vancouver, BC
CLIENT 2001 Communications, Ltd.
DESIGN 1984
CONSTRUCTION 1985
DESIGN TEAM
Perkins+Will (formerly Peter Busby Architect):
  • P. Busby

Architectural Institute of British Columbia, Vancouver, BC (1997-1998)

PROJECT Architectural Institute of British Columbia (AIBC) Headquarters
LOCATION Vancouver, BC
CLIENT 440 Cambie Street Development Group
DESIGN 1997
CONSTRUCTION 1997-1998
DESIGN TEAM
Perkins+Will (formerly Busby + Associates Architects):
  • A. Brown, P. Busby, T. Mullock, M. Nielsen, D. Thiruchittampalam, A. Waugh, B. Welty
Robert Lemon Architecture & Preservation:
  • R. Lemon
PROJECT MANAGER J. Anderson & B. Davis
STRUCTURAL ENGINEER Rockingham Engineering
MECHANICAL ENGINEER Keen Engineering
ELECTRICAL ENGINEER Reid Crowther
COST CONSULTANT Locke McKinnon Domingo Gibson
CONTRACTOR Willow Spring Construction
INTERIOR DESIGNER Roger Hughes Architects
PHOTOGRAPHER Martin Tessler
AWARDS RECEIVED
  • City of Vancouver, Heritage Award of Honour, 1999
REFERENCE TO PUBLICATIONS
  • "The AIBC moves to The Architecture Centre at 440 Cambie Street," *AIBC Newsletter,* June 9, 1998.
  • "Architecture Centre preserves past the right way," *Vancouver Sun,* June 3, 1998

Association of Professional Engineers and Geoscientists of British Columbia (APEGBC), Burnaby, BC (1994-1995)

PROJECT Association of Professional Engineers and Geoscientists of British Columbia (APEGBC) Headquarters
LOCATION Burnaby, BC
CLIENT APEGBC
DESIGN 1994
CONSTRUCTION 1994-1995
SIZE 21,500 sf /1,997 sm
DESIGN TEAM
Perkins+Will (formerly Busby Bridger Architects):
  • A. Brown, P. Busby, T. Mullock, M. Nielsen, S. Schou, D. Thiru chittampalam, G. Tovey, A. Waugh, B. Welty
PROJECT MANAGER Degelder Construction, Ltd.
STRUCTURAL ENGINEER Read Jones Christoffersen
MECHANICAL ENGINEER Keen Engineering
ELECTRICAL ENGINEER Reid Crowther & Partners
LANDSCAPE ARCHITECT Reeve MacDougall
PHOTOGRAPHER Martin Tessler
AWARDS RECEIVED
  • Lieutenant Governor of British Columbia Award of Merit, Medal in Architecture, 1998
  • Governor General of Canada, Medal for Excellence in Architecture, 1997
  • Canadian Institute of Steel Construction, BC Steel Design Award, Honorable Mention, 1996
  • Consulting Engineers of BC, Award of Excellence, Building Engineering Projects, 1996
  • BC Hydro Power Smart Award of Excellence, Commercial Buildings, 1996
REFERENCE TO PUBLICATIONS
  • "APEGBC Building highlights both engineering, architectural efforts," *Business in Vancouver,* September 24, 1996

BC Rail Yard Offices and Control Tower, North Vancouver, BC (1993-1995)

PROJECT BC Rail Yard Offices and Control Tower
LOCATION North Vancouver, BC
CLIENT British Columbia Rail Corporation
DESIGN 1993
CONSTRUCTION 1994-1995
SIZE 7,728 sf / 718 sm
DESIGN TEAM
Perkins+Will (formerly Busby Bridger Architects):
  • P. Bridger, A. Brown, P. Busby, H. Goodland, S. Gushe, J. Huffman, B. Welty
CONTRACTOR Regatta Construction
STRUCTURAL ENGINEER Fast + Epp
MECHANICAL ENGINEER Reid Crowther & Partners
ELECTRICAL ENGINEER Reid Crowther & Partners
CIVIL ENGINEER Reid Crowther & Partners
FIRE CODE ENGINEER Protection Engineering
LANDSCAPE ARCHITECT Wendt Land Planning
SUBSOIL INVESTIGATIONS Golder Associates
PHOTOGRAPHER Unknown
AWARDS RECEIVED
  • Corporation of the District of North Vancouver, Award of Excellence, 1996
  • Consulting Engineers of British Columbia, Building Engineering Projects, Award of Excellence, 1996
REFERENCE TO PUBLICATIONS
  • "Design erection of BC Rail Yard control tower" PCI Journal, January 1998
  • Sensible, solid aesthetics for BC Rail control tower, *Journal of Commerce,* November 7, 1994

Blatchford Redevelopment, Edmonton, AB (2010-2040)

PROJECT Blatchford Redevelopment
LOCATION Former Municipal Airport, Edmonton, AB
CLIENT City of Edmonton, City Centre Redevelopment
DESIGN 2010-2013
SIZE 531 acres / 215 hectares
DESIGN TEAM
Perkins+Will:
- P. Busby, A. Charisius, J. Drohan, N. Friedman, C. Gomes, B. McCarry, M. Nielsen, P. Pinto, G. Silwal, Y. Sun, P. Vaucheret

COMMUNITY PLANNING Civitas Urban Design and Planning
LOCAL ARCHITECTURE AND URBAN DESIGN Group 2 Architecture Engineering Ltd.
TRANSPORTATION ENGINEER Nelson\Nygaard
SUSTAINABLE BUILDING DESIGN Archineers; Integral Group
GEOTECHNICAL AND ENVIRONMENTAL CONSULTANT Golder Associates
LOCAL MUNICIPAL PLANNING ISL Engineering and Land Services
LAND ECONOMICS Pro Forma Advisors
PUBLIC CONSULTATION Soles and Co.
MECHANICAL ENGINEER Integral Group
ELECTRICAL ENGINEER Integral Group
HERITAGE CONSULTANT Alberta Western Heritage
LANDSCAPE ARCHITECT Phillips Farevaag Smallenberg
RENDERINGS Foyd Architects
AWARDS RECEIVED
- Canadian Urban Institute Brownie Award, 2014
- Royal Architectural Institute of Canada, (RAIC) National Urban Design Awards, 2014
- Globe Awards - Excellence in Urban Sustainability, 2014

SUSTAINABILITY RATINGS Beyond carbon neutral
REFERENCE TO PUBLICATIONS
- Gorden Kent, "Trash vacuum, stormwater irrigation on the table in Blatchford project," *Edmonton Journal,* March 21, 2014.
- Blair McCarry, "Blatchford Redevelopment," *SABMag,* December 24, 2013: http://

www.*sabmagazino*.com/blog/2013/12/24/blatchford-redevelopment/
- Alix Kemp, "Downtown or Bust: Calgary and Edmonton attempt to revitalize their downtown cores," *Alberta Venture,* November 18, 2013.

URL City of Edmonton, Blatchford Redevelopment website: http://www.edmonton.ca/blatchford.aspx

Brentwood Skytrain Station, Burnaby, BC (1999-2001)

PROJECT Brentwood Skytrain Station
LOCATION Burnaby, BC
CLIENT Rapid Transit Project Office
DESIGN 1999
CONSTRUCTION 2000-2001
SIZE 22,000 sf / 2,045 sm
DESIGN TEAM
Perkins+Will (formerly Busby + Associates, Architects):
- B. Billingsley, M. Bonaventura, P. Busby, S. Edwards, T. Mullock, M. Nielsen, R. Peck, S. Schou, A. Slawinski

CONTRACTOR Dominion Construction
STRUCTURAL ENGINEER Fast + Epp
MECHANICAL ENGINEER Klohn Crippen
ELECTRICAL ENGINEER Agra Simons
LANDSCAPE ARCHITECT Durante Kreuk
PUBLIC ARTIST Jill Anholt
PHOTOGRAPHER Nic Lehoux
AWARDS RECEIVED
- AIA 8th Annual Business Week/Architectural Record Finalist, 2004
- Governor General of Canada, Medal in Architecture, 2004
- Lieutenant Governor of BC, Medal in Architecture, 2004
- UK Institute of Structural Engineers, Structural Achievement Commendation, 2003
- Award of Excellence for Building Engineering, Consulting Engineers of BC, 2003
- Illuminating Engineering Society of North America, IIDA and Vision Awards, Section Award, 2003
- CISC Awards for Excellence, 2002
- IStructE Supreme Award for Structural Engineering Excellence, UK, 2003
- Canadian Institute of Steel Construction, BC Steel Design Awards, Honourable Mention for an Outstanding Steel Structure, 2002
- BC Art of CAD, Applied Rendering, Honorable Mention, 2001
- Bentley Success Award, Transportation Design and Engineering, 2000

REFERENCE TO PUBLICATIONS
- Canadian Wood Council, *Wood in Transportation,* December 2010.

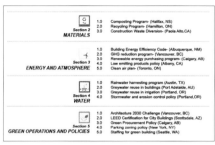

Section 2 MATERIALS	1.0 2.0 3.0	Composting Program- (Halifax, NS) Recycling Program- (Hamilton, ON) Construction Waste Diversion- (Paola Alto,CA)
Section 3 ENERGY AND ATMOSPHERE	1.0 2.0 3.0 4.0 5.0	Building Energy Efficiency Code- (Albuquerque, NM) GHG reduction program- (Vancouver, BC) Renewable energy purchasing program- (Calgary, AB) Low emitting products policy (Albany, CA) Clean air plan- (Toronto, ON)
Section 4 WATER	1.0 2.0 3.0 4.0	Rainwater harvesting program (Austin, TX) Greywater reuse in buildings (Port Adelaide, AU) Greywater reuse in irrigation (Portland, OR) Stormwater and erosion control policy (Portland,OR)
Section 5 GREEN OPERATIONS AND POLICIES	1.0 2.0 3.0 4.0 5.0	Architecture 2030 Challenge (Vancouver, BC) LEED Certification for City Buildings (Scottsdale, AZ) Green Procurement Policy (Calgary, AB) Parking zoning policy (New York, NY) Staffing for green building (Seattle, WA)

- David Sokol, "Shedding Weight," *GreenSource,* September/October 2008, p. 50.
- "Brentwood Town Centre Station," *Urban Land,* January 2008, p. 45.
- Brentwood Skytrain Station, *Canadian Architect,* May 2004.
- Russell, James. S., "Architect Busby + Associates stretched a curving canopy over passengers, giving an iconic image to the new Brentwood Skytrain Station," *Architectural Record,* January 2003, Vol. 191 Issue 1, p. 104.

Canada Line Skytrain Stations, Richmond, BC (2007-2009)

PROJECT Canada Line Skytrain Stations
LOCATION Richmond, BC
CLIENT InTransitBC
DESIGN 2007
CONSTRUCTION 2008-2009
SIZE 15,000 sf / 1,395 sm
DESIGN TEAM
Perkins+Will:
- P. Busby, T. Grimwood, I. Ilic, K. Robertson, M. Nielsen, E. Stedman

CONTRACTOR SNC Lavalin
CIVIL ENGINEER Cochrane Group
STRUCTURAL ENGINEER Fast + Epp
MECHANICAL ENGINEER Stantec
ELECTRICAL ENGINEER Stantec
PHOTOGRAPHER Martin Tessler
AWARDS RECEIVED
- Schreyer Award, 2010
- International Association of Lighting Designers Award of Merit, 2010

REFERENCE TO PUBLICATIONS
- Canadian Wood Council, *Wood in Transportation,* December 2010.
- Duane Palibroda, "Wood: Sustainable with or without LEED," *SABMag*, September 25, 2010: p. 41-46.
- Katharine Logan "Total Lighting Solutions lights the way for Vancouver's new transit system," *Architectural Record,* February 2010: p. 96-98.
- Kelly Sinoski, "Opportunity to build around new train lines" *Vancouver Sun,* August 15, 2009: K19.

Canadian Cities in a Climate of Change, Throughout Canada (2007-2008)

PROJECT Canadian Cities in a Climate of Change
LOCATION Presented throughout Canada
CLIENT Self-directed research and presentations
DESIGN 2007-2008
DESIGN TEAM
Perkins+Will:
- P. Busby, M. Driedger, K. Wardle

REFERENCE TO PUBLICATIONS
- Peter Busby and Michael Driedger, "Canadian Cities in a Climate of Change" *Municipal World,* November 2008, p. 9-12.

ENVIRONMENTAL SITE PLANNING Cape Roger Curtis

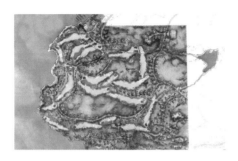

Design, and Rezoning, Bowen Island, BC (1989-1992)

PROJECT Cape Roger Curtis Site Planning, Environmental Design, and Rezoning
LOCATION Bowen Island, BC
CLIENT Burke and Frith Families
DESIGN 1989-1992
SIZE 649 acres / 262 hectares
DESIGN TEAM
Perkins+Will (formerly Busby Bridger Architects):
  • P. Busby, T. Hubel, R. Maas, C. Odinga, J. Taggart, B. Welty
GOLF COURSE DESIGNER Robinson Carrick & Associates
LANDSCAPE ARCHITECT Durante & Partners
CIVIL ENGINEER Hub Engineering
GEOTECHNICAL CONSULTANT Robinson S. R. K
ENVIRONMENTAL CONSULTANT Robin Gardener
QUANTITY SURVEYORS Hanscomb Consultants, Inc.
HYDROLOGY ANALYSIS NovaTech Consultants

Center for Urban Waters, Tacoma, WA (2005-2010)

PROJECT Center for Urban Waters
LOCATION Tacoma, WA
CLIENT National Development Council
SIZE 51,000 sf / 4738 sm
DESIGN 2005-2006
CONSTRUCTION 2009-2010
DESIGN TEAM
Perkins+Will:
  • P. Busby, T. DeEulio, D. Kleiner, K. Kornovich, D. Seng
DEVELOPER Lorig Associates
CONTRACTOR Turner Construction
STRUCTURAL ENGINEER AHBL, Inc.
MECHANICAL ENGINEER WSP Flack + Kurtz
ELECTRICAL ENGINEER WSP Flack + Kurtz
LANDSCAPE ARCHITECT Swift Company
COMMISSIONING AGENT Rushing
PHOTOGRAPHER Benjamin Benschneider
AWARDS RECEIVED
  • AIA Seattle Regional Top Ten Green Award, 2008
  • AIA Washington Civic Design, Merit Award, 2008
SUSTAINABILITY RATINGS LEED Platinum
REFERENCE TO PUBLICATIONS
  • "Center for Urban Waters," *Arch Daily,* February 23, 2011, http://www.archdaily.com/112190/center-for-urban-waters-perkins-will/
URLS http://www.urbanwaters.org/

Centre for Interactive Research on Sustainability (CIRS), University of British Columbia, Vancouver, BC (2008-2011)

PROJECT Centre for Interactive Research on Sustainability
LOCATION Vancouver, BC
CLIENT University of British Columbia
SIZE 61,085 sf / 5,675 sm
DESIGN 2008-2009
CONSTRUCTION 2009-2011
DESIGN TEAM
Perkins+Will:
  • P. Busby, M. Cocivera, W. Dahl, R. Drew, B. Gasmena, J. Gravenstein, R. Holt, H. Lai, B. McCarry, T. Miller, M. Nielsen, J. Peacock, A. Pilon, R. Rheaume, M. Richter, S. Schou, Z. Smith, K. Wardle
PROJECT MANAGER Alberto Cayuela, P. Eng., PMP, University of British Columbia
CONSTRUCTION MANAGEMENT Heatherbrae Construction
STRUCTURAL ENGINEER Fast + Epp
MECHANICAL ENGINEER Stantec
ELECTRICAL ENGINEER Stantec
LANDSCAPE ARCHITECT PWL Partnership
CIVIL ENGINEER Core Group Consultants
GEOTECHNICAL CONSULTANT Trow Associates, Inc
INTERIOR DESIGN Perkins+Will Canada
BUILDING ENVELOPE Morrison Hershfield Limited
CODE CONSULTANT LMDG Building Code Consultants
ACOUSTIC CONSULTANT BKL Consultants
QUANTITY SURVEYOR Spiegel Skillen
AUDIO VISUAL CONSULTANT MC Squared System Group
FURNITURE, FIXTURES AND EQUIPMENT Haworth
OWNER REPRESENTATIVE UBC Properties Trust
WASTEWATER CONSULTANT Eco-Tek Ecological Technologies
RAINWATER CONSULTANT NovaTec Consultants
PHOTOGRAPHER Martin Tessler
AWARDS RECEIVED
  • SAB Magazine, 2014 Canadian Green Building Award, 2014
  • Wood WORKS! BC Wood Design Awards, Green Building Award, 2013
  • Delta Management Group, Clean50, Top 5

Project, 2013
- World Architecture News WAN Sustainable Building of the Year, Longlist, 2013
- North American Wood Design Award, Canadian Wood Council Award, 2012
- IStructE (Institute of Structural Engineering) Commendation - Award for Education or Healthcare Structures, 2012
- National Council of Structural Engineering Associations Awards, $30-100 Million Category, 2012
- AIBC Innovation Award, 2012
- GLOBE Awards for Environmental Excellence, Excellence in Urban Sustainability Finalist, 2012
- Treehugger Best of Green: Best Office or Commercial Design & Reader's Choice Winner, 2012
- Treehugger Best of Green: Design and Architecture, 2010

SUSTAINABILITY RATINGS LEED Platinum with a strong score of 56 points. Pursuing Petal Recognition through the Living Building Challenge v1.3. The building has completed the Preliminary Audit process, and expects to finalize certification when one year of operations monitoring is complete.

REFERENCE TO PUBLICATIONS
- Zachary Edelson, "Architecture That Drives Ecological Innovation" *Architizer,* August 13, 2013.
- "Centre for Interactive Research on Sustainability," *Arch Daily,* March 13, 2013. http://www.archdaily.com/343442/centre-for-interactive-research-on-sustainability-perkins-will/
- Paige Magarrey, "Higher Learning," *Azure,* November/December 2012, p. 72-73.
- "Centre for Interactive Research on Sustainability," Wood Design & Building, September 6, 2012, p. 15-17.
- Suzanna Morphet, "Making a Positive Impression," *Innovation Magazine,* July/August 2012, p. 16-19.
- Paula Melton, "Whole-Building Life-Cycle Assessment: Taking the Measure of a Green Building" *BuildingGreen.com,* May 6, 2012.
- Frances Bula, "The Building that's Beyond Green," *Globe and Mail,* April 20, 2012, E6-E7.Sean Ruthen, "Regenerative Design,"

Canadian Architect, March 1, 2012, p. 26-33.
- Edward Keegan, "Centre for Interactive Research on Sustainability," *Architect,* March 2012. http://www.architectmagazine.com/sustainability/the-centre-for-interactive-research-on-sustainabi.aspx?dfpzone=projects.sustainability
- "UBC - Educating today to ensure tomorrow, "*Canadian Journal of Green Building and Design,* January/February 2012.
- "The Centre for Interactive Research on Sustainability opens at the University of British Columbia," *Canadian Architect,* November 8, 2011.
- Heather Amos, "UBC opens North America's most sustainable building," *UBC Report,* November 1, 2011.
- Michael Cockram, "The Living Lab," *GreenSource,* September/October 2011, p. 100-106.

URLS CIRS Handbook – A Technical Manual and website (www.cirs.ubc.ca) further disseminate information with lessons learned, ongoing updates, and actual performance data from the project.

The process of creating CIRS has reshaped UBC's vision for its campus and its role as an institution; the results from CIRS are helping move the world toward a more sustainable future.
http://cirs.ubc.ca/building/building-history

https://www.youtube.com/watch?v=uz_au8JvCO8

Chaudière; Les Isles, Ottawa, ON-Gatineau, QC metropolitan area (2013-2030)

PROJECT Chaudière; Les Isles
LOCATION Ottawa-Gatineau metropolitan area. The site is located on both sides of the Ottawa River and falls partly within the City of Ottawa, Ontario and partly within The City of Gatineau, Quebec.
CLIENT Windmill Development Group
DESIGN June 2013 through April 2014
CONSTRUCTION 2015 through 2030
SIZE Site Area 38 acres/15 hectares Proposed Development 3,000,000 sf / 279,000 sm mixed-use
DESIGN TEAM
Perkins+Will:
- P. Busby, D. Dornan, N. Friedman, L. Shifley, R. Song, J. Yong
LANDSCAPE ARCHITECT PFS
PLANNING CONSULTANT Fotenn
CIVIL ENGINEER DSEL (Civil)
HERITAGE ASSETS Rubin Rotmann
TRAFFIC ENGINEER Delcan
SUSTAINABILITY ADVISOR Archineers
RENDERINGS Chris Foyd
SUSTAINABILITY RATINGS The project is designed to be the first One Planet Community in North America. In keeping with Windmill's sustainability commitments, all buildings will pursue the certification goal of LEED Platinum.
REFERENCE TO PUBLICATIONS
- "Windmill unveils plans for 'world's most sustainable community' for former Domtar lands," *Ottawa Citizen,* April 22, 2014.

**Concord Pacific Pavilions, Vancouver, BC
(1993-2000)**

PROJECT Concord Pacific Pavilions
LOCATION Vancouver, BC
CLIENT Concord Pacific Developments
DESIGN 1993-1994
Construction:
- Building A: 1994
- Building B: 1996
- Building C: 2000
SIZE
- Building A: 5,307 sf / 493 sm
- Building B: 5,963 sf / 554 sm
- Building C: 3,714 sf / 345 sm
DESIGN TEAM
Perkins+Will (formerly Busby Bridger
Architects):
- P. Busby, R. Maas, M. McColl, E. Stedman,
  B. Welty
STRUCTURAL ENGINEER Fast + Epp
MECHANICAL/ELECTRICAL ENGINEER D.W.
Thomson Consultants
MECHANICAL ENGINEER Sterling Cooper
MECHANICAL ENGINEER Yoneda & Associates
ELECTRICAL ENGINEER Arnold Nemetz &
Associates
Building CONTRACTOR Centreville Construction
Moving CONTRACTOR Nickel Bros. House
Moving, Ltd.

**Crossroads Mixed-use Development,
Vancouver, BC (2004-2009)**

PROJECT Crossroads Mixed-use Development
LOCATION Vancouver, BC
CLIENT PCI Developments
DESIGN 2004 - 2006
CONSTRUCTION 2006 -2009
SIZE 293,000 sf / 27,000 sm
DESIGN TEAM
Perkins+Will:
- P. Busby, K. Bismanis, D. Dove, J. Doble,
  J. Foit, J. Gravenstein, T. Grimwood, K.
  Meissner, T. Miller, R. Piccolo, D. Roberts,
  S. Schou, N. Shuttleworth, A. Slawinski, A.
  Wolanski
CONTRACTOR Ledcor Group
STRUCTURAL ENGINEER Glotman Simpson
Consulting Engineers
MECHANICAL ENGINEER Perez Engineering
ELECTRICAL ENGINEER Nemetz and Associates,
Ltd.
LANDSCAPE ARCHITECT Eckford + Associates
INTERIOR DESIGN Scott Trepp Interior Design
BUILDING ENVELOPE Aqua-Coast Engineering,
Ltd.
ACOUSTIC CONSULTANT Brown Strachan
TRAFFIC CONSULTANT ND Lea
CERTIFIED PROFESSIONAL CFT Engineering, Inc.
GEOTECHNICAL CONSULTANT Geo-Pacific
ENVIRONMENTAL CONSULTANT Keystone
Environmental
COMMISSIONING AUTHORITY KD Engineering Co.
SURVEYOR Butler Sundvick & Associates
HYDROLOGIST Hay and Company
PHOTOGRAPHER Martin Tessler
AWARDS RECEIVED
- VRCA Awards of Excellence - General
  Contractor over $50 million, Mechanical
  Contractor over $3 million, 2009
SUSTAINABILITY RATINGS LEED Gold
REFERENCE TO PUBLICATIONS
- Jean Sorensen, "Crossroads helps turn its
  area into a community" *Journal of Commerce,*
  October 5, 2009, p. AE-12.

**District of North Vancouver City Hall, North
Vancouver, BC (1989-1995)**

PROJECT District of North Vancouver City Hall
LOCATION North Vancouver, BC
CLIENT The Corporation of the District of North
Vancouver
DESIGN 1989-1991
CONSTRUCTION 1992-1995
SIZE 65,660 sf / 6,100 sm
DESIGN TEAM
Perkins+Will (formerly Busby Bridger
Architects):
- P. Bridger, A. Brown, P. Busby, M. Carter, R.
  Maas, U. Mueller, R. Pacheco, A. Slawinski, T.
  Waters, B. Welty, P. Zieth
Frits de Vries Architects, Ltd.
CONTRACTOR Marbella Pacific Construction
West, Ltd.
STRUCTURAL ENGINEER Fast + Epp
MECHANICAL ENGINEER Yoneda & Associates
ELECTRICAL ENGINEER Reid Crowther &
Partners
LANDSCAPE ARCHITECT Wendt Land Planning
PHOTOGRAPHER Martin Tessler
AWARDS RECEIVED
- Lieutenant Governor of British Columbia,
  Award of Merit, 1995

Dockside Green, Victoria, BC (2004-2009)

PROJECT Dockside Green
LOCATION Victoria, BC
CLIENT Windmill West, VanCity Enterprises
SIZE
- Site: 15 acres / 6 hectares
- Total Development: 30,000 sm of built mixed-use space
- Synergy (Phase I): 178,680 sf / 16,600 sm
- Balance (Phase II): 155,215 sf / 14,420 sm
- Inspiration (Phase III): 20,160 sf / 1,874 sm

DESIGN AND CONSTRUCTION
- Synergy (Phase I): Design 2004-2005; CONSTRUCTION 2006-2008
- Balance (Phase II): Design 2005-2006; CONSTRUCTION 2007-2009
- Inspiration (Phase III): Design 2007-2008; CONSTRUCTION 2008-2009

DESIGN TEAM
Perkins+Will:
- P. Busby, L. Chester, P. Cowcher, R. Drew, A. Fawkes, D. Kitazaki, R. Maas, S. Patterson, J. Skinner, A. Slawinski, T. Williams, B. Wakelin, G. Underhill

STRUCTURAL ENGINEER Read Jones Christoffersen
MECHANICAL ENGINEER Stantec
ELECTRICAL ENGINEER Stantec
CIVIL ENGINEER Worley Parsons Komex
CIVIL ENGINEER RCL Consulting
ECOLOGY/STORMWATER Aqua-Tex Scientific Consulting
GREEN BUILDING BuildGreen Consulting
COST CONSULTANT Payne Group
LANDSCAPE ARCHITECT PWL Partnership
ENVIRONMENTAL SOILS Quantum Environmental Remediation
SURVEYOR Focus Group
GEOTECHNICAL CONSULTANT C.N. Ryzuk & Associates
TRAFFIC CONSULTANT Boulevard Transportation Group
CONTRACTOR Farmer Constructors, Inc.
INTERIOR DESIGNER False Creek Design
CODE CONSULTANT Gage-Babcock & Associates
ENVELOPE CONSULTANT Morrison Hershfield
PHOTOGRAPHER Vince Klassen
AWARDS RECEIVED
- Dockside Green was named one of the first carbon neutral projects by the Clinton Climate Development Initiative, 2009
- Architectural Institute of British Columbia Special Jury Award, 2009
- AIA Committee on the Environment (COTE), Top Ten Green Projects, 2009
- Royal Architectural Institute of Canada, Green Building Award of Excellence, 2009
- AIA Seattle Committee on the Environment (COTE), What Makes it Green?, Regional Top 10 Green Project, 2009
- GLOBE Awards for Environmental Excellence in Urban Sustainability, 2008
- BC Hydro Power Smart Excellence Award, Innovation in Sustainable Design, 2007
- Smart Growth of British Columbia Awards, Process/Proposal Award, 2006
- RAIC National Urban Design Awards, Merit Award, Approved or Adopted Urban Design Plan, 2006
- *Canadian Architect,* Award of Excellence, 2005
- Canadian Urban Institute, Brownie Award, Best Overall Project, 2005
- Canadian Urban Institute, Brownie Award, Green Design and Technology, 2005
- Planning Institute of BC Innovation in Site Planning and Design Award, 2005

SUSTAINABILITY RATINGS
- Synergy (Phase I): LEED Platinum. This phase reached LEED Platinum at 63 points, making it the highest-scoring LEED Platinum Certified project in the world at the time.
- Inspiration (Phase II): LEED Platinum
- Balance (Phase III): LEED Platinum

REFERENCE TO PUBLICATIONS
- Kaid Benfield, "Is this the world's greenest neighborhood?" *The Atlantic,* August 24, 2011.
- Sara Hart, "Dockside Green: A Platinum Setting,"*GreenSource,* January 2009.
- "Dockside Green," *Metropolis,* October 2008, p. 134.
- "Dockside Green," *Urban Land,* October 2008, p. 71.
- Dockside Green Achieves Highest LEED Score Ever," *SABMag,* September/October 2008, p. 7.
- Zach Mortice, "Busby Perkins+Will's Dockside Green Places Its Bets on Record-Shattering Sustainability," *Architect,* September 26, 2008.
- "Dockside Green's integrated design team celebrates groundbreaking achievement," *Canadian Architect,* July 23, 2008.
- "Dockside Green recognized for sustainable design," *Globe Net,* June 22, 2006.

Dubai International Financial Centre, Dubai, United Arab Emirates (2006-2008)

PROJECT Dubai International Financial Centre (DIFC)
LOCATION Dubai, United Arab Emirates
CLIENT DIFC Central Complex
DESIGN 2006-2008
SIZE 3,000,000 sf / 279,000 sm
DESIGN TEAM
Perkins+Will:
- P. Busby, A. Charisius, J. Deutscher, B. Engel-Folchert, B. Greig, F. Jungen, I. Ilic, H. Lai, E. Lee, M. Nielsen, J. Rudd, A. Slawinski, Y. Sun, R. Maas, M. Visram, L. Woofter
STRUCTURAL ENGINEER MKA and Fast+Epp
MECHANICAL ENGINEER Integral Group (formerly Cobalt)
ELECTRICAL ENGINEER Integral Group (formerly Cobalt)
SUSTAINABILITY RATINGS Registered with the certification goal of LEED Gold.

Earth Sciences Building, University of British Columbia (UBC), Vancouver, BC (2009-2011)

PROJECT Earth Sciences Building, University of British Columbia
LOCATION Vancouver, BC
CLIENT UBC Properties Trust
DESIGN 2009-2010
CONSTRUCTION 2010-2011
SIZE 170,005 sf / 15,794 sm
DESIGN TEAM
Perkins+Will:
- S. Bergen, P. Busby, A. Chmiel, J. Deutscher, J. Gravenstein, J. Foit, H. Kao, S. Schou, E. Stedman
CONSTRUCTION MANAGER Bird Construction
CIVIL ENGINEER Core Group Consultants
STRUCTURAL ENGINEER Equilibrium Consulting
MECHANICAL ENGINEER Stantec Consulting
ELECTRICAL ENGINEER Acumen Engineering
PLUMBING ENGINEER Stantec Consulting
LANDSCAPE ARCHITECT Eckford + Associates
GEOTECHNICAL CONSULTANT Geo Pacific
CODE CONSULTANT GHL Consultants, Ltd.
ACOUSTICS CONSULTANT Brown Strachan
BUILDING ENVELOPE CONSULTANT JRS Engineering
AUDIO VISUAL CONSULTANT Mc Squared System Design Group
LABORATORY DESIGN Maples Argo Architects
COMMISSIONING AUTHORITY Airmec Systems, Ltd.
HAZARDOUS MATERIALS ABATEMENT ACM Environmental Corp.
PHOTOGRAPHER Martin Tessler
AWARDS RECEIVED
- AIBC Innovation Award, 2013
- AIA-CAE / SCUP Merit Award, Excellence in Architecture for a New Building, 2013
- Wood WORKS! BC Wood Design Awards, Institutional Wood Design – Large, 2013
- Forest Products Society / American Wood Council, Wood Innovation Engineering Award, 2012
SUSTAINABILITY RATINGS LEED Gold
REFERENCE TO PUBLICATIONS
- "Earth Sciences Building," *Arch Daily,* March 16, 2013: http://www.archdaily.com/343465/earth-sciences-building-perkins-will/

- James Gauer, "Earth Sciences Building," *GreenSource,* March/April 2013, p. 44-49
- "New Earth Sciences Building Opens at UBC," *Canadian Architect,* February 9, 2013.
URLS https://www.youtube.com/watch?v=z5beJygbTKO

Eau Claire Market Redevelopment, Calgary, AB (2013-2025)

PROJECT Eau Claire Market Redevelopment
LOCATION Calgary, AB
CLIENT Harvard Developments, Inc.
Design 2013-2017
CONSTRUCTION 2015-2025 (three phases)
SIZE 2,500,000 sf / 232,000 sm overall
(950,000 sf / 88,300 sm for Phase I)
DESIGN TEAM
Perkins+Will:
  • J. Bamberger, R. Beal, S. Bryce, P. Busby,
    A. Chan, J. Chang, K. Donaldson, R. Drew,
    J. Drohan, D. Hawthorne, G. Tierney, J. Till,
    S. Yu
ARCHITECTURAL CONSULTANT MBAC, Gibbs
Gage Architects
STRUCTURAL ENGINEER JC Kenyon Engineering,
Read Jones Christoffersen, Fast+Epp
MECHANICAL ENGINEER WSP Group
ELECTRICAL ENGINEER SMP Engineering
RENDERINGS Atchain
SUSTAINABILITY RATINGS Registered with the
certification goal of LEED Gold.
REFERENCE TO PUBLICATIONS
  • Rhiannon M. Kirkland, "New proposed plan for
    Eau Claire Market," *Avenue Calgary,* online,
    November 15, 2013.
URLS https://www.youtube.com/
watch?v=VWZM1wdWV5c

Ebco Aerospace Centre, Delta, BC (1986-1987)

PROJECT Ebco Aerospace Centre
LOCATION Delta, BC
CLIENT Ebco Industries, Ltd.
DESIGN 1986-1987
CONSTRUCTION 1987
SIZE 43,000 sf / 3,995 sm
DESIGN TEAM
Perkins+Will (formerly Busby Bridger
Architects):
  • J. Breshears, P. Bridger, A. Brown, P. Busby,
    B. Welty
STRUCTURAL ENGINEER Fast + Epp
AWARDS RECEIVED
  • Association of Consulting Engineers of
    Canada, Award of Excellence, 1990

Ebco Table, Delta, BC (1988)

PROJECT Ebco Table
LOCATION Delta, BC
CLIENT Ebco Aerospace
DESIGN 1988
DESIGN TEAM Designlines Canada
  • P. Barber, P. Busby, H. Eng, V. Nishi
CONTRACTOR Designlines Canada
STRUCTURAL ENGINEER Richard Smart
PHOTOGRAPHER Designlines Canada

EcoDensity, Vancouver, BC (2008)

PROJECT EcoDensity
LOCATION Vancouver, BC
CLIENT Perkins+Will
DESIGN 2008
DESIGN TEAM
Perkins+Will:
- R. Bragg, P. Busby, D. Dove, M. Driedger, V. Gilles, M. Hague, J. Huffman, M. Nielsen, M. Sachs, A. Slawinski, Z. Smith, E. Stedman, B. Wakelin, K. Wardle

ENERGY. ENVIRONMENT. EXPERIENTIAL LEARNING (EEEL), University of Calgary, Calgary, AB (2008-2011)

PROJECT ENERGY. ENVIRONMENT. EXPERIENTIAL LEARNING (EEEL), University of Calgary
LOCATION Calgary, AB
CLIENT University of Calgary
DESIGN 2008-2010
CONSTRUCTION 2010-2011
SIZE 264,050 sf / 24,531 sm
DESIGN TEAM
Perkins+Will:
- P. Busby, A. Chmiel, A. McCumber, R. Piccolo, S. Schou, E. Stedman
DESIGN PARTNER DIALOG
CONSTRUCTION MANAGEMENT Ellis Don Construction
PROJECT MANAGERS Duke Evans, Inc.
STRUCTURAL ENGINEER RJC Engineers and DIALOG
MECHANICAL ENGINEER DIALOG
ELECTRICAL ENGINEER Stebnicki + Partners
LANDSCAPE ARCHITECT O2 Planning + Design
CIVIL ENGINEER AECOM
BUILDING ENVELOPE Building Envelope Engineering
CODE CONSULTANT Senez Reed Calder
ACOUSTIC CONSULTANT FFA
QUANTITY SURVEYOR Spiegel Skillen
PHOTOGRAPHER Tom Arban
AWARDS RECEIVED
- The City of Calgary Mayors Urban Design Award, Civic Design Projects Category, 2013
- AIBC Special Jury Award For Animating the Program, 2013
- AIA-CAE/SCUP, Excellence in Architecture for a New Building, Honor Award, 2012
- The Alberta Association of Architects, The Saskatchewan Association of Architects and The Manitoba Association of Architects, Prairie Design Award of Merit, 2012
- Consulting Engineers of Alberta, Award of Excellence–Building Engineering Category, 2012
SUSTAINABILITY RATINGS LEED Platinum
REFERENCE TO PUBLICATIONS
- Alexandra McIntosh, "Bedazzled Box - A shiny addition to the University of Calgary provides a vibrant meeting place for students while achieving ambitious sustainability goals," *Canadian Architect,* October 2013.
- "Energy Environment Experiential Learning / Perkins+Will + DIALOG," ArchDaily, April 9, 2013. http://www.archdaily.com/356805/energy-environment-experiential-learning-perkins-will/?utm_source=dlvr.it&utm_medium=twitter
- Edward Keegan, "Energy.Environment. Experiential Learning," *Architect,* March 2012, p. 92-98.

EyeMasters Stores, various locations across Canada (1990-1992)

PROJECT EyeMasters Stores
LOCATION Vancouver, BC; Calgary, AB; Toronto, ON; Edmonton, AB
CLIENT Eyemasters Canada, Ltd.
DESIGN 1990-1992
CONSTRUCTION 1990-1992
DESIGN TEAM
Perkins+Will (formerly Busby Bridger Architects):
• M. Beckett, P. Busby, A. Feldman, J. Huffman, K. Humphreys, C. Odinga, D. Salk, S. Verbeek
CONTRACTOR Designlines Canada
PHOTOGRAPHER Martin Tessler

Fremont Warm Springs, Fremont, CA

PROJECT Fremont Warm Springs Community Plan
LOCATION Fremont, CA
CLIENT City of Fremont
SIZE 879 acres
DESIGN 2010-2014
DESIGN TEAM
Perkins+Will:
• K. Alschuler, D. Dornan, N. Friedman, R. Song
CIVIL ENGINEER BKF
ECONOMIC CONSULTANT EPS
TRAFFIC CONSULTANTS Fehr & Peers
ENVIRONMENTAL CONSULTANT First Carbon Solutions
RENDERINGS Chris Foyd
REFERENCE TO PUBLICATIONS
• John King, "Fremont's Imaginative Planning puts San Francisco's to Shame," *San Francisco Chronicle,* September 20, 2014.

Future of Gardiner Expressway: Environmental Assessment and Urban Design Study, Toronto, ON (2010-2015)

PROJECT Future of Gardiner Expressway: Urban Design Study and Environmental Assessment
LOCATION Toronto, ON
CLIENT Waterfront Toronto
DESIGN 2010-2015
DESIGN TEAM
Perkins+Will:
• K. Alschuler, L. Giaramidaro, G. Silwal, K. Oh
ENVIRONMENTAL ENGINEER Dillon Consulting Limited
CIVIL ENGINEER Morrison Hershfield
LANDSCAPE ARCHITECT Hargreaves Associates
ECONOMIST HR&A Advisors
URLS http://www.gardinereast.ca/

Gilmore Skytrain Station, Burnaby, BC (1999-2001)

PROJECT Gilmore Skytrain Station
LOCATION Burnaby, BC
CLIENT Rapid Transit Project Office
SIZE 24,700 sf / 2,294 sm
DESIGN 1999
CONSTRUCTION 2000-2001
DESIGN TEAM
Perkins+Will (formerly Busby + Associates Architects):
  • B. Billingsley, P. Bodonarus, M. Bonaventura, P. Busby, S. Chevalier, T. Mullock, M. Nielsen, R. Peck, A. Slawinski
CONTRACTOR Dominion Construction
STRUCTURAL ENGINEER Fast + Epp
MECHANICAL ENGINEER Klohn-Crippen
ELECTRICAL ENGINEER Agra Simons
LANDSCAPE ARCHITECT Durante Kreuk
PUBLIC ARTIST Muse Atelier
PHOTOGRAPHER Nic Lehoux
AWARDS RECEIVED
  • The Wood Design Awards, Citation Award, 2002

Giraf Table (1998)

PROJECT Giraf Table
CLIENT Busby + Associates Architects and Componance, Inc.
DESIGN AND CONSTRUCTION 998
DESIGN TEAM
Componance, Inc.:
  • P. Busby, S. Schou
PHOTOGRAPHER Busby + Associates Architects

Great Northern Way Business Park, Vancouver, BC (1998-1999)

PROJECT Great Northern Way Technology Park
LOCATION Vancouver, BC
CLIENT Finning International, Inc.
DESIGN 1998-1999
SIZE 3,500,000 sf / 325,160 sm
DESIGN TEAM
Perkins+Will (formerly Busby + Associates Architects):
  • B. Billingsley, P. Bodnarus, P. Busby, J. Huffman, S. Ockwell, S. Schou, A. Slawinski
ARCHITECTURAL CONSULTANTS MBT
PLANNING CONSULTANT Moodie Consultants, Arkle Development Services, Spaxman Consulting Group
CIVIL ENGINEER Robertson Planning Services
LANDSCAPE ARCHITECT EDAW
TRAFFIC PLANNING ND Lea
RENDERINGS Ron Love

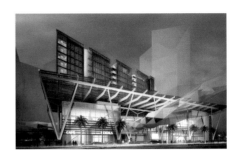

Great River Energy Headquarters, Maple Grove, MN (2005-2008)

PROJECT Great River Energy Headquarters
LOCATION Maple Grove, MN
CLIENT Great River Energy
DESIGN 2005-2006
CONSTRUCTION 2006-2008
DESIGN TEAM
Perkins+Will:
- T. Beck, D. Dimond, J. Foran, M. Hammer, M. Hayes-Gordon, E. Heinen, D. Koenen, T. Layne, D. Little, K. Martenson, R. Philstrom, D. Pierce, L. Pool, D. Sachs, G. Voermans, J. Wollak
ENERGY MODELING The Weidt Group
STRUCTURAL ENGINEER BKBM Engineers
MECHANICAL ENGINEER Dunham
ELECTRICAL ENGINEER Dunham
CIVIL ENGINEER RLK Incorporated
LIGHTING DESIGN Dunham
INTERIOR DESIGN Perkins+Will
CONSTRUCTION MANAGEMENT McGough Construction
LANDSCAPE ARCHITECT Close Landscape Architects
PHOTOGRAPHER Perkins+Will
AWARDS RECEIVED
- Members Choice Award, IIDA Northland Chapter FAB Awards, 2010
- Sustainable Design, IIDA Northland Chapter FAB Awards, 2010
- AIA/COTE Top Ten Green Projects Award, 2009
- AIA MN Honor Award, 2009
- SARA National Design Award of Excellence, 2009
- AIA-Minneapolis Merit Award Winner, 2009
- American Planning Association, Minnesota Chapter, Public Education Category Honor Award, 2008
- Consulting-Specifying Engineering New CONSTRUCTION Gold ARC Award, 2008
- Building Excellence Awards, Aggregate & Ready Mix Large Commercial Building project Award 2008
- TEKNE Green Award, 2008
- Minnesota Governor's Award for Pollution Control, 2008

- Minnesota Waste Wise Leader Award, 2008
SUSTAINABILITY RATINGS LEED Platinum
REFERENCE TO PUBLICATIONS
- "Geoexchange Systems Drill Into Clean Energy," *Building Magazine,* October 2011.
- "Underfloor air distribution, how to get the details right," *Building Design +Construction,* August 2011.
- "Great River Energy HQ," *Minnesota Real Estate Journal,* 27(1). January 2011.
- "Perkins+Will at 75: Sustaining Sustainability,"*GoProfile,* Winter 2011, p. 12-14
- "Evolving Efficiency," *High Performing Buildings,* Summer 2011, p. 52-57.
- "Great River Energy Headquarters," *Traveler,* No.17, April 2010. (Chinese)
- "Display Case," *Architecture Minnesota,* March/April 2010, p. 32-51
- Carlo Broto, *Eco-Friendly Architecture,* Linksbooks: Barcelona, Spain (2010): p. 190
- "Peer recognition, engaged clients motivate and inspire architect," *Minneapolis Business Journal,* December 4, 2009, p. 11.
- "Setting a Green Example,"*GreenSource.* July/August 2009, p. 69-71.
- "MEP Technologies for Eco-Effective Buildings," *Building Design +Construction,* July 2009.
- "Headquarters Case Study: Powerful Paradigm," *Today's Facility Manager,* June 2009.
- "Platinum Dreams," *Consulting-Specifying Engineer,* December 2008, p. 26-28
- "Great River Energy HQs in Maple Grove achieved LEED Certification," *Minnesota Real Estate Journal,* November 2008, p. 21
- "Great River Energy Seeks LEED Platinum Status for New Maple Grove Headquarters," *USGBC Mississippi Headwater Chapter Transformation,* v (2), Summer 2008.
- "Energy Star," Architecture Minnesota. January/February 2008, p. 44-47.
- "Great River Energy's High-Performance Headquarters Will Set New Standards in Sustainable Design," *Twin Cities Business,* September 2006, p. 129.
- "Maple Grove approves 1st phase of GRE headquarters." *Press & News,* September 20, 2006.

King Abdullah Financial District Mixed-Use Tower, Riyadh, Saudi Arabia (2009-2015)

PROJECT Confidential Mixed-Use Tower
LOCATION Riyadh, Saudi Arabia
CLIENT Ministry of Finance
DESIGN 2009-2012
Construction): 2012-2015
SIZE 521,511 sf / 48,450 sm
DESIGN TEAM
Perkins+Will:
- L. Briney, P. Busby, W. Dahl, J. Deutscher, A. Espinoza, B. Greig, J. Huffman, J. Meyer, R. Maas, Y. Madkour, J. Wong, L. Woofter, J. Yum, F. Zahr
CONTRACTOR Saudi Binladin Group
STRUCTURAL ENGINEER Dar Al-Handasah (Shair and Partners)
MECHANICAL ENGINEER Dar Al-Handasah (Shair and Partners)
ELECTRICAL ENGINEER Dar Al-Handasah (Shair and Partners)
SUSTAINABILITY RATINGS LEED Gold

 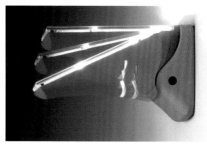 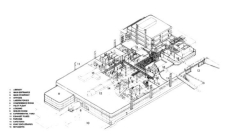

Kingsway Pedestrian Bridge, Burnaby, BC (2007-2008)

PROJECT Kingsway Pedestrian Bridge
LOCATION Burnaby, BC
CLIENT City of Burnaby
DESIGN 2007
CONSTRUCTION 2008
DESIGN TEAM
Perkins+Will:
• P. Busby, J. Huffman, D. Kitazaki, R. Maas
CONTRACTOR Dominion CONSTRUCTION
STRUCTURAL ENGINEER Fast + Epp
MECHANICAL ENGINEER Yoneda & Associates
ELECTRICAL ENGINEER RFA Consulting Electrical Engineers
LANDSCAPE ARCHITECT PWL Partnership Landscape Architects
CIVIL ENGINEER R.F. Binnie & Associates, Ltd.
GEOTECHNICAL CONSULTANT Trow Associates, Inc.
PHOTOGRAPHER Martin Tessler
AWARDS RECEIVED
• The Consulting Engineers of British Columbia, Award of Excellence in Transportation, 2009
• Wood Design and Building Award Winner, 2009
• Outstanding Project -National Council of Structural Engineers Association, 2009
REFERENCE TO PUBLICATIONS
• Canadian Wood Council, *Wood in Transportation,* December 2010.

L-01 'Gill' Wall Sconce (1991)

PROJECT L-01 'Gill' Wall Sconce
CLIENT Designlines Canada
DESIGN 1991
DESIGN TEAM
Designlines Canada
• P. Busby, A. Feldman, K. Humphreys, D. Salk
PHOTOGRAPHER Designlines Canada
AWARDS RECEIVED
• 1992 VIRTU Canadian Industrial Design Prize, 1992

MacMillan Bloedel Research and Development Centre, Burnaby, BC (1987-1989)

PROJECT MacMillan Bloedel Research and Development Centre
LOCATION Burnaby, BC
CLIENT MacMillan Bloedel, Ltd.
DESIGN 1987-1988
CONSTRUCTION 1988-1989
SIZE 129,167 sf / 12,000 sm
DESIGN TEAM
Perkins+Will (formerly Busby Bridger Architects):
• R. Bremer, P. Bridger, P. Busby, S. F. Hu-Moore, U. Mueller, P. Pierce, A. Slawinski
CONTRACTOR Farmer Construction
PROJECT MANAGEMENT Hanscomb Consultants
STRUCTURAL ENGINEER Paul Fast & Associates
MECHANICAL ENGINEER D.W. Thomson Consultants
ELECTRICAL ENGINEER Mahanti Engineering
FIRE CODE ENGINEER Rolf Jensen Associates

Marine Gateway, Vancouver, BC (2005-2015)

PROJECT Marine Gateway
LOCATION Vancouver, BC
CLIENT PCI Developments
DESIGN 2005-2009
CONSTRUCTION 2012-2015
SIZE 860,000 sf / 81,300 sm
DESIGN TEAM
Perkins+Will:
 • A. Baldwin, A. Boivin, R. Bragg, L. Briney, P.
   Busby, A. Charisius, D. Dove, M. Haberli, J.
   Ho, H. Lai, D. Newby, R. Piccolo, M. Richter,
   K. Rowe, J. Rudd, S. Schou, A. Shum, N.
   Shuttleworth, J. Tomas Nunez, Y. Watanabe,
   E. Wolpin
STRUCTURAL ENGINEER Glotman Simpson
MECHANICAL ENGINEER MCW Engineering
ELECTRICAL ENGINEER Nemetz S/A &
Associates, Ltd.
LANDSCAPE ARCHITECT PWL Partnership
CONTRACTOR Ledcor Group
ACOUSTIC CONSULTANT Brown Strachan
GEOTECHNICAL CONSULTANT MMM Group
TRAFFIC CONSULTANT MMM Group
WIND/ODOR CONSULTANT RWDI
AWARDS RECEIVED
 • Precast Concrete Architectural Recognition
   Firm Award, Canadian Precast/Pre-stressed
   Concrete Institute, 2012
SUSTAINABILITY RATINGS Registered with the
certification goal of LEED Gold
URLS http://marinegateway.com

**City of Vancouver Materials Testing
Laboratory, Vancouver, BC (1997-1999)**

PROJECT City of Vancouver Materials Testing
Laboratory
LOCATION Vancouver, BC
SIZE 4,284 sf / 398 sm
CLIENT City of Vancouver, Engineering Services
DESIGN 1997-1998
CONSTRUCTION 1998-1999
DESIGN TEAM
Perkins+Will (formerly Busby + Associates
Architects):
 • P. Busby, S. Chevalier, M. McColl, D.
   Thiruchittampalam
STRUCTURAL ENGINEER Fast + Epp
MECHANICAL ENGINEER Keen Engineering
ELECTRICAL ENGINEER Reid Crowther &
Partners
PHOTOGRAPHER Martin Tessler
AWARDS RECEIVED
 • Innovation Award, Architecture Institute of BC,
   2001
 • International Design Resource Award, 2001
 • Award of Merit (Structural), Consulting
   Engineers of British Columbia, 2000
 • American Institute of Architects, "What Makes
   it Green" Exhibit, 2000
REFERENCE TO PUBLICATIONS
 • "Building Vancouver's new materials testing
   facility presented challenges," *Business in
   Vancouver,* March 7 - 13, 2000.

**Metro McNair Clinical Laboratory and Office,
Burnaby, BC (1994-1996)**

PROJECT Metro McNair Clinical Laboratory and
Office
LOCATION Burnaby, BC
SIZE 46,300 sf / 4,300 sm
CLIENT MDS Metro
DESIGN 1994
CONSTRUCTION 1995-1996
DESIGN TEAM
Perkins+Will (formerly Busby Bridger
Architects):
 • P. Bridger, P. Busby, S. Gushe, E. Maifredi, A.
   Slawinski, A. Vaughan
DESIGN BUILD CONTRACTOR Ledcor Industries
STRUCTURAL ENGINEER Fast + Epp
MECHANICAL ENGINEER D.W. Thomson
ELECTRICAL ENGINEER Reid Crowther &
Partners
LANDSCAPE ARCHITECT Reeve MacDougall
INTERIOR DESIGNER Gittens Mason
PHOTOGRAPHER Martin Tessler
AWARDS RECEIVED
 • BC Hydro Power Smart Award of Excellence,
   Commercial Building, 1996
REFERENCE TO PUBLICATIONS
 • "Clinical Precision - Research Buildings"
   Canadian Architect, June 1996, p. 26-28

Mount Pleasant Centre, Vancouver, BC (2004-2009)

PROJECT Mount Pleasant Centre
LOCATION Vancouver, BC
CLIENT City of Vancouver Corporate Services, Vancouver Park Board, Vancouver Public Library, City of Vancouver Social Planning Department
DESIGN 2003-2004
CONSTRUCTION 2004-2009
SIZE 135,528 sf / 12,591 sm
DESIGN TEAM
Perkins+Will (formerly Busby + Associates Architects):
  • K. Abraham, R. Bens, J. Belisle, S. Brent, P. Busby, J. Doble, D. Dove, S. Mani, T. Maunu, G. Miu, D. Pepin, K. Robertson, S. Schou
STRUCTURAL ENGINEER CY Loh and Associates
MECHANICAL ENGINEER Keen Engineering
ELECTRICAL ENGINEER Schenke Bawol Engineers
CODE CONSULTANT Gage Babcock
TRAFFIC CONSULTANT Hamilton Associates
COST CONSULTANT Jim Bush & Associates
ENVELOPE CONSULTANT BC Building Science
LANDSCAPE ARCHITECT Durante Kreuk
GEOTECHNICAL CONSULTANT Trow Associates, Inc.
ENVIRONMENTAL CONSULTANT Keystone Environmental, Ltd.
ACOUSTICAL CONSULTANT Brown Strachan Associates
COMMISSIONING AUTHORITY KD Engineering Co.
PHOTOGRAPHER Martin Tessler
AWARDS RECEIVED
  • Precast Concrete Architectural Recognition Firm Award Canadian Precast/Pre-stressed Concrete Institute, 2012
  • Georgia Straight Best of Vancouver Awards, Best Community Centre, Second Place, 2010
SUSTAINABILITY RATINGS LEED Gold
REFERENCE TO PUBLICATIONS
  • Jim Taggart, "Mount Pleasant Centre," *SABMag*, December 2010, 20-27.
  • Claudia Kwan, "Centre directs community to its centre," *Vancouver Sun,* November 7, 2009.
  • Cheryl Mah, "Serving a community," *Design Quarterly*, Summer 2009, 12-13.

Nicola Valley Institute of Technology, Merritt, BC (1999-2001)

PROJECT Nicola Valley Institute of Technology (NVIT)
LOCATION Merritt, BC
CLIENT Nicola Valley Institute of Technology/ University College of the Cariboo
DESIGN 1999
CONSTRUCTION 2000-2001
SIZE 48,631 sf / 4,520 sm
DESIGN TEAM
Perkins+Will (formerly Busby + Associates Architects):
  • P. Busby, R. Drew, V. Gilles, S. Gushe, R. Maas, S. Schou, A. Slawinski, A. Waugh, B. Wakelin, N. Webster, T. Winkler
STRUCTURAL ENGINEER Equilibrium Consulting, Inc.
MECHANICAL ENGINEER Keen Engineering
ELECTRICAL ENGINEER Earth Tech Canada
CODE CONSULTANT Pioneer Consultants
CIVIL ENGINEERING AND LANDSCAPE ARCHITECTURE True Engineering
PHOTOGRAPHER Nic Lehoux
AWARDS RECEIVED
  • AIA Committee on Education/SCUP, Excellence in Architecture Award, 2005
  • Canadian Wood Council, Wood Works High-Performance Building Award, 2005
  • Vancouver Regional Construction Association Awards of Excellence, General Contractors Award of Merit (under $10 Million category), 2002
  • Governor General of Canada, Medal for Excellence in Architecture, 2002
  • International Green Building Challenge, 2002
  • Lieutenant Governor of British Columbia, Medal for Excellence, 2002
  • The Wood Design Awards, Citation Award, 2002
  • AIA "What Makes it Green?" Exhibit, 2001
REFERENCE TO PUBLICATIONS
  • "Nicola Valley Institute of Technology," *Design Exchange,* May 2009, p. 35.
  • "Nicola Valley Institute of Technology in Merritt," *Archinnovations,* October 21, 2008, online.

Normand Maurice Building, Montreal, QC (2002-2006)

PROJECT Normand Maurice Building
LOCATION Montreal, QC
CLIENT Public Works and Government Services Canada (PWGSC)
DESIGN 2002
CONSTRUCTION 2003-2006
SIZE 169,000 sf / 15,700 sm
DESIGN TEAM
Perkins+Will (formerly Busby + Associate Architects):
  • P. Busby, M. Galloway, R. Glover, S. Gushe, M. Labrie, D. Petrovic, S. Schou, A. Slawinski, B. Wakelin
ABCP Architecture & Urbanisme:
  • S. Allaire, R. Baril, A. Bergeron, F. Berthiaume, C. Genest, A. King
Beauchamp-Bourbeau Architectes:
  • F. Belair, G. Beauchamp, C. Bourbeau, G. Cardinal, I. Chan, A. Desroches, D. Dewar, J. Gauthier, S. Girard, L. Houde, D. Lacombe, S. Leclerc, P. Lessard, B. Paquet, C. Pitre, D. Savage, A. Sideco, H. Proulx, R. Zamarato
MECHANICAL ENGINEER Pageau Morel et Associés
ELECTRICAL ENGINEER Pageau Morel et Associés
STRUCTURAL ENGINEER Saia Deslauriers Kadanoff
STRUCTURAL ENGINEER Fast + Epp
CODE CONSULTANT Serge Arsenault
GREEN MECHANICAL CONSULTANT Keen Engineering
CONTRACTOR Decarel, Inc.
PHOTOGRAPHER Marc Cramer
PHOTOGRAPHER Nic Lehoux
AWARDS RECEIVED
  • ASHRAE Technology Award International Award, First place in New Institutional Building category, 2009
  • Excellence and Leadership Award from Canadian GeoExchange Coalition, 2008
  • Energia Award, Sustainable buildings - Green buildings category, 2007
  • Canadian Institute of Steel Construction, Award of Excellence in Steel Construction, Green Building Category, 2005
  • Contech Awards, Innovation in Sustainable Development, 2003
SUSTAINABILITY RATINGS LEED Gold

REFERENCE TO PUBLICATIONS
- David Sokol, "Normand Maurice Building" *GreenSource,* September/October, 2008, p. 56-61.
- Brian Wakelin, "Quebec LEED project hail government direction in sustainability," *SABMag*, March-April 2008, p. 27-32.

Oltremare Marine Theme Park, Riccione, Italy (1999-2004)

PROJECT Oltremare Marine Theme Park
LOCATION Riccione, Italy
CLIENT Oltremare, s.r.l.
DESIGN 1999-2001
CONSTRUCTION 2001-2004
SIZE 215,278 sf / 20,000 sm
DESIGN TEAM
Perkins+Will (formerly Busby + Associates Architects):
- M. Bonaventura, P. Busby, S. Chevalier, S. Edwards, V. Gillies, J. Huffman, G. Lorenzon, R. Maas, T. Mullock, M. Nielsen, R. Peck, D. Petrovic, A. Slawinski, S. Vannini, B. Wakelin

EXHIBIT DESIGNER Aldrich Pears Associates
LIFE SUPPORT SPECIALIST Ted Maranda
STRUCTURAL ENGINEER Read Jones Christoffersen
MECHANICAL ENGINEER Keen Engineering
ELECTRICAL ENGINEER Reid Crowther & Partners
ANIMAL HUSBANDRY Joe Geraci
CONCEPT MANAGER Leandro Stanzani
AWARDS RECEIVED
- Canadian Architect Award of Excellence, 2000

REFERENCE TO PUBLICATIONS
- "Parco Oltremare a Riccione," *TSPORT,* September/October 2004.

One Wall Centre, Vancouver, BC (1996-2001)

PROJECT One Wall Centre
LOCATION Vancouver, BC
CLIENT Wall Financial Corporation
DESIGN 1996-1998
CONSTRUCTION 1998-2001
SIZE 462,000 sf / 42,900 sm
DESIGN TEAM
Perkins+Will (formerly Busby + Associates Architects):
- P. Busby, B. Billingsley, B. Ellis, C. Eveleigh, J. Heinen, J. Huffman, M. Nielsen, S. Palmier, R. Piccolo, S. Schou, A. Slawinski

Wall Design Group:
- R. Emslie, B. Wall, P. Wall

CONSTRUCTION MANAGER Siemens Development Corp.
STRUCTURAL ENGINEER Glotman Simpson
MECHANICAL ENGINEER Keen Engineering
ELECTRICAL ENGINEER Arnold Nemetz & Assoc.
LANDSCAPE ARCHITECT Phillips Farevaag Smallenberg
CERTIFIED PROFESSIONAL Pioneer Consultants
GEOTECHNICAL CONSULTANT Geopacific Consultants
TRAFFIC CONSULTANT Bunt & Associates
INTERIOR DESIGNER Mitchell Freedland Design
TRAFFIC CONSULTANT Bunt & Associates
PHOTOGRAPHER Nic Lehoux / Martin Tessler
AWARDS RECEIVED
- Association of Canadian Consulting Engineering Awards, First Place, 2002
- Consulting Engineers of BC, Award of Excellence, 2002
- Skyscrapers.com Award, Skyscraper of the Year, 2001

REFERENCE TO PUBLICATIONS
- "Towering Wall Centre breaks ground and rules," *Westender*, June 10-16, 1999.

Ottawa Confederation LRT Line, Ottawa, ON (2010-2017)

PROJECT Ottawa Confederation Line
LOCATION Ottawa, ON
CLIENT Capital Transit Partners
DESIGN 2010-2012
CONSTRUCTION 2014-2017
AREA 13 stations (10 above / 3 below grade), 394 f / 120 m platforms each
DESIGN TEAM
Perkins+Will:
- J. Belisle, J. Bielun, L. Briney, S. Briney, S. Bryce, P. Busby, M. Cunningham, J. Doble, B. Engle-Folchert, L. Espino, M. Haberli, A. Knorr, S. Kohut, M. Lampard, E. Ma, Y. Madkour, T. Martin, M. Nielsen, C. Osbourne, R. Piccolo, M. I. Thicke, E. Wolpin, J. Yum, F. Zahr
STRUCTURAL ENGINEER URS
MECHANICAL ENGINEER URS
ELECTRICAL ENGINEER URS
RENDERINGS Atchain
AWARDS RECEIVED
- Gold Award for Transportation Innovation, Canadian Council for Public-Private Partnerships, 2013
REFERENCE TO PUBLICATIONS
- "Realism And Excellence / Awards of Excellence 2013," *Canadian Architect,* December 2013: p. 11-18: http://www.canadianarchitect.com/news/awards-of-excellence-2013-realism-and-excellence/1002793990/?&er=NA
URLS http://ww.confederationline.ca

Pemberton Air Terminal, Pemberton, BC (1987-1989)

PROJECT Pemberton Air Terminal
LOCATION Pemberton, BC
SIZE 12,917 sf / 1,200 sm
CLIENT Municipality of Pemberton
DESIGN 1987-1989
DESIGN TEAM
Perkins+Will (formerly Busby Bridger Architects)
- P. Busby, R. Bremer, C. Phillips, J. Huffman, A. Slawinski
COST CONSULTANT Hanscomb
TRANSPORTATION CONSULTANT N.D. Lea Consultants, Ltd.
STRUCTURAL, MECHANICAL, ELECTRICAL, AND CIVIL ENGINEER Fenco Lavalin, Inc.

Pier 1, San Francisco, CA (1999-2001)

PROJECT Pier 1
LOCATION San Francisco, California
CLIENT AMB Property Corporation + Port of San Francisco
DESIGN 1999-2000
CONSTRUCTION 2000-2001
DESIGN TEAM
Perkins+Will (formerly SMWM):
- J. Long, C. Simon
HISTORIC PRESERVATION ARCHITECT Page & Turnbull, Inc.
ASSOCIATED ARCHITECT Tom Bloszies Aguila (for Port of San Francisco offices and Pier One Deli)
MECHANICAL ENGINEER Flack & Kurtz
STRUCTURAL ENGINEER Rutherford & Chekene
CIVIL ENGINEER Olivia Chen Consultants
ELECTRICAL ENGINEER C+N Engineers
MARITIME ENGINEER Moffatt & Nichol
PHOTOGRAPHER Tim Hursley and Richard Barnes
AWARDS RECEIVED
- AIA Committee on the Environment Award, 2002
- AIA SF Green Design Award, 2004
REFERENCE TO PUBLICATIONS
- "Pier 1, San Francisco," *Architettura OFX International Magazine Architecture Design Contract,* no.68, 2002.
URLS http://prologispier1.com/

Pioneer Pedestrian Bridge, Surrey, BC (2009-2011)

PROJECT Pioneer Pedestrian Bridge
LOCATION Surrey, BC
CLIENT City of Surrey
DESIGN 2009-2010
CONSTRUCTION 2010-2011
DESIGN TEAM
Perkins+Will:
- P. Busby, R. Bremer, C. Phillips, J. Huffman, A. Slawinski

PROJECT ENGINEER Associated Engineering
GEOTECHNICAL CONSULTANT Thurber Engineering, Ltd.
LANDSCAPE ARCHITECT space2place
ARTISTIC LIGHTING EOS Light Media
PHOTOGRAPHER Perkins+Will
URLS https://www.youtube.com/watch?v=ntVCwLgbEyY#t=107
https://www.youtube.com/watch?v=mG7lF55kGw8

Plan Abu Dhabi, Abu Dhabi, United Arab Emirates (2005-2007)

PROJECT Plan Abu Dhabi 2030
LOCATION Abu Dhabi, United Arab Emirates
CLIENT Abu Dhabi Executive Affairs Authority Development Co., Ltd
DESIGN 2006-2010
DESIGN TEAM
Perkins+Will:
- P. Busby, M. Cocievera, J. Loewen, M. Nielsen, A. Slawinski

DESIGN PARTNERS
- L. Beasley, Beasley and Associates, Vancouver, BC
- Civitas Urban Design and Planning, Vancouver, BC
- John Buck, John Buck Company, Chicago, USA
- David Camp, London, UK
- Herbert Dreiseitl, Atelier Dreisleitl, Ueberlingen, Germany
- David Fields, Nelson/Nygaard Associates, New York, USA
- Michael Flanigan, City of Vancouver, Vancouver, Canada
- Jacquie Forbes-Roberts, City of Vancouver, Vancouver, Canada
- Robert France, Harvard Graduate School of Design, Cambridge, USA
- Alan Jacobs, Cityworks, San Francisco, USA
- Huub Juurlink, Juurlink & Geluk, Rotterdam, The Netherlands
- Lon LaClaire, City of Vancouver, Vancouver, Canada
- Elizabeth MacDonald, Cityworks / University of California at Berkeley, Berkeley, USA
- Paul Murphy, ARUP, Manchester, England
- Jaakko van't Spijker, Sputnik, Rotterdam, The Netherlands
- Jeffrey Tumlin, Nelson/Nygaard Consulting Associates, San Francisco, USA

AWARDS RECEIVED
- Planning Institute of British Columbia Award, 2008
- Canadian Institute of Planners Award, 2008
- GLOBE Award, Excellence in Urban Sustainability Finalist, 2008

REFERENCE TO PUBLICATIONS
- Kathryn Engle, "The Canadians," *Slick World,* September/October 2010, p. 20-25.

Point Wells, Snohomish County, WA (2009-2015)

PROJECT Point Wells
LOCATION Unincorporated Snohomish County, WA
CLIENT BSRE Point Wells, affiliated with Blue Square Real Estate
SIZE 61 acres / 25 hectares; 3081 Units
DESIGN 2009-2011
CONSTRUCTION Projected to start in 2015
DESIGN TEAM
Perkins+Will:
- P. Busby, K. Kornovich, D. Seng, G. Smith, C. Stinn, D. Streeter

CONTRACTOR TBD
STRUCTURAL ENGINEER Coughlin Porter Lundeen
ELECTRICAL ENGINEER Sparling
LANDSCAPE ARCHITECT Peter Walker Partners
CIVIL ENGINEER SvR, Inc.
ENVIRONMENTAL, TRAFFIC ENGINEER David Evans Associates
RENDERING Tim Wells
SUSTAINABILITY RATINGS Designed to meet Net Zero carbon and Puget Sound Regional Council Vision 2040 goals. The planned development will take on the remediation of this brown-field site, convert it to a visionary community and move towards sustainable prosperity by striving for a 'carbon neutral' status.
REFERENCE TO PUBLICATIONS
- Noah Haglund, "High-rise waterfront planned for Woodway shoreline," *Herald Net (Seattle),* January 28, 2011.

URL http://pointwells.com/

Princess Nora Bint Abdulrahman University, Riyadh, Saudi Arabia (2009-2011)

PROJECT Princess Nora Bint Abdulrahman University (PNU)
LOCATION Riyadh, Saudi Arabia
CLIENT Kingdom of Saudi Arabia - Ministry of Higher Education
DESIGN AND CONSTRUCTION 2009-2011
SIZE 32,000,000 sf / 3,000,000 sm
DESIGN TEAM
Perkins+Will:
Designated Design Leads:
- Master Plan, Campus Architecture: J. Hajjar, Director Architecture – Dar Al-Handasah (Shair and Partners), D. Hansen
- Administration Buildings: D. Hansen
- K-12 School:S. Miller
- Academic Campus:P. Bosch
- Student Union: S. Miller
- Health Sciences Campus: A. Williams
- Research Center: A. Williams
- Sports & Recreation: D. Hansen, C. Knutson
- Academic Medical Center: D. Hansen, R. Stelmarski
CONTRACTOR Saudi Binladin Group
STRUCTURAL ENGINEER Dar Al-Handasah (Shair and Partners)
MECHANICAL ENGINEER Dar Al-Handasah (Shair and Partners)
ELECTRICAL ENGINEER Dar Al-Handasah (Shair and Partners)
PHOTOGRAPHER Bill Lyons
SUSTAINABILITY RATINGS The majority of the Princess Nora University campus buildings are registered with certification goals of LEED Gold and LEED Certified. At the time the projects were registered, they doubled the number of LEED projects in Saudi Arabia.
REFERENCE TO PUBLICATIONS
- Jean Nayar, "Princess Nora Bint Abdulrahman University," *Contract,* March 6, 2014.
- Lamar Anderson, "Perkins+Will Completes Women's University in Saudi Arabia," *Architectural Record,* November 5, 2013.

Profile X F1 Podium (1999-2000)

PROJECT Profile X F1 Podium
CLIENT Profile Projex International, Inc.
DESIGN 1999-2000
DESIGN TEAM
Perkins+Will (formerly Busby + Associates Architects):
- P. Busby, S. Schou, A. Slawinski
STRUCTURAL ENGINEER Fast + Epp
URLS http://www.youtube.com/watch?v=Ev3n-5JXRsE http://www.youtube.com/watch?v=E6hFDqBZoQc

Regenerative Design Framework (2009-ongoing)

PROJECT Regenerative Design Framework
CLIENT Collaborative research with the University of British Columbia
DESIGN 2009 -ongoing
DESIGN TEAM
Perkins+Will:
- L. Briney, P. Busby, R. Guenther, T. Layne, P. McEvoy, D. Pierce, A. Pilon, P. Syrett, J. Till, K. Wardle
- University of British Columbia: R. Cole, and students

Resilient San Francisco, RDoC (2013)

PROJECT Resilient San Francisco - Rapidly Deployable Health Clinic "RDoC"
CLIENT Public Architecture
DESIGN 2013
DESIGN TEAM
Perkins+Will:
- M. Bardin, A. Chikhale, A. Iwan, B. Janak, A. Killgore, K. Macosko, K. Raines, G. Srapyan, R. Walters
STRUCTURAL ENGINEER Degenkolb Engineers
MEP ENGINEER Mazzetti Engineers
HEALTHCARE PARTNER UCSF Alliance Health Project
URLS http://blog.perkinswill.com/building_resilient_communities_rdoc/

Revenue Canada Office, Surrey, BC (1997-1998)

PROJECT Revenue Canada Office
LOCATION Surrey, BC
SIZE 120,000 sf / 11,150 sm
CLIENT Public Works and Government Services Canada
DESIGN 1997
CONSTRUCTION 1997-1998
DESIGN TEAM
Perkins+Will (formerly Busby + Associates Architects)
- P. Busby, S. Chevalier, J. Heinen, J. Huffman, M. McColl, S. Ockwell, S. Schou, A. Waugh
STRUCTURAL ENGINEER Jones, Kwong, Kishi Consulting
MECHANICAL ENGINEER Keen Engineering
ELECTRICAL ENGINEER Reid Crowther & Partners
DEVELOPMENT ADVISOR Mitchell Kim Thompson
FIRE CODE CONSULTANT Protection Engineering
LANDSCAPE ARCHITECT Site Design Solutions
WORKPLACE STRATEGIST KLR Consulting
PHOTOGRAPHER Martin Tessler
AWARDS RECEIVED
- Lieutenant Governor of British Columbia, Medal in Architecture, 2000
- American Institute of Architects, "What Makes it Green?" 2000
- Governor General of Canada, Medal in Architecture, 1999
- Vancouver Regional Construction Association, Award of Excellence, 1999
- Building Owners and Managers Association, Earth Award, 1999
- Project Management Institute, Project of the Year, 1999
- International Green Building Challenge, 1998
REFERENCE TO PUBLICATIONS
- "Revenue Canada building a refreshing modern example of green engineering," *Vancouver Sun,* March 3, 1999.

Riyadh Bus Rapid Transit, Riyadh, Saudi Arabia (2013-2017)

PROJECT Riyadh Bus Rapid Transit
LOCATION Riyadh, Saudi Arabia
CLIENT Riyadh Development Authority
DESIGN 2013
CONSTRUCTION 2014-2017 (projected)
DESIGN TEAM
Perkins+Will:
• L. Arreola, A. Baldwin, A. Boivin, S. Bryce, P. Busby, A. Chan, P. Cowcher, J. Deutscher, S. Diaz, J. Doble, P. Grzybek, J. Huffman, R. Maas, Y. Makour, K. McGuinness, J. Nunez, M. Richter, C. Rivard, S. Schou, A. Slawinski, A. Tsay-Jacobs
SIZE 878,000 sf / 81,600 sm total
10,979 sf / 1,020 sm per station
72 stations, 8 interchange stations,
PLATFORM SIZE 230 f / 70 m
STRUCTURAL ENGINEER Dar Al-Handasah (Shair and Partners)
MECHANICAL ENGINEER Dar Al-Handasah (Shair and Partners)
ELECTRICAL ENGINEER Dar Al-Handasah (Shair and Partners)
SUSTAINABILITY RATINGS Registered with the certification goal of LEED Silver
REFERENCE TO PUBLICATIONS
• Matthew Carcak, "Inside the Future of Public Transit Design," *curbingcars.com,* March 19, 2014, online.
• Eric Jaffe, "How Design Can Help Build a 'Transit Culture,'" *The Atlantic Cities,* March 14, 2014, online.

Riyadh Metro Stations, Riyadh, Saudi Arabia (2004-2018)

PROJECT Riyadh LRT Stations
LOCATION Riyadh, Saudi Arabia
CLIENT Riyadh Development Authority
DESIGN 2004-2012;
CONSTRUCTION 2014-2018 (projected)
SIZE
AREA 10,979 sf / 1,020 sm per station / 72 stations, 8 interchange stations, 81,600 sm total (878,000 sf)
PLATFORM SIZE 230f / 70 m
DESIGN TEAM
Perkins+Will:
• S. Bryce, P. Busby, W. Dahl, S. Diaz, J. Deutscher, J. Doble, A. Espinoza, C. Gomes, M. Haberli, A. Knorr, R. Maas, T. Miller, J. Sampson, S. Schou, A. Slawinski, Y. Sun, E. Wolpin
STRUCTURAL ENGINEER Fast + Epp
MECHANICAL ENGINEER Dar Al-Handasah (Shair and Partners)
ELECTRICAL ENGINEER Dar Al-Handasah (Shair and Partners)
PHOTOGRAPHER Martin Tessler
REFERENCE TO PUBLICATIONS
• Eric Jaffe, "How Design Can Help Build a 'Transit Culture,'" The Atlantic Cities online, March 14, 2014.
• Matthew Carcak "Inside the Future Of Public Transit Design" *curbingcars.com* online, March 20, 2014.

Royal Academy Kiosk, London, UK (1986)

PROJECT Royal Academy Kiosk, competition entry
LOCATION London, UK
CLIENT Royal Academy
DESIGN 1986
DESIGN TEAM
Perkins+Will (formerly Peter Busby Architect):
• P. Busby

St. Mary's Hospital, Sechelt, BC (2008-2012)

PROJECT St. Mary's Hospital
LOCATION Sechelt, BC
CLIENT Vancouver Coastal Health
DESIGN 2008- 2010
CONSTRUCTION 2010- 2012
SIZE New addition: 51,667 sf / 4,800 sm
Renovated Space: 16,146 sf / 1,500 sm
DESIGN TEAM
Perkins+Will:
  • S. Bergen, P. Busby, B. Greig, E. Latreille, R.
    Maas, T. McAuley, K. Meissener, G. Miu
JOINT VENTURE ARCHITECT Farrow Partnership
STRUCTURAL ENGINEER Fast + Epp
MECHANICAL ENGINEER Integral Group (formerly
Cobalt Engineering)
ELECTRICAL ENGINEER Acumen Consulting
Engineers
TECHNOLOGY CONSULTANT Acumen Consulting
Engineers
LANDSCAPE ARCHITECT Sharp & Diamond
CIVIL ENGINEER Stantec
CODE CONSULTANT CFT Engineering
QUANTITY SURVEYOR Altus Group
PHOTOGRAPHER Latreille Delage Photography
AWARDS RECEIVED
  • The Design & Health International Academy
    Awards, Award for Sustainable Design, 2014
  • The Design & Health International Academy
    Awards, Award for Use of Art in the Patient
    Environment, 2014
SUSTAINABILITY RATINGS LEED Gold
REFERENCE TO PUBLICATIONS
  • Kristen Avis, "Canada's Greenest Hospital,"
    Design Build Source AU, May 16, 2013, online.
  • Frances Bula, "Hospital uses power of
    architecture to promote healing," Globe and
    Mail, May 6, 2012, p. B10.
  • "Island Hospital," Journal of Commerce, May
    26, 2010.

Samuel Brighouse Elementary School, Richmond, BC (2009-2011)

PROJECT Samuel Brighouse Elementary School
LOCATION Richmond, BC
CLIENT Richmond School District No. 38
DESIGN 2009-2010
CONSTRUCTION 2010-2011
SIZE 50,590 sf / 4,700 sm
DESIGN TEAM
Perkins+Will:
  • E. Brossy de Dios, P. Busby, R. Drew, R.
    Maas, J. Rudd, A. Shum, W. Vaughn, J.
    Verville, C. Waight, C. Wang, L. Woofter
STRUCTURAL ENGINEER Fast + Epp
MECHANICAL ENGINEER Integral Group (formerly
Cobalt Engineering)
ELECTRICAL ENGINEER Acumen Consulting
Engineers
TECHNOLOGY CONSULTANT Acumen Consulting
Engineers
LANDSCAPE ARCHITECT Durante Kreuk, Ltd.
CIVIL ENGINEER Hub Engineering
ECOLOGIST Raincoast Applied Ecology
BUILDING ENVELOPE CONSULTANT Morrison
Hershfield
ACOUSTICAL CONSULTANT BKL Consultants
GEOTECHNICAL CONSULTANT Trow Associates
TRANSPORTATION CONSULTANT Bunt &
Associates
SURVEYOR Matson Peck & Topliss
COST CONSULTANT Jim Bush & Associates
CODE CONSULTANT CFT Engineering
CONSTRUCTION MANAGER EllisDon Corporation
PHOTOGRAPHER Nic Lehoux
AWARDS RECEIVED
  • Wood Design Awards, Canadian Wood
    Council Wood WORKS! BC, Honorable
    Mention, 2014
  • Vancouver Regional Construction Association,
    Silver Award in the category of Sustainable
    Construction, Gold Award in the category of
    General Contractor up to $15 million
  • AIA Pasadena & Foothill Chapter Honor
    Award, Institutional / Educational, 2012,
  • Lieutenant-Governor of British Columbia Merit
    Recipient, 2012
  • BC Hydro Power Smart Excellence Awards,
    New Construction Category, Finalist, 2012
  • Wood Design Awards Canadian Wood Council

    Wood WORKS! BC Engineering Category,
    2012
  • Vancouver Regional Construction Association,
    Gold Award in the category of General
    Contractor up to $15 Million, 2013
  • Vancouver Regional Construction Association
    Silver Award in the category of Sustainable
    Construction, 2013
SUSTAINABILITY RATINGS LEED Gold
REFERENCE TO PUBLICATIONS
  • Linda C. Lentz, "Schools of the 21st Century,"
    Architectural Record, January 3, 2012, http://
    archrecord.construction.com/features/schools/
  • Brian Salgado, "Learning Curve," Building &
    Construction, Fall 2010, p. 115-116

Smart Development, Vancouver, BC (2005-2009)

PROJECT Smart Development
LOCATION Vancouver, BC
CLIENT Concord Pacific
DESIGN 2005-2006
CONSTRUCTION 2007-2009
SIZE 124,000 sf / 11,520 sm
DESIGN TEAM
Perkins+Will:
- P. Busby, R. Drew, J. Gravenstein, J. Huffman, D. Kitazaki, H. Lai, T. Miller, A. Minard, K. Robertson, J. Skinner
STRUCTURAL ENGINEER Jones Kwong Kishi
MECHANICAL ENGINEER Yoneda & Associates
ELECTRICAL ENGINEER Nemetz S/A & Associates, Ltd.
LANDSCAPE ARCHITECT PWL Partnership
CONTRACTOR JRS Engineering
INTERIOR DESIGNER Perkins+Will
CODE CONSULTANT B.R. Thorson Consulting, Ltd.
ENVELOPE CONSULTANT JRS Engineering

The Squamish Lil'wat Cultural Centre, Whistler, BC (2003-2006)

PROJECT Squamish Lil'wat Cultural Centre
LOCATION Whistler, BC
SIZE 50,000 sf / 4,645 sm
CLIENT Squamish Nation and Lil'wat Nation
DESIGN 2003
CONSTRUCTION 2004-2006
DESIGN TEAM
Waugh Busby Architects:
- R. Bens, P. Busby, S. Ockwell, A. Slawinski, A. Waugh, N. Webster
CONSTRUCTION ADMINISTRATION ARCHITECT
Ratio Architecture (formerly Toby Russell Buckwell + Partners Architects)
STRUCTURAL ENGINEER Equilibrium Consulting
MECHANICAL ENGINEER Stantec
ELECTRICAL ENGINEER Acumen Consulting Engineers
CIVIL ENGINEER CJ Andersen Civil Engineering, Inc.
LANDSCAPE ARCHITECT Philips Wuori Long, Inc.
CODE CONSULTANT Pioneer Consultants
GEOTECHNICAL CONSULTANT Thurber Engineering
SNOW CONSULTANT Snow Country Consultants
MUSEUM CONSULTANT University of British Columbia, Museum of Anthropology
PHOTOGRAPHER Michael Bednar
AWARDS RECEIVED
- Canadian Wood Council, Western Red Cedar Award, Non-Residential, 2009
SUSTAINABILITY RATINGS Registered with the certification goal of LEED Gold.
REFERENCE TO PUBLICATIONS
- Katherine McIntyre, "Rocky Mountain Green: Squamish Lil'wat Cultural Centre Cuts a Green Swath in British Columbia," *Legacy Magazine,* November 2008.
- Jim Taggart, "New Building Based On Traditions, and Modern Application of LEED Principles," *SABMagazine blog,* April 2009, online: http://www.*sab*magazine.com/blog/2009/04/10/squamish/

Stanley Park Tropical Complex, Vancouver, BC (1986-1987)

PROJECT Stanley Park Tropical Complex
LOCATION Vancouver, BC
CLIENT Vancouver Parks Board
DESIGN 1986-1987
SIZE 2,700 sf / 250 sm
DESIGN TEAM
Perkins+Will (formerly Busby Bridger Architects):
- P. Bridger, P. Busby, N. Shearing
ARCHITECTURAL CONSULTANTS Perkins+Will (formerly SMWM), C. Simon
ZOOLOGICAL J. Stephen McCusker, General Curator, Washington Park Zoo
STRUCTURAL ENGINEER Rockingham Engineering, Ltd.
MECHANICAL ENGINEER D.W. Thompson
ELECTRICAL ENGINEER Peter Scott & Associates, Ltd
LANDSCAPE ARCHITECT Christopher Phillips & Associates, Inc.
SURVEYOR Thornley White & Associates, Ltd.
AWARDS RECEIVED
- *Canadian Architect,* Award of Excellence, 1986

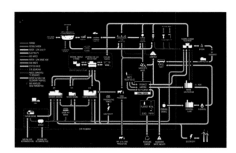

Sustainable Campus Design in a Climate of Change

PROJECT Sustainable Campus Design in a Climate of Change (2008)
CLIENT Self-directed research, Perkins+Will
DATE 2008
DESIGN TEAM
Perkins+Will:
  • P. Busby, M. Driedger, K. Wardle, B. Wakelin
REFERENCE TO PUBLICATIONS
  • Brian Wakelin and Kathy Wardle, "Universities in a climate of change," *Academic Matters,* April/May 2008, p. 18-21.

Sustainable Condo, Mobile Exhibit, (2004)

PROJECT Sustainable Condo
LOCATION Mobile Exhibit
SIZE 750 sf / 70 sm
CLIENT EcoSmart Foundation
DESIGN 2004
CONSTRUCTION 2004
DESIGN TEAM
Perkins+Will (formerly Busby + Associates Architects):
  • O. Arbel, M. Bonaventura, P. Busby, J. Johansen, R. Maas, G. Miller, M. Nielsen, K. Wardle
CONTRACTOR Ledcor Construction
STRUCTURAL ENGINEER Fast+Epp
MECHANICAL ENGINEER Keen Engineering
ELECTRICAL ENGINEER Keen Engineering
DEVELOPER The Shelter Group
EXHIBIT DESIGN D. Jensen & Associates
INTERIOR DESIGN Penner & Associates Interior Design
PHOTOGRAPHER Martin Tessler
AWARDS RECEIVED
  • Environmental Design & Construction Excellence in Design Award, Honorable Mention, 2005
  • AIBC Innovation Award, 2005
  • RAIC Award of Excellence for Innovation in Architecture, 2005
  • Canadian Institute of Energy (BC) Energy Research & Development Award, 2004
REFERENCE TO PUBLICATIONS
  • "Sustainable condo on road to promote green building," *Vancouver Sun,* October 29, 2005.
  • "Busby reveals 'world's first sustainable condo' in Vancouver; makes AIA list" *Construction Canada,* September 2004.

TELUS House Revitalization/William Farrell Building, Vancouver, BC (1998-2001)

PROJECT TELUS House Revitalization/William Farrell Building
LOCATION Vancouver, BC
CLIENT TELUS Corporation
DESIGN AND CONSTRUCTION 1998-2001
SIZE 130,000 sf / 12,077 sm
DESIGN TEAM
Perkins+Will (formerly Busby + Associates Architects):
  • R. Bens, B. Billingsley, M. Bonaventura, P. Busby, D. Dove, R. Drew, S. Edwards, M. Elkan, R. Glover, J. Huffman, M. Johnston, S. Khattak, M. McColl, T. Mullock, D. Nielsen, M. Nielsen, S. Ockwell, S. Palmier, R. Peck, D. Petrovic, S. Schou, J. South, B. Wakelin, A. Waugh, B. Welty, T. Winkler
STRUCTURAL ENGINEER Read Jones Christoffersen
MECHANICAL ENGINEER Keen Engineering
ELECTRICAL ENGINEER Reid Crowther & Partners
COST CONSULTANT James Bush & Associates
ENVIRONMENTAL CONSULTANT PHH Environmental
CODE CONSULTANT Pioneer Consultants
INTERIOR DESIGNER Perkins+Will, Smart Design Group/Gowling + Gibb
PHOTOGRAPHER Martin Tessler
AWARDS RECEIVED
  • Great Canadian Curtainwall Contest, Canadian Glass Magazine First Place, 2002
  • International Design Resource Award, Honorable Mention, 2001
  • American Institute of Architects, "What Makes it Green?" Exhibit, 2001
  • National Energy Efficiency Award, 2000
  • International Green Building Challenge, 2000
  • Consulting Engineers of British Columbia, Award of Excellence, 2000
  • One of three projects selected to represent Canada at the Green Building Challenge in Maastricht, Netherlands.
REFERENCE TO PUBLICATIONS
  • Matthew Soules, "Open-Faced," *Canadian Architect,* January 2008, p. 31-34.

Ten Big Ideas to Make Vancouver the Greenest City in the World, Vancouver, BC (2010)

PROJECT Ten Big Ideas to Make Vancouver the Greenest City in the World
LOCATION Vancouver, BC
CLIENT Self-directed research, Perkins+Will
DESIGN 2010
DESIGN TEAM
Perkins+Will:
- R. Bragg, P. Busby, D. Dove, M. Driedger, M. Sachs, K. Wardle

Tenderloin Museum, San Francisco, CA (2009-2015)

PROJECT Tenderloin Museum
LOCATION San Francisco, CA
CLIENT Uptown Tenderloin, Inc.
DESIGN 2009-2014
CONSTRUCTION 2014-2015
DESIGN TEAM
Perkins+Will:
- S. Meisler, Y. Matsushita, J. Chang, R. Sandoval, J. Mallery
CONTRACTOR Webcor
STRUCTURAL ENGINEER Santos & Urrutia Structural Engineers
MECHANICAL ENGINEER Design Build
ELECTRICAL ENGINEER Design Build
EXHIBIT DESIGN West Office Exhibition Design
RENDERING Perkins+Will
URLS http://www.uptowntl.org/museum.php

Treasure Island, San Francisco, CA (2009-2030)

PROJECT Treasure Island
LOCATION San Francisco, CA
CLIENT Treasure Island Development Corporation
DESIGN 2009-2012
CONSTRUCTION 2015-2030 (projected)
SIZE 730,000 sf / 67,819 sm
DESIGN TEAM
Perkins+Will:
- K. Alschuler, N. Friedman, J. Lee, Y. Liu, P. Pinto, E. Reifenstein, C. Simon, G. Silwal, K. Subbarayan, G. Tierney, P. Vaucheret, J. Xiao
Associated Architects: Skidmore, Owings & Merrill
AWARDS RECEIVED
- American Institute of Architects, National, Honor Award, 2009
- American Institute of Architects, California Council, Urban Design Merit Award, 2008
- American Institute of Architects, San Francisco Chapter, Urban Design Merit Award, 2006
SUSTAINABILITY RATINGS Neighborhood development is registered with LEED for Neighborhood Development with the certification goal of Gold. Per City of San Francisco requirements, all buildings will be LEED certified to the Gold level at a minimum. 2009 Clinton Climate Initiative's "Climate Positive Development Program" participant.
URLS http://sftreasureisland.org/approved-plans-and-documents

University of British Columbia, Evaluation of Green Building Rating Systems for UBC: Greenhouse Gas Conservation Measure Recommendations, Vancouver, BC (2007-2008)

PROJECT University of British Columbia, Evaluation of Green Building Rating Systems for UBC: Greenhouse Gas Conservation Measure Recommendations
LOCATION Vancouver, BC
CLIENT University of British Columbia
DESIGN 2007-2008
DESIGN TEAM
Perkins+Will:
- P. Busby, M. Driedger, Z. Smith, K. Wardle

University of Texas at Dallas Student Services Building, Dallas, TX (2008-2011)

PROJECT University of Texas at Dallas Student Services Building
LOCATION Dallas, TX
CLIENT University of Texas System
DESIGN 2008
CONSTRUCTION 2008-2011
SIZE 74,343 sf / 6,907 sm
DESIGN TEAM
Perkins+Will:
- R. Bragg, D. Burns, P. Busby, L. Cavallin, B. Cay, P. Cowcher, S. Curry, D. Day, H. Kao, E. Latreille, R. Miller, S. Schou, A. Toney

STRUCTURAL ENGINEER Jaster Quintanilla & Associates
MECHANICAL ENGINEER Infrastructure Associates
ELECTRICAL ENGINEER Infrastructure Associates
CIVIL ENGINEER URS
LANDSCAPE ARCHITECT Kendall Landscape Architecture
CODE CONSULTANT Schirmer Engineering Corporation
QUANTITY SURVEYOR Halford Busby
COST CONSULTANT Halford Busby
PHOTOGRAPHER Charles Davis Smith
AWARDS RECEIVED
- USGBC Central Texas Board Chapter Green School Design Awards, School of the Year Award (Higher Education), 2011
- Association for the Advancement of Sustainability in Higher Education/USGBC Innovation in Green Building Award, Inaugural Award, 2011
- Accessibility Professionals Association / Texas Governor's Committee on People with Disabilities, Accessibility Award, 2011
- Green Project Award of Merit (ENR Texas & Louisiana magazine, 2011
- College Planning & Management Magazine, Judge's Choice Award - Education Design Showcase, The Sustainability & Innovation Award, 2011
- Dallas Business Journal Best Real Estate Deals, Best Green Project - Public Award, 2011
- University of Texas System, Outstanding HUB Participation Award, 2010

SUSTAINABILITY RATINGS LEED Platinum

REFERENCE TO PUBLICATIONS
- Candice Carlisle, "University of Dallas at Texas Student Services Center," *Dallas Business Journal,* February 25, 2011, p. B42.

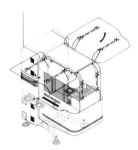

University of Washington, Husky Union Building, Seattle, WA (2008-2013)

PROJECT University of Washington, Husky Union Building (HUB)
LOCATION Seattle, WA
CLIENT University of Washington
DESIGN 2008-2010
CONSTRUCTION 2011-2013
DESIGN TEAM
Perkins+Will:
- P. Busby, R. Bussard, S. Chan, A. DeEulio, J. Geringer, A. Gianopoulos, L. Leland, F. Long, J. Stebar, A. Wu

CONTRACTOR Skanska Construction
STRUCTURAL/CIVIL ENGINEER Coughlin Porter Lundeen
MECHANICAL ENGINEER AEI
ELECTRICAL ENGINEER AEI
LANDSCAPE ARCHITECT Gustafson Guthrie Nichol
PHOTOGRAPHER Lara Swimmer; Ben Benschneider
AWARDS RECEIVED
- Association of College Unions International (ACUI) 2014 Facility Design Award of Excellence, 2014
- *AIA Washington Council,* Civic Design Awards, Honor Award, 2013,
- Architectural Woodwork Institute, Award of Excellence, 2013

SUSTAINABILITY RATINGS LEED Gold
REFERENCE TO PUBLICATIONS
- "Civic Design Awards Interview with Ryan Bussard, AIA, Perkins+Will," *AIA Washington Council,* February 10, 2014: http://aiawa.org/2014/02/10/civic-design-awards-interview-ryan-bussard-aia-perkinswill/

Urban Expresso Kiosk, Vancouver, BC (1985-1987)

PROJECT Urban Expresso Kiosk
LOCATION Various Locations, Vancouver, BC
SIZE 34 sf / 3.2 sm
CLIENT Urban Expresso, Inc.
DESIGN 1985-1986
CONSTRUCTION 1986-1987
DESIGN TEAM
Perkins+Will (formerly Peter Busby Architect):
- P. Busby, I. Douglas

STRUCTURAL ENGINEER C.Y. Loh
AWARDS RECEIVED
- British Columbia Premier's Award for Excellence in Accessible Design, 1988

REFERENCE TO PUBLICATIONS
- "The portable espresso bars," *Tandem,* July 11, 1999.

The Vale Living With Lakes Centre for Applied Research in Environmental Restoration and Sustainability, Laurentian University, Sudbury, ON (2006-2011)

PROJECT The Vale Living With Lakes Centre for Applied Research in Environmental Restoration and Sustainability
LOCATION Sudbury, ON
CLIENT Laurentian University
DESIGN 2006-2009
CONSTRUCTION 2009-2011
SIZE Site **AREA** 440,610 sf / 40,934 sm
PROJECT AREA 28,441 sf / 2,643 sm
DESIGN TEAM
Perkins+Will:
- P. Busby, S. Bergen, R. Holt, G. Lim, N. Shuttleworth, S. Schou, B. Wakelin

JOINT VENTURE ARCHITECT J.L. Richards & Associates Limited
STRUCTURAL ENGINEER Fast + Epp / J.L. Richards
MECHANICAL ENGINEER Stantec Engineering / J.L. Richards
ELECTRICAL ENGINEER K.L. Engineering
CIVIL ENGINEER J.L. Richards
PHOTOGRAPHER Tom Arban
AWARDS RECEIVED
- Wood WORKS! Ontario Green Building Wood Design Award, 2012
- Canadian Consulting Engineers (CCE) Award of Excellence Building Category, 2012
- Holcim Award for Sustainable Construction, Bronze Award, 2008

SUSTAINABILITY RATINGS LEED Platinum. The Vale Living With Lakes Centre is designed to be adaptable to a 2050 climate.
URLS http://www3.laurentian.ca/livingwithlakes/community/video/

Vancouver Dunsmuir Viaducts Study, Vancouver, BC (2012)

PROJECT Vancouver Dunsmuir Viaducts Study
LOCATION Vancouver, BC
SIZE 74 acres / 30 hectares
CLIENT City of Vancouver
DESIGN AND CONSTRUCTION 2012
DESIGN TEAM
Perkins+Will:
  • P. Busby, J. Drohan, C. Gomes, A. Espinoza, Y. Madkour, A. Slawinski
STRUCTURAL ENGINEER Fast+Epp
TRANSPORTATION ENGINEER Bunt + Associates Engineering
LANDSCAPE ARCHITECT Phillips Farevaag Smallenberg
CIVIL ENGINEER HUB Engineering
COST CONSULTANT Coriolis Consulting Corporation
REFERENCE TO PUBLICATIONS
  • Jeff Lee, "Vancouver unveils plan to replace viaducts with 'super road'" *Vancouver Sun,* July 25, 2012.

Vancouver Street Furnishings, Vancouver, BC (2000-2002)

PROJECT Vancouver Street Furnishings
LOCATION Vancouver, BC
CLIENT Pattison Outdoor
DESIGN 2000-2002
DESIGN TEAM
Perkins+Will (formerly Busby + Associates Architects):
  • P. Busby, S. Khattak, S. Schou, A. Slawinski
CONTRACTOR Enseicom
STRUCTURAL ENGINEER Fast + Epp/ Enseicom
MECHANICAL ENGINEER Enseicom
ELECTRICAL ENGINEER Enseicom

Vancouver View Study, Vancouver, BC (1988-1989)

PROJECT Vancouver View Study
LOCATION Vancouver, BC
CLIENT City of Vancouver Manager's Office
DESIGN 1988-1989
DESIGN TEAM
Perkins+Will (formerly Busby Bridger Architects):
  • P. Busby, C. Leung, R. Maas, U. Mueller
PUBLIC CORPORATION MTR Consultants
ECONOMIC IMPACTS Coriolis Consultants Corporation
SURVEY INFORMATION Brenda Farrell Associates

VanDusen Botanical Garden Visitor Centre, Vancouver, BC (2007-2012)

PROJECT VanDusen Botanical Garden Visitor Centre
LOCATION Vancouver, BC
CLIENT Vancouver Board of Parks and Recreation
SIZE
PROJECT AREA 183,000 sf / 17,000 sm
BUILDING AREA 19,483 sf / 1,810 sm
DESIGN 2007-2008
CONSTRUCTION 2009-2012
DESIGN TEAM
Perkins+Will:
  • S. Bergen, P. Busby, P. Cowcher, R. Drew, R. Glover, H. Grusko, J. Ho, R. Holt, J. Huffman, P. Martyn, J. Peacock, M. Richter, S. Schou
GENERAL CONTRACTOR Ledcor Construction
STRUCTURAL ENGINEER Fast + Epp
MECHANICAL ENGINEER Integral Group
ELECTRICAL ENGINEER Integral Group
CIVIL ENGINEER R.F. Binnie & Associates
CODE CONSULTANT B.R. Thorson, Ltd.
COST CONSULTANT BTY Group
ENVELOPE CONSULTANT Morrison Hershfield
LANDSCAPE ARCHITECT Sharp & Diamond Landscape Architecture, Inc. with Cornelia Hahn Oberlander
LIGHTING DESIGN Total Lighting Solutions
ECOLOGY CONSULTANT Raincoast Applied Ecology
ACOUSTICAL CONSULTANT BKL Consultants
COMMISSIONING AGENT KD Engineering Co.
COMMISSIONING AUTHORITY KD Engineering Co.
PHOTOGRAPHER Nic Lehoux
AWARDS RECEIVED
  • World Architecture News (WAN), Sustainable Building of the Year, 2014
  • SAB Magazine, 2014 Canadian Green Building Award, 2014
  • International Green Roof Association, Green Roof Leadership Award, 2013
  • Metal Architecture Design Award, Metal Roofing Category, 2013
  • Wood WORKS! BC Wood Design Awards, Wood Innovation Award, 2013,
  • Globe Award for Excellence in Urban Sustainability, Finalist, 2013
  • World Architecture News (WAN) Engineering Awards, Winner, 2012
  • Lieutenant-Governor of British Columbia Merit Recipient, 2012
  • Lieutenant Governor's Award for Engineering Excellence, ACEC-BC, 2012
SUSTAINABILITY RATINGS LEED Platinum. Pursuing certification through the Living Building Challenge v.1.3.
REFERENCE TO PUBLICATIONS
  • Peter Busby and Harley Grusko, "How Does Your Building Grow? The VanDusen Botanical Garden Visitor Centre, *Trim Tab,* v 2.1, April 2014.
  • "VanDusen Botanical Garden Visitor Centre, *Arch Daily,* March 20, 2012. http://www.archdaily.com/215855/vandusen-botanical-garden-visitor-centre-perkinswill/
  • Edward Keegan, "VanDusen Botanical Garden Visitor Centre," *Architect,* March 2012.
URLS https://vancouver.ca/parks-recreation-culture/vandusen-botanical-garden.aspx

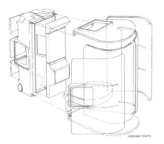

Video Recording Kiosk, Vancouver, BC (1987-1989)

PROJECT Video Recording Kiosk
LOCATION Vancouver, BC
CLIENT Videogram International Corp.
DESIGN AND CONSTRUCTION 1987-1989
DESIGN TEAM
Perkins+Will (formerly Busby Bridger Architects):
  • M. Barber, P. Busby, G. Cannon, H. Eng, K. Humphreys, V. Nishi, A. Slawinski, K. Sturton
ELECTRO-MECHANICAL SYSTEMS Bill Kitchen
ELECTRONICS Pthalo Systems

White Rock Operations Centre, White Rock, BC (2001-2003)

PROJECT White Rock Operations Centre
LOCATION White Rock, BC
CLIENT City of White Rock
DESIGN 2001
CONSTRUCTION 2002-2003
Size 6,545 sf / 608 sm
DESIGN TEAM
Perkins+Will (formerly Busby + Associates Architects):
- R. Bens, P. Busby, D. Dove, M. Elkan, R. Glover, M. Labrie, R. MacPherson, M. McColl, S. Ockwell, D. Petrovic, R. Piccolo, J. South, B. Wakelin, N. Webster, T. Winkler
GENERAL CONTRACTOR KDS Construction
STRUCTURAL ENGINEER Fast + Epp
MECHANICAL ENGINEER Keen Engineering
ELECTRICAL ENGINEER Flagel Lewandowski
LANDSCAPE ARCHITECT Wendy Grandin
IAQ CONSULTANT Pacific Environmental Consulting Services
PHOTOGRAPHER Colin Jewall / Enrico Dagostini
AWARDS RECEIVED
- Lieutenant Governor of BC, Medal in Architecture, 2004
- Design Exchange Awards/National Post, Gold Medal Winner, 2004
- AIA/COTE Top Ten Green Projects, Winner, 2004
- Architecture Institute of BC, Innovation Award, 2004
- Community Energy Association, Energy Aware Award, 2003
SUSTAINABILITY RATINGS LEED Gold
REFERENCE TO PUBLICATIONS
- Jim Taggart, "The Cedar Book 2008," Janam Publications, Inc., 2008, p. 52-57.
- John Riordan and Kirsten Becker, *The Good Office, Green Design on the Cutting Edge,* Grayson Publishing, LLC and Collins Design, 2008, p. 83-89.
- "A City Operations Center Creates Gold with Green Techniques," *Eco-Structure,* January/February 2005.

York University, Computer Science Building, Toronto, ON (1998-2001)

PROJECT York University Computer Science Building
LOCATION Toronto, ON
CLIENT York University
DESIGN 1998
CONSTRUCTION 2000-2001
SIZE 104,400 sf / 9,699 sm
DESIGN TEAM
Perkins+Will (formerly Busby + Associates Architects):
- P. Busby, V. Gillies, M. McColl, A. Waugh, S. Ockwell
van Nostrand DiCastri Architects:
- W. Bettio, A. DiCastri, J. van Nostrand, B. Zee
BNIM:
- B. Berkebile
STRUCTURAL ENGINEER Yolles Partnership, Inc.
MECHANICAL ENGINEER Keen Engineering
ELECTRICAL ENGINEER Carinci Burt Rogers
LANDSCAPE ARCHITECT Robert Packham Design, Inc.
ENVIRONMENTAL CONSULTANT RWDI
COST CONSULTANT Hanscomb Consultants
PHOTOGRAPHER Steven Evans
AWARDS RECEIVED
- Natural Resources Canada, Energy Efficiency, Honorable Mention, 2004
- Association of Canadian Consulting Engineers, Award of Excellence, Second Place, 2002
- Governor General of Canada, Medal for Excellence, 2002
- Lieutenant Governor of British Columbia, Medal in Architecture, 2002
- International Green Building Challenge Representative, 2002
- World Architecture, International Green Building Award, 2002
REFERENCE TO PUBLICATIONS
- "York University's Computer Science Building," *Architectural Record,* February 7, 2003.

ECOtone
publishing company

Ecotone Publishing - International Living Future Institute

Founded by green building experts in 2004, Ecotone Publishing is dedicated
to meeting the growing demand for authoritative and accessible books on
sustainable design, materials selection and building techniques in North America
and beyond. Located in the Cascadia region, Ecotone is well positioned to play
an important part in the green design movement. Ecotone searches out and
documents inspiring projects, visionary people and vital trends that are leading
the design industry to transformational change toward a healthier planet.

Ecotone Publishing is an imprint of the International Living Future Institute - an
environmental NGO committed to catalyzing the transformation toward
communities that are socially just, culturally rich and ecologically restorative.